English-French
French-English

Word to Word®
Bilingual Dictionary

Compiled by:
C. Sesma M.A.

Translated by:
Vanessa Munsch

Bilingual Dictionaries, Inc.

French Word to Word® Bilingual Dictionary
2nd Edition © Copyright 2011

Published in the United States by:

Bilingual Dictionaries, Inc.
PO Box 1154
Murrieta, CA 92562
T: (951) 461-6893 • F: (951) 461-3092
www.BilingualDictionaries.com

ISBN13: 978-0-933146-36-5
ISBN: 0-933146-36-1

Preface

Bilingual Dictionaries, Inc. is committed to providing schools, libraries and educators with a great selection of bilingual materials for students. Along with bilingual dictionaries we also provide ESL materials, children's bilingual stories and children's bilingual picture dictionaries.

Sesma's French Word to Word® Bilingual Dictionary was created specifically with students in mind to be used for reference and testing. This dictionary contains approximately 19,000 entries targeting common words used in the English language.

List of Irregular Verbs

present - past - past participle

arise - arose - arisen
awake - awoke - awoken, awaked
be - was - been
bear - bore - borne
beat - beat - beaten
become - became - become
begin - began - begun
behold - beheld - beheld
bend - bent - bent
beseech - besought - besought
bet - bet - betted
bid - bade (bid) - bidden (bid)
bind - bound - bound
bite - bit - bitten
bleed - bled - bled
blow - blew - blown
break - broke - broken
breed - bred - bred
bring - brought - brought
build - built - built
burn - burnt - burnt *
burst - burst - burst
buy - bought - bought
cast - cast - cast
catch - caught - caught
choose - chose - chosen
cling - clung - clung
come - came - come
cost - cost - cost
creep - crept - crept
cut - cut - cut
deal - dealt - dealt

dig - dug - dug
do - did - done
draw - drew - drawn
dream - dreamt - dreamed
drink - drank - drunk
drive - drove - driven
dwell - dwelt - dwelt
eat - ate - eaten
fall - fell - fallen
feed - fed - fed
feel - felt - felt
fight - fought - fought
find - found - found
flee - fled - fled
fling - flung - flung
fly - flew - flown
forebear - forbore - forborne
forbid - forbade - forbidden
forecast - forecast - forecast
forget - forgot - forgotten
forgive - forgave - forgiven
forego - forewent - foregone
foresee - foresaw - foreseen
foretell - foretold - foretold
forget - forgot - forgotten
forsake - forsook - forsaken
freeze - froze - frozen
get - got - gotten
give - gave - given
go - went - gone
grind - ground - ground
grow - grew - grown
hang - hung * - hung *
have - had - had

hear - heard - heard	**ring** - rang - rung
hide - hid - hidden	**rise** - rose - risen
hit - hit - hit	**run** - ran - run
hold - held - held	**saw** - sawed - sawn
hurt - hurt - hurt	**say** - said - said
hit - hit - hit	**see** - saw - seen
hold - held - held	**seek** - sought - sought
keep - kept - kept	**sell** - sold - sold
kneel - knelt * - knelt *	**send** - sent - sent
know - knew - known	**set** - set - set
lay - laid - laid	**sew** - sewed - sewn
lead - led - led	**shake** - shook - shaken
lean - leant * - leant *	**shear** - sheared - shorn
leap - lept * - lept *	**shed** - shed - shed
learn - learnt * - learnt *	**shine** - shone - shone
leave - left - left	**shoot** - shot - shot
lend - lent - lent	**show** - showed - shown
let - let - let	**shrink** - shrank - shrunk
lie - lay - lain	**shut** - shut - shut
light - lit * - lit *	**sing** - sang - sung
lose - lost - lost	**sink** - sank - sunk
make - made - made	**sit** - sat - sat
mean - meant - meant	**slay** - slew - slain
meet - met - met	**sleep** - sleep - slept
mistake - mistook - mistaken	**slide** - slid - slid
must - had to - had to	**sling** - slung - slung
pay - paid - paid	**smell** - smelt * - smelt *
plead - pleaded - pled	**sow** - sowed - sown *
prove - proved - proven	**speak** - spoke - spoken
put - put - put	**speed** - sped * - sped *
quit - quit * - quit *	**spell** - spelt * - spelt *
read - read - read	**spend** - spent - spent
rid - rid - rid	**spill** - spilt * - spilt *
ride - rode - ridden	**spin** - spun - spun

spit - spat - spat
split - split - split
spread - spread - spread
spring - sprang - sprung
stand - stood - stood
steal - stole - stolen
stick - stuck - stuck
sting - stung - stung
stink - stank - stunk
stride - strode - stridden
strike - struck - struck (stricken)
strive - strove - striven
swear - swore - sworn
sweep - swept - swept
swell - swelled - swollen *
swim - swam - swum
take - took - taken
teach - taught - taught
tear - tore - torn

tell - told - told
think - thought - thought
throw - threw - thrown
thrust - thrust - thrust
tread - trod - trodden
wake - woke - woken
wear - wore - worn
weave - wove * - woven *
wed - wed * - wed *
weep - wept - wept
win - won - won
wind - wound - wound
wring - wrung - wrung
write - wrote - written

**Those tenses with an * also
have regular forms.**

English-French

Bilingual Dictionaries, Inc.

Abbreviations

a - article
n - noun
e - exclamation
pro - pronoun
adj - adjective
adv - adverb
v - verb
iv - irregular verb
pre - preposition
c - conjunction

a *a* un, une
abandon *v* abandonner
abandonment *n* abandon
abbey *n* abbaye
abbot *n* abbé
abbreviate *v* abréger
abbreviation *n* abréviation
abdicate *v* abdiquer
abdication *n* abdication
abdomen *n* abdomen
abduct *v* enlever
abduction *n* enlèvement
aberration *n* aberration
abhor *v* abhorer
abide by *v* se conformer à
ability *n* talent
ablaze *adj* en feu
able *adj* être capable de
abnormal *adj* anorma
abnormality *n* anormalité
aboard *adv* à bord
abolish *v* abolir
abort *v* avorter
abortion *n* avortement
abound *v* abonder
about *pre* à propos de
about *adv* environ
above *pre* au-dessus de
abreast *adv* côte à côte

abridge *v* abréger
abroad *adv* à l'étranger
abrogate *v* abroger
abruptly *adv* abruptement
absence *n* absence
absent *adj* absent
absolute *adj* absolut
absolution *n* absolution
absolve *v* absoudre
absorb *v* absorber
absorbent *adj* absorbant
abstain *v* abstenir
abstinence *n* abstinence
abstract *adj* abstrait
absurd *adj* absurde
abundance *n* abondance
abundant *adj* abondant
abuse *v* abuser
abuse *n* abus
abusive *adj* abusif
abysmal *adj* abyssal
abyss *n* abîme
academic *adj* universitaire
academy *n* académie
accelerate *v* accélérer
accelerator *n* accélérateur
accent *n* accent
accept *v* accpter
acceptable *adj* acceptable
acceptance *n* acceptation
access *n* accès
accessible *adj* accessible

accident *n* accident
accidental *adj* accendentel
acclaim *v* acclamer
acclimatize *v* aclimatiser
accommodate *v* satisfaire
accompany *v* renir compagnie
accomplice *n* complice
accomplish *v* accomplir
accord *n* accord
according to *pre* selon
accordion *n* accordéon
account *n* compte
account for *v* expliquer
accountable *adj* responsible pour
accountant *n* comptable
accumulate *v* accumuler
accuracy *n* exactitude
accurate *adj* exact
accusation *n* accusation
accuse *v* accuser
accustom *v* acoutumer
ace *n* as
ache *n* douleur
achieve *v* accomplir
acid *n* acide
acidity *n* acidité
acorn *n* glan
acoustic *adj* acoustique
acquaint *v* informer
acquaintance *n* connaissance
acquire *v* aquérir
acquisition *n* acquisition

acquit *v* absolver
acquittal *n* acquitement
acre *n* acre
acrobat *n* acrobate
across *pre* à travers
act *v* agir
action *n* action
activate *v* activer
activation *n* activation
active *adj* actif
activity *n* activité
actor *n* acteur
actress *n* actrice
actual *adj* actuel
actually *adv* en fait
acute *adj* vif; grave
adamant *adj* catégorique
adapt *v* adapter
adaptable *adj* adaptable
adaptation *n* adaptation
adapter *n* adaptateur
add *v* ajouter
addicted *adj* dépendant
addiction *n* addiction
addition *n* addition
additional *adj* additionel
address *n* adresse
address *v* adresser
addressee *n* destinataire
adequate *adj* adéquat
adhere *v* adhérer
adhesive *adj* adhésif

adjacent *adj* adjacent
adjective *n* adjectif
adjoin *v* toucher
adjoining *adj* adjacent
adjourn *v* ajourner
adjust *v* ajuster
adjustable *adj* ajustable
adjustment *n* ajustement
administer *v* administrer
admirable *adj* admirable
admiral *n* admiral
admiration *n* admiration
admire *v* admirer
admirer *n* admirateur
admissible *adj* admissible
admission *n* entrée, aveu
admit *v* admettr
admittance *n* entrée
admonish *v* admonester
admonition *n* admonestation
adolescence *n* adolescence
adolescent *n* adolescent
adopt *v* adopter
adoption *n* adoption
adoptive *adj* adoptif
adorable *adj* adorable
adoration *n* adoration
adore *v* adorer
adorn *v* orner
adrift *adv* à la dérive
adulation *n* adulation
adult *n* adulte

adulterate *v* dénaturer
adultery *n* adultère
advance *v* avancer
advance *n* avance
advantage *n* avantage
Advent *n* avent
adventure *n* aventure
adverb *n* adverbe
adversary *n* adversaire
adverse *adj* adverse
adversity *n* adversité
advertising *n* publicité
advice *n* conseil
advisable *adj* recommandé
advise *v* conseiller
adviser *n* conseiller
advocate *v* recommander
aeroplane *n* aéroplane
aesthetic *adj* ésthetique
afar *adv* de loin
affable *adj* affable
affair *n* liaison, situation
affect *v* affecter
affection *n* affection
affectionate *adj* affectioné
affiliate *v* affilier
affiliation *n* affiliation
affinity *n* affinité
affirm *v* affirmer
affirmative *adj* affirmative
affix *v* apposer
afflict *v* affliger

affliction *n* affliction
affluence *n* affluence
affluent *adj* affluent
affordable *adj* abordable
affront *v* affronter
affront *n* affront
afloat *adv* à flot
afraid *adj* avoir peur
afresh *adv* à nouveau
after *pre* après
afternoon *n* après-midi
afterwards *adv* plus tard
again *adv* encore
against *pre* contre
age *n* âge
agency *n* agence
agenda *n* agenda
agent *n* agent
agglomerate *v* aggloméré
aggravate *v* aggravé
aggravation *n* aggravation
aggregate *v* regrouper
aggression *n* aggression
aggressive *adj* aggressif
aggressor *n* aggresseur
aghast *adj* effaré
agile *adj* agile
agitator *n* agitateur
agnostic *n* agnostique
agonize *v* agoniser
agonizing *adj* agonisant
agony *n* agonie

agree *v* convenir de
agreeable *adj* agréable
agreement *n* accord
agricultural *adj* agriculturel
agriculture *n* agriculture
ahead *pre* en avant
aid *n* aide
aid *v* aider
aide *n* assistance
ailing *adj* souffrant
ailment *n* maladie
aim *v* viser
aimless *adj* sans but
air *n* air
air *v* aérer,exprimer
aircraft *n* avion
airfield *n* aérodrome
airliner *n* avion commercial
airmail *n* par avion
airplane *n* avion
airport *n* aéroport
airspace *n* espace aérien
airtight *adj* étanche
aisle *n* allée
ajar *adj* entrouvert
akin *adj* parent
alarm *n* alarme
alarm clock *n* reveil
alarming *adj* inquiétant
alcoholic *adj* alcolique
alcoholism *n* alcolisme
alert *n* alerte

alert *v* alerter
algebra *n* algèbre
alien *n* étranger
alight *adv* allumé
align *v* aligner
alignment *n* alignement
alike *adj* pareil
alive *adj* vivant
all *adj* tout
allegation *n* allégation
allege *v* alléguer
allegedly *adv* prétendument
allegiance *n* allégeance
allegory *n* allégorie
allergic *adj* allergique
allergy *n* allergie
alleviate *v* soulager
alley *n* allée
alliance *n* alliance
allied *adj* allié
alligator *n* alligator
allocate *v* afecter
allot *v* attribuer
allotment *n* allocation
allow *v* permettre
allowance *n* argent de poche
alloy *n* alliage
allure *n* allure
alluring *adj* attirant
allusion *n* allusion
ally *n* allié
ally *v* s'allier

almanac *n* almanac
almighty *adj* tout puissant
almond *n* amande
almost *adv* presque
alms *n* aumône
alone *adj* seul
along *pre* le long de
aloof *adj* distant
aloud *adv* a haute voix
alphabet *n* alphabet
already *adv* déjà
alright *adv* d'accord
also *adv* aussi
altar *n* autel
alter *v* changer
alteration *n* modification
altercation *n* altercation
alternate *v* alterner
alternate *adj* en alternance
alternative *n* alternative
although *c* bien que
altitude *n* altitude
altogether *adj* ensemble
aluminum *n* aluminum
always *adv* toujours
amass *v* amasser
amateur *adj* amateur
amaze *v* surprendre
amazement *n* surprise
amazing *adj* surprenant
ambassador *n* ambassadeur
ambiguous *adj* ambigu

ambition *n* ambition
ambitious *adj* ambitieux
ambivalent *adj* ambivalent
ambulance *n* ambulance
amenable *adj* accommodant
amend *v* modifier
amendment *n* amendement
amenities *n* commodités
American *adj* Américain
amiable *adj* amiable
amicable *adj* amical
ammonia *n* ammoniaque
ammunition *n* munition
amnesia *n* amnésie
amnesty *n* amnéstie
among *pre* parmis
amoral *adj* immoral
amorphous *adj* amorphe
amortize *v* amortir
amount *n* quantité
amount to *v* équivaloir à
amphibious *adj* amphibien
amphitheater *n* amphithéâtre
ample *adj* ample
amplifier *n* amplificateur
amplify *v* amplifier
amputate *v* amputer
amputation *n* amputation
amuse *v* s'amuser
amusement *n* distraction
amusing *adj* amusant
an *a* un

analogy *n* analogie
analysis *n* analyse
analyze *v* analyser
anarchist *n* anarchiste
anarchy *n* anarchie
anatomy *n* anatomie
ancestor *n* ancêtre
ancestry *n* ascendance
anchor *n* ancre
anchovy *n* anchois
ancient *adj* ancient
and *c* et
anecdote *n* anecdote
anemia *n* anémie
anemic *adj* anémique
anesthesia *n* anésthésie
anew *adv* encore
angel *n* ange
angelic *adj* angélique
anger *v* s'énerver
anger *n* colère
angina *n* angine
angle *n* angle
Anglican *adj* Anglican
angry *adj* en colere
anguish *n* angoisse
animal *n* animal
animate *v* animer
animation *n* animation
animosity *n* animosité
ankle *n* cheville
annex *n* annexe

annexation *n* annexion
annihilate *v* anéantir
annihilation *n* anéantissement
anniversary *n* anniversaire
annotate *v* annoter
annotation *n* annotation
announce *v* annonce
announcement *n* annoncement
announcer *n* annonceur
annoy *v* embêter
annoying *adj* embêtant
annual *adj* annuel
annul *v* annuler
annulment *n* annulation
anoint *v* oindre
anonymity *n* anonimat
anonymous *adj* anonyme
another *adj* other
answer *v* répondre
answer *n* réponse
ant *n* fourmis
antagonize *v* antagoniser
antecedent *n* antécédent
antecedents *n* antécédents
antelope *n* antilope
antenna *n* antenne
anthem *n* hymne
antibiotic *n* antibiotique
anticipate *v* anticiper
anticipation *n* anticipation
antidote *n* antidote
antipathy *n* antipathie

antiquated *adj* vétuste
antiquity *n* antiquité
anvil *n* enclume
anxiety *n* anxiété
anxious *adj* anxieux
anybody *pro* quelqu'un
anyhow *pro* n'importe comment
anyone *pro* n'importe qui
anything *pro* n'importe quoi
apart *adv* à part
apartment *n* appartement
apathy *n* apathie
ape *n* singe
aperitif *n* apéritif
apex *n* sommet
aphrodisiac *adj* aphrodisiaque
apiece *adv* chacun
apocalypse *n* apocalypse
apologize *v* s'excuser
apology *n* excuse
apostle *n* apôtre
apostolic *adj* apostolique
apostrophe *n* apostrophe
appall *v* scandaliser
appalling *adj* révoltant
apparel *n* habillement
apparent *adj* apparent
apparently *adv* apparemment
apparition *n* apparition
appeal *n* appel, charme
appeal *v* faire appel
appealing *adj* attirant

appear *v* apparaître
appearance *n* apparence
appease *v* appaiser
appeasement *n* appaisement
appendicitis *n* appendicite
appendix *n* appendice
appetite *n* appétit
appetizer *n* entrée
applaud *v* applaudir
applause *n* applaudissement
apple *n* pomme
appliance *n* électroménager
applicable *adj* applicable
applicant *n* applicant
application *n* candidature
apply *v* s'appliquer
apply for *v* postuler
appoint *v* nommer
appointment *n* nomination
appraisal *n* estimation
appraise *v* estimer
appreciate *v* apprécier
appreciation *n* remerciement
apprehend *v* appréhender
apprehensive *adj* appréhensif
apprentice *n* apprenti
approach *v* approcher
approach *n* approche
approachable *adj* abordable
approbation *n* approbation
appropriate *adj* approprié
approval *n* approbation

approve *v* approuver
approximate *adj* approximatif
apricot *n* abricot
April *n* avril
apron *n* tablier
aptitude *n* aptitude
aquarium *n* aquarium
aquatic *adj* aquatique
aqueduct *n* aqueduc
Arabic *adj* Arabique
arable *adj* arable
arbiter *n* arbitre
arbitrary *adj* arbitraire
arbitrate *v* arbitrer
arbitration *n* arbitrage
arc *n* arc
arch *n* arche
archaeology *n* archaéologie
archaic *adj* archaïque
archbishop *n* archevêque
architect *n* architecte
architecture *n* architecture
archive *n* archive
arctic *adj* arctique
ardent *adj* ardent
ardor *n* ardeur
arduous *adj* ardu
area *n* région
arena *n* arène, domaine
argue *v* discuter
argument *n* argument
arid *adj* aride

arise *iv* survenir
aristocracy *n* aristocracie
aristocrat *n* aristocrate
arithmetic *n* arithmétique
ark *n* arc
arm *n* arme
arm *v* armer
armaments *n* armements
armchair *n* fauteuil
armed *adj* armé
armistice *n* armistice
armor *n* armure
armpit *n* aisselle
army *n* armée
aromatic *adj* aromatique
around *pre* autour
arouse *v* éveiller, exciter
arrange *v* arranger
arrangement *n* arrangement
array *n* étalage
arrest *v* arrêter
arrest *n* arrestation
arrival *n* arrivée
arrive *v* arriver
arrogance *n* arrogance
arrogant *adj* arrogant
arrow *n* flèche
arsenal *n* arsenal
arsenic *n* arsenique
arson *n* incendie criminel
arsonist *n* pyromane
art *n* art

artery *n* artère
arthritis *n* arthrite
artichoke *n* artichaut
article *n* article
articulate *v* articuler
articulation *n* articulation
artificial *adj* artificiel
artillery *n* artillerie
artisan *n* artisant
artist *n* artiste
artistic *adj* artistique
artwork *n* œuvre d'art
as *c* comme
as *adv* aussi, autant
ascend *v* gravir
ascendancy *n* ascendance
ascertain *v* établir
ascetic *adj* ascétique
ash *n* cendre, frêne
ashamed *adj* honteux
ashore *adv* à terre
ashtray *n* cendrier
aside *adv* à part
aside from *adv* à part
ask *v* demander
asleep *adj* endormi
asparagus *n* asperge
aspect *n* aspect
asphalt *n* bitume
asphyxiate *v* asphyxier
asphyxiation *n* asphyxie
aspiration *n* aspiration

aspire v aspirer
aspirin n aspirine
assail v assaillir
assailant n assaillant
assassin n assassin
assassinate v assassiner
assassination n assassinat
assault n assaut
assault v assaillir
assemble v assembler
assembly n assemblée
assent v consentir
assert v affirmer
assertion n déclaration
assess v estimer, contrôler
assessment n contrôle
asset n atout
assets n bien
assign v assigner
assignment n devoir
assimilate v assimiler
assimilation n assimilation
assist v assister
assistance n assistance
associate v s'associer
association n association
assorted adj assorti
assortment n assortiment
assume v assumer
assumption n supposition
assurance n assurance
assure v assurer

asterisk n astérisque
asteroid n astéroïde
asthma n asthme
asthmatic adj asthmatique
astonish v étonner
astonishing adj étonnant
astound v stupéfier
astounding adj stupéfiant
astray v s'égarer
astrologer n astrologiste
astrology n astrologie
astronaut n astronaute
astronomer n astronome
astronomic adj astronomique
astronomy n astronomie
astute adj astucieux
asunder adv en pièces
asylum n asyle
at pre a
atheism n athéisme
atheist n athée
athlete n athlète
athletic adj athlètique
atmosphere n atmosphère
atmospheric adj atmosphèrique
atom n atome
atomic adj atomique
atone v expier
atonement n expiation
atrocious adj atroce
atrocity n atrocité
atrophy v atrophier

attach v attacher
attached adj attaché
attachment n attachment
attack n attaque
attack v attaquer
attacker n attaquant
attain v atteindre
attainable adj accessible
attainment n accomplissement
attempt v tenter
attempt n tentative
attend v assister
attendance n présence
attendant n gardien
attention n attention
attentive adj attentif
attenuate v attenué
attenuating adj attenuant
attest v attester
attic n grenier
attitude n comportement
attorney n avocat
attract v attirer
attraction n attraction
attractive adj séduisant
attribute v attribuer
auction n enchères
auctioneer n commissaire
audacious adj audacieux
audacity n audace
audible adj audible
audience n audience

audit v auditer
auditorium n auditorium
augment v augmenter
August n août
aunt n tante
auspicious adj prometteur
austere adj austère
austerity n austèrité
authentic adj authentique
authenticate v authentifier
authenticity n authenticité
author n auteur
authoritarian adj autoritaire
authority n autorité
authorization n autorisation
authorize v autoriser
auto n auto
autograph n autographe
automatic adj automatique
automobile n automobile
autonomous adj autonome
autonomy n autonomie
autopsy n autopsie
autumn n automne
auxiliary adj auxiliaire
avail v profiter
availability n disponibilité
available adj disponible
avalanche n avalanche
avarice n avarice
avaricious adj avare
avenge v venger

avenue *n* avenue
average *n* moyenne
averse *adj* inverse
aversion *n* aversion
avert *v* éviter
aviation *n* aviation
aviator *n* aviateur
avid *adj* avide
avoid *v* éviter
avoidable *adj* évitable
avoidance *n* évasion
avowed *adj* avoué
await *v* attendre
awake *iv* se reveiller
awake *adj* eveillé
awakening *n* reveil
award *v* attribuer
award *n* prix
aware *adj* conscient
awareness *n* conscience
away *adv* loin
awe *n* crainte
awesome *adj* grandiose
awful *adj* affreux
awning *n* auvent
ax *n* hache
axiom *n* axiome
axis *n* axe
axle *n* essieu

babble *v* babiller
baby *n* bébé
babysitter *n* babysitter
bachelor *n* célibataire, licence
back *n* dos
back *adv* de retour
back *v* soutenir
back down *v* reculer
back up *v* sauvegarder
backbone *n* colonne vertébrale
backdoor *n* porte de derrière
backfire *v* se retourner contre
background *n* milieu; arrière-plan
backing *n* soutien
backlash *n* réaction violente
backlog *n* réserve
backpack *n* sac à dos
backup *n* sauvegarde
backward *adj* arriéré
backwards *adv* en arrière
backyard *n* jardin
bacon *n* bacon
bacteria *n* bactérie
bad *adj* mauvais
badge *n* badge
badly *adv* mal, gravement
baffle *v* confondre
bag *n* sac
baggage *n* valise

baggy *adj* ample
baguette *n* baguette
bail *n* caution
bail out *v* dépanner
bailiff *n* huissier
bait *n* appât
bake *v* cuire au four
baker *n* boulanger
bakery *n* boulangerie
balance *v* balancer
balance *n* balance, équilbre
balcony *n* balcon
bald *adj* chauve
bale *n* balle
ball *n* ball, boule
balloon *n* montgolfière
ballot *n* scrutin
ballroom *n* salle de danse
balm *n* baume
balmy *adj* doux; dingue
bamboo *n* bambou
ban *n* interdiction
ban *v* bannir
banality *n* banalité
banana *n* banane
band *n* groupe; bandeau
bandage *n* bandage
bandage *v* bander
bandit *n* bandit
bang *v* heurter
banish *v* bannir
banishment *n* bannissement

bank *n* banque
bankrupt *v* faire faillite
bankrupt *adj* ruiné
bankruptcy *n* faillite
banner *n* banderole
banquet *n* banquet
baptism *n* baptême
baptize *v* baptiser
bar *n* bar; barre
bar *v* barrer
barbarian *n* barbare
barbaric *adj* barbarique
barbarism *n* barbarisme
barbecue *n* barbecue
barber *n* barbier
bare *adj* nu
barefoot *adj* pied nu
barely *adv* presque
bargain *n* bonne affaire
bargain *v* négocier
bargaining *n* négociation
barge *n* péniche
bark *v* écorce
bark *n* aboyer; s'écorcher
barley *n* orge
barmaid *n* serveuse
barman *n* serveur
barn *n* ferme
barometer *n* baromètre
barracks *n* caserne
barrage *n* barrage
barrel *n* tonneau

barren *adj* désertique; nu
barricade *n* barricade
barrier *n* barrière
barring *pre* à moins de
bartender *n* serveur
barter *v* troquer
base *n* base
base *v* baser
baseball *n* baseball
baseless *adj* sans fondement
basement *n* sous-sol
bashful *adj* pudique
basic *adj* élémentaire
basin *n* bol; bassin; lavabo
basis *n* base
bask *v* se dorer
basket *n* panier
basketball *n* basketball
bastard *n* bâtard
bat *n* chauve-souris; batte
batch *n* convoi, groupe
bath *n* bain
bathe *v* se baigner
bathrobe *n* robe de chambre
bathroom *n* salle de bains
bathtub *n* baignoire
baton *n* bâton
battalion *n* batalion
batter *v* frapper
battery *n* pile, batterie
battle *n* bataille
battle *v* batailler

battleship *n* cuirassé
bay *n* baie
bayonet *n* baïonnette
bazaar *n* bazar
be *iv* être, se trouver
be born *v* être né
beach *n* plage
beacon *n* balise
beak *n* bec
beam *n* rayon
bean *n* haricot
bear *n* ours
bear *iv* supporter, aller
bearable *adj* supportable
beard *n* barbe
bearded *adj* barbu
bearer *n* porteur
beast *n* bête
beat *iv* battre
beat *n* rythme; battement
beaten *adj* battu
beating *n* bastonnade
beautiful *adj* magnifique
beautify *v* embellir
beauty *n* beauté
beaver *n* castor
because *c* parce que
because of *pre* à cause de
beckon *v* dfaire signe
become *iv* devenir
bed *n* lit, fond
bedding *n* literie

bedroom *n* chambre
bedspread *n* dessus de lit
bee *n* abeille
beef *n* boeuf
beef up *v* renforcer
beehive *n* ruche
beer *n* bière
beet *n* betterave
beetle *n* scarabée
before *adv* avant
before *pre* avant
beforehand *adv* auparavant
befriend *v* se lier d'amitié
beg *v* mendier
beggar *n* mendiant
begin *iv* commencer
beginner *n* débutant
beginning *n* début
beguile *v* charmer
behalf (on) *adv* au nom de
behave *v* se comporter
behavior *n* comportement
behead *v* décapiter
behind *pre* derrière
behold *iv* voir
being *n* être
belated *adj* tardif
belch *v* vomir
belch *n* renvoi, rot
belfry *n* beffroi
Belgian *adj* Belge
Belgium *n* Belgique

belief *n* croyance
believable *adj* croyable
believe *v* croire
believer *n* croyant
belittle *v* rabaisser
bell *n* cloche; sonnette
bell pepper *n* poivron
belligerent *adj* belligérant
belly *n* ventre
belly button *n* nombril
belong *v* appartenir
belongings *n* effets personnels
beloved *adj* bien-aimé
below *adv* au dessous
below *pre* du dessous
belt *n* ceinture
bench *n* banc
bend *iv* tourner, plier
bend down *v* se pencher
beneath *pre* sous
benediction *n* bénédiction
benefactor *n* bienfaiteur
beneficial *adj* bénéfique
beneficiary *n* bénéficiaire
benefit *n* bénéfice
benefit *v* bénéficier
benevolence *n* bienveillance
benevolent *adj* bienveillant
benign *adj* bénin
bequeath *v* léguer
bereaved *adj* endeuillé
bereavement *n* deuil

B

beret *n* béret
berserk *adv* fou furieux
berth *n* couchette
beseech *iv* conjurer
beset *iv* assaillir
beside *pre* à côté de
besides *pre* de plus
besiege *iv* assiéger
best *adj* meilleur
best man *n* témoin
bestial *adj* bestial
bestiality *n* bestialité
bestow *v* accorder
bet *iv* parier
bet *n* pari
betray *v* trahir
betrayal *n* trahison
better *adj* améliorer
between *pre* entre
beverage *n* boisson
beware *v* attention!
bewilder *v* déconcerter
bewitch *v* ensorceler
beyond *adv* au-delà de
bias *n* penchant
bible *n* bible
biblical *adj* biblique
bibliography *n* bibliographie
bicycle *n* bicyclette
bid *n* enchère
bid *iv* enchèrir
big *adj* grand

bigamy *n* bigamie
bigot *adj* bigot
bigotry *n* bigoterie
bike *n* vélo; moto
bile *n* bile
bilingual *adj* bilingue
bill *n* facture; affiche
billiards *n* billiard
billion *n* millard
billionaire *n* millardaire
bimonthly *adj* bimestriel
bin *n* poubelle
bind *iv* attacher
binoculars *n* jumelles
biography *n* biographie
biological *adj* biologique
biology *n* biologie
bird *n* oiseau
birth *n* naissance
birthday *n* anniversaire
biscuit *n* biscuit
bishop *n* évêque
bison *n* bison
bit *n* morceau; un peu
bite *iv* mordre
bite *n* morsure
bitter *adj* amer
bitterly *adv* amèrement
bitterness *n* amertume
bizarre *adj* bizarre
black *adj* noir
blackberry *n* mûre

B

blackboard *n* tableau noir
blackmail *n* chantage
blackmail *v* faire du chantage
blackness *n* noirceur
blackout *n* panne de courrant
blacksmith *n* forgeron
bladder *n* vessie
blade *n* lame
blame *n* faute
blame *v* blâmer
blameless *adj* irréprochable
bland *adj* fade
blank *adj* vide
blanket *n* couverture
blaspheme *v* blasphémerer
blasphemy *n* blasphème
blast *n* explosion
blaze *v* brûler
bleach *v* décolorer
bleach *n* javel
bleak *adj* désolé
bleed *iv* saigner
bleeding *n* hémorragie
blemish *n* imperfection
blemish *v* ternir; souiller
blend *n* mélange
blend *v* mélanger
blender *n* mixeur
bless *v* bénir
blessed *adj* béni
blessing *n* bénidiction
blind *v* aveugler

blind *adj* aveugle
blindfold *n* bandeau
blindfold *v* bander les yeux
blindly *adv* aveuglément
blindness *n* cécité
blink *v* cligner
bliss *n* bonheur
blissful *adj* bienheureux
blister *n* ampoule
blizzard *n* blizzard
bloat *v* enfler
bloated *adj* enflé
block *n* bloc, cube
block *v* bloquer
blockade *v* bloquer
blockade *n* blocus
blockage *n* obstruction
blond *adj* blond
blood *n* sang
bloodthirsty *adj* sanguinaire
bloody *adj* sanglant
bloom *v* fleurir; s'épanouir
blossom *v* fleurir; s'épanouir
blot *n* tache
blot *v* tacher
blouse *n* blouse
blow *n* coup
blow *iv* souffler
blow out *iv* souffler
blow up *iv* exploser
blowout *n* crevaison
bludgeon *v* tuer

blue *adj* bleu; triste
blueprint *n* plan
bluff *v* bluffer
blunder *n* bourde
blunt *adj* émoussé; direct
blur *v* brouiller
blurred *adj* flou
blush *v* rougir
blush *n* blush
boar *n* sanglier
board *n* plache; panneau
board *v* monter à bord
boast *v* vantardise
boat *n* bateau
bodily *adj* corporel
body *n* corps, cadavre
bog *n* bourbier
bog down *v* s'embourber
boil *v* bouillir
boil down to *v* porter à ébullition
boil over *v* déborder
boiler *n* chaudière
boisterous *adj* chahuteur
bold *adj* vif, audacieux
boldness *n* audace
bolster *v* soutenir
bolt *n* verrou, boulon
bolt *v* engouffrer
bomb *n* bombe
bomb *v* bombarder
bombing *n* bombardement
bombshell *n* bombe

bond *n* lien, obligation
bondage *n* esclavage
bone *n* os
bone marrow *n* moelle
bonfire *n* feu de joie
bonus *n* bonus
book *n* livre
bookcase *n* bibliothèque
bookkeeper *n* comptable
bookkeeping *n* comptabilité
booklet *n* brochure
bookseller *n* libraire
bookstore *n* librairie
boom *n* détonation
boom *v* prospérer
boost *v* stimuler
boost *n* stimulation
boot *n* botte
booth *n* cabine
booty *n* butin
booze *n* alcool
border *n* frontière, bord
border on *v* border
borderline *adj* limite
bore *v* ennuyer
bored *adj* ennuyé
boredom *n* ennui
boring *adj* ennuyant
born *adj* né
borough *n* arrondissement
borrow *v* emprunter
bosom *n* poitrine

boss *n* patron
boss around *v* mener
bossy *adj* autoritaire
botany *n* botanie
botch *v* bâcler
both *adj* les deux
bother *v* embêter
bothersome *adj* embêtant
bottle *n* bouteille
bottle *v* embouteiller
bottleneck *n* embouteillage
bottom *n* dessous
bottomless *adj* sans fond
bough *n* branche maîtresse
boulder *n* roche
boulevard *n* boulevard
bounce *v* rebondir
bounce *n* rebondissement
bound *adj* lié
bound for *adj* en route
boundary *n* limite
boundless *adj* sans limite
bounty *n* récompense
bourgeois *adj* bourgeois
bow *n* arc; noeud
bow *v* saluer
bow out *v* tirer sa révérence
bowels *n* entrailles
bowl *n* bol, saladier
box *n* boite
box office *n* guichet
boxer *n* boxeur

boxing *n* boxe
boy *n* garçon
boycott *v* boycotter
boyfriend *n* petit ami
boyhood *n* enfance
bra *n* soutien gorge
brace for *v* se préparer
bracelet *n* bracelet
bracket *n* crochet
brag *v* se vanter
braid *n* natte
brain *n* cerveau
brake *n* frein
brake *v* freiner
branch *n* branche
branch out *v* se diversifier
brand *n* marque
brand-new *adj* nouveau
brandy *n* eau-de-vie
brat *n* marmot
brave *adj* brave
bravely *adv* bravement
bravery *n* bravoure
brawl *n* bagarre
breach *n* infraction
bread *n* pain
breadth *n* largeur
break *n* freins; pause
break *iv* se casser
break away *v* s'échaper
break down *v* s'effondrer
break free *v* se libérer

B

break in *v* dresser
break off *v* rompre
break open *v* enfoncer
break out *v* éclater
break up *v* rompre
breakable *adj* cassable
breakdown *n* panne
breakfast *n* petit déjeuner
breakthrough *n* percée
breast *n* sein
breath *n* respiration; haleine
breathe *v* respirer
breathing *n* respiration
breathtaking *adj* époustouflant
breed *iv* se reproduire
breed *n* race
breeze *n* brise
brethren *n* frères
brevity *n* brièveté
brew *v* brasser
brewery *n* brasserie
bribe *v* soudoyer
bribe *n* pot-de-vin
bribery *n* corruption
brick *n* brique
bricklayer *n* maçon
bridal *adj* nuptial
bride *n* mariée
bridegroom *n* marié
bridge *n* pont
bridle *n* bride
brief *adj* bref

brief *v* informer
briefcase *n* serviette
briefing *n* briefing
briefly *adv* brièvement
briefs *n* slip
brigade *n* brigade
bright *adj* vif
brighten *v* illuminer
brightness *n* clarté
brilliant *adj* brilliant
brim *n* bord
bring *iv* apporter
bring back *v* rapporter
bring down *v* réduire
bring up *v* élever, parler de
brink *n* bord
brisk *adj* vif
Britain *n* Grande Betagne
British *adj* Britanique
brittle *adj* fragile
broad *adj* large
broadcast *v* diffuser
broadcast *n* émission
broadcaster *n* animateur
broaden *v* élargir
broadly *adv* largement
broadminded *adj* large d'esprit
brochure *n* brochure
broil *v* griller
broiler *n* rôtissoire
broke *adj* fauché
broken *adj* cassé

bronchitis *n* bronchite
bronze *n* bronze
broom *n* balais
broth *n* bouillon
brothel *n* bordel
brother *n* frère
brotherhood *n* fraternité
brother-in-law *n* beau-frère
brotherly *adj* fraternel
brow *n* sourcil
brown *adj* brun
browse *v* parcourir
browser *n* navigateur
bruise *n* bleu
bruise *v* se faire un bleu
brunch *n* brunch
brunette *adj* brune
brush *n* brosse
brush *v* brosser
brush aside *v* repousser
brush up *v* se remettre à
brusque *adj* brusque
brutal *adj* brutal
brutality *n* brutalité
brutalize *v* brutaliser
brute *adj* simple
bubble *n* bulle
bubble gum *n* chewing gum
buck *n* dollar
bucket *n* seau
buckle *n* boucle
buckle up *v* boucler

bud *n* bourgeon, boutton
buddy *n* copain
budge *v* bouger
budget *n* budget
buffalo *n* buffle
bug *n* insecte
bug *v* embêter
build *iv* construire
builder *n* constructeur
building *n* immeuble
buildup *n* accumulation
built-in *adj* encastré
bulb *n* ampoule; buble
bulge *n* bosse; gonflement
bulk *n* essentiel; vrac
bulky *adj* encombrant
bull *n* taureau
bull fight *n* corrida
bull fighter *n* toréador
bullet *n* balle
bulletin *n* bulletin
bully *adj* tyran
bulwark *n* sabord
bum *n* derrière
bump *n* bosse; dos-d'âne
bump into *v* heurter
bumper *n* pare-chocs
bumpy *adj* irrégulier
bun *n* petit pain; chignon
bunch *n* groupe; régime
bundle *n* paquet; botte
bundle *v* empaqueter

bunk bed *n* lit superposé
bunker *n* fosse
buoy *n* balise
burden *n* fardeau
burden *v* encombrer
burdensome *adj* encombrant
bureau *n* bureau, commode
bureaucracy *n* bureaucratie
bureaucrat *n* bureaucrate
burger *n* hamburger
burglar *n* cambrioleur
burglarize *v* cambrioler
burglary *n* cambriolage
burial *n* enterrement
burly *adj* solide
burn *iv* brûler
burn *n* brûlure
burp *v* roter
burp *n* rot
burrow *n* terrier
burst *iv* exploser
burst into *v* faire irruption
bury *v* enterrer
bus *n* bus
bush *n* buisson
busily *adv* activement
business *n* commerce
bust *n* buste
bustling *adj* animé
busy *adj* occupé
but *c* mais
butcher *n* boucher

butchery *n* boucherie
butler *n* majordome
butt *n* fesses; coup
butter *n* beurre
butterfly *n* papillon
button *n* bouton
buttonhole *n* boutonnière
buy *iv* acheter
buy off *v* racheter
buyer *n* acheteur
buzz *n* bourdonnement
buzz *v* bourdonner
buzzard *n* buse
buzzer *n* sonnerie
by *pre* par
bye *e* au revoir
bypass *n* rocade
bypass *v* detourner
by-product *n* dérivé
bystander *n* passant

C

cab *n* taxi
cabbage *n* chou
cabin *n* cabane; chalet
cabinet *n* placard; vitrine
cable *n* cable
cafeteria *n* cafétéria
caffeine *n* caféine
cage *n* cage
cake *n* gâteau
calamity *n* calamité
calculate *v* calculer
calculation *n* calcul
calculator *n* calculatrice
calendar *n* calendrier
calf *n* veau
caliber *n* calibre
calibrate *v* calibrer
call *n* appel; cri
call *v* appeller; nommer
call off *v* annuler
call on *v* visiter
call out *v* appeller
calling *n* vocation
callous *adj* inhumain
calm *adj* calme
calm *n* calme
calm down *v* se calmer
calorie *n* calorie
calumny *n* calomnie

camel *n* chameau
camera *n* appareil photo
camouflage *v* camoufler
camouflage *n* camouflage
camp *n* camp
camp *v* camper
campaign *n* campagne
campfire *n* feu de camp
can *iv* pouvoir; savoir
can *v* mettre en conserve
can *n* boîte
can opener *n* ouvre boîte
canal *n* canal
canary *n* canarie
cancel *v* annuler
cancellation *n* annulation
cancer *n* cancer
cancerous *adj* cancereux
candid *adj* candide
candidacy *n* candidature
candidate *n* candidat
candle *n* bougie
candlestick *n* chandelier
candor *n* candeur
candy *n* bonbon
cane *n* canne; rotin
canned *adj* en boîte
cannibal *n* cannibale
cannon *n* canon
canoe *n* canoë
canonize *v* canoniser
cantaloupe *n* melon

C

canteen *n* gourde; cantine

canvas *n* canevas

canvas *v* canevaser

canyon *n* canyon

cap *n* casquette

capability *n* capabicité

capable *adj* capable

capacity *n* capacité

cape *n* cape; cap

capital *n* capitale

capital letter *n* lettre capitale

capitalism *n* capitalisme

capitalize *v* capitaliser

capitulate *v* capituler

capsize *v* chavirer

capsule *n* capsule

captain *n* capitaine

captivate *v* captiver

captive *n* captif

captivity *n* captivité

capture *v* capturer

capture *n* capture

car *n* voiture

carat *n* carat

caravan *n* caravane

carburetor *n* carburateur

carcass *n* carcasse

card *n* carte; fiche

cardboard *n* carton

cardiac *adj* cardiaque

cardiac arrest *n* arrêt cardiaque

cardiology *n* cardiologie

care *n* soin

care *v* se soucier

care about *v* se soucier

care for *v* s'occuper

career *n* carrière

carefree *adj* insouciant

careful *adj* prudent

careless *adj* négligent

carelessness *n* négligence

caress *n* caresse

caress *v* caresser

cargo *n* cargo

caricature *n* caricature

caring *adj* affectueux

carnage *n* carnage

carnal *adj* charnel

carnation *n* œillet

carol *n* chant de Noël

carpenter *n* menuisier

carpentry *n* menuiserie

carpet *n* moquette; tapis

carriage *n* chariot; carosse

carrot *n* carotte

carry *v* porter

carry on *v* continuer

carry out *v* effectuer

cart *n* charrette

cart *v* transporter

cartoon *n* dessin animé

cartridge *n* cartouche

carve *v* graver; couper

cascade *n* cascade

case *n* cas; valise
cash *n* liquide
cashier *n* caissier
casino *n* casino
casket *n* cerceuil
casserole *n* cocotte
cassock *n* soutane
cast *iv* jeter; lancer
castaway *n* naufragé
caste *n* caste
castle *n* chateau
casual *adj* décontracté
casualty *n* victime
cat *n* chat
cataclysm *n* cataclisme
catacomb *n* catacombe
catalog *n* catalogue
catalog *v* cataloguer
cataract *n* cataracte
catastrophe *n* catastrophe
catch *iv* s'accrocher
catch up *v* ratrapper
catching *adj* contagieux
catechism *n* catéchisme
category *n* catégorie
cater to *v* pourvoir
caterpillar *n* chenille
cathedral *n* cathédrale
catholic *adj* catholique
Catholicism *n* Catholicisme
cattle *n* troupeau
cauliflower *n* chou fleur

cause *n* cause
cause *v* causer
caution *n* prudence
cautious *adj* prudent
cavalry *n* cavalerie
cave *n* cave
cave in *v* s'effondrer; céder
cavern *n* caverne
cavity *n* cavité
cease *v* cesser
cease-fire *n* cessez-le-feu
ceaselessly *adv* sans cesse
ceiling *n* plafond
celebrate *v* célébrer
celebration *n* célébration
celebrity *n* célébrité
celery *n* céleri
celestial *adj* céleste
celibacy *n* célibat
celibate *adj* chaste
cellar *n* cave
cement *n* ciment
cemetery *n* cimetière
censorship *n* censure
censure *v* censurer
census *n* recensement
cent *n* centime
centenary *n* centenaire
center *n* centre
center *v* centrer
centimeter *n* centimètre
central *adj* centrale

C

C

centralize _v_ centraliser
century _n_ siècle
ceramic _n_ céramique
cereal _n_ céréale
cerebral _adj_ cérébrale
ceremony _n_ cérémonie
certain _adj_ certain
certainty _n_ certitude
certificate _n_ certificat
certify _v_ certifier
chagrin _n_ chagrin
chain _n_ chaine
chain _v_ enchainer
chainsaw _n_ tronçonneuse
chair _n_ chaise
chair _v_ présider
chairman _n_ président
chalet _n_ chalet
chalice _n_ calice
chalk _n_ craie
chalkboard _n_ tableau noir
challenge _v_ défier
challenge _n_ challenge; défi
chamber _n_ chambre; cabinet
champ _n_ champion
champion _n_ champion
champion _v_ déféndre
chance _n_ chance; occasion
chancellor _n_ chancelier
chandelier _n_ lustre
change _v_ changer
change _n_ changement

channel _n_ chaîne
chant _n_ chant scandé
chaos _n_ chaos
chaotic _adj_ chaotique
chapel _n_ chapel
chaplain _n_ chapelain
chapter _n_ chapitre
character _n_ caractère
characteristic _adj_ caractèristique
charade _n_ charade
charcoal _n_ charbon
charge _v_ facturer; inculper
charge _n_ frais; charge
charisma _n_ charisme
charismatic _adj_ charismatique
charitable _adj_ charitable
charity _n_ charité
charm _v_ charmer
charm _n_ charme
charming _adj_ charmant
chart _n_ tableau, graphique
charter _n_ charter; charte
charter _v_ affréter
chase _n_ poursuite
chase _v_ poursuivre
chase away _v_ poursuivre
chasm _n_ gouffre
chaste _adj_ chaste
chastise _v_ châtier
chastisement _n_ châtiment
chastity _n_ chasteté
chat _v_ discuter

chauffeur *n* chauffeur
cheap *adj* bon marché
cheat *v* tromper; tricher
cheater *n* tricheur
check *n* contrôle; chèque
check *v* contrôler
check in *v* enregistrer
check up *n* check-up
checkbook *n* chèquier
cheek *n* joue
cheekbone *n* pommette
cheeky *adj* effronté
cheer *v* acclamer
cheer up *v* égayer
cheerful *adj* gai
cheers *n* acclamation
cheese *n* fromage
chef *n* chef
chemical *adj* chimique
chemist *n* chimiste
chemistry *n* chimie
cherish *v* chérir
cherry *n* cerise
chess *n* échec
chest *n* poitrine, commode
chestnut *n* marron
chew *v* mastiquer
chick *n* poussin; nana
chicken *n* poulet
chicken out *v* se dégonfler
chicken pox *n* varicelle
chide *v* réprimander

chief *n* chef
chiefly *adv* surtout
child *n* enfant
childhood *n* enfance
childish *adj* enfantin
childless *adj* sans enfants
children *n* enfants
chill *n* fraîcheur, froid
chill *v* rafraîchir
chill out *v* décompresser
chilly *adj* froid
chimney *n* cheminée
chimpanzee *n* chimpanzé
chin *n* menton
chip *n* puce; fragement
chisel *n* ciseau
chocolate *n* chocolat
choice *n* choix
choir *n* chorale
choke *v* étrangler
cholera *n* choléra
cholesterol *n* choléstérole
choose *iv* choisir
choosy *adj* difficile
chop *v* couper
chop *n* côtelette
chopper *n* hélicopter
chore *n* tâche
chorus *n* chœur
christen *v* baptiser
christening *n* baptême
christian *adj* chrétien

Christianity *n* christianisme
Christmas *n* Noël
chronic *adj* chronique
chronicle *n* chronique
chronology *n* chronologie
chubby *adj* potelé
chuckle *v* glousser
chunk *n* morceau
church *n* église
chute *n* toboggan
cider *n* cidre
cigar *n* cigare
cigarette *n* cigarette
cinder *n* cendre
cinema *n* cinéma
cinnamon *n* cannelle
circle *n* cercle
circle *v* encercler
circuit *n* circuit
circular *adj* circulaire
circulate *v* circuler
circulation *n* circulation
circumcise *v* circonciser
circumcision *n* circoncision
circumstance *n* circonstance
circumstantial *adj* indirect
circus *n* cirque
cistern *n* citerne
citizen *n* citoyen
citizenship *n* citoyenneté
city *n* ville
city hall *n* mairie

civic *adj* civique
civil *adj* civil
civilization *n* civilisation
civilize *v* civiliser
claim *v* soutenir
claim *n* revendication
clam *n* palourde
clamor *v* réclamer
clamp *n* étau
clan *n* clan
clandestine *adj* clandestin
clap *v* applaudir
clarification *n* clarification
clarify *v* clarifier
clarinet *n* clarinette
clarity *n* clarté
clash *v* s'opposer
clash *n* affrontement
class *n* classe; cours
classic *adj* classique
classify *v* classifier
classmate *n* camarade de classe
classroom *n* salle de classe
classy *adj* élégant
clause *n* clause
claw *n* griffe
claw *v* griffe
clay *n* argile
clean *adj* propre
clean *v* nettoyer
cleanliness *n* propreté
cleanse *v* nettoyer

cleanser *n* nettoyant
clear *adj* claire; net
clear *v* effacer; évacuer
clearance *n* autorisation
clear-cut *adj* net
clearly *adv* clairement
clearness *n* clarté
cleft *n* fêlure
clemency *n* clémence
clench *v* serrer
clergy *n* clérgé
clergyman *n* ecclésiastique
clerical *adj* clérical
clerk *n* employé
clever *adj* intelligent
click *v* cliquer
client *n* client
clientele *n* clientèle
cliff *n* cliff
climate *n* climat
climatic *adj* climatique
climax *n* sommet
climb *v* escalader
climbing *n* escalade
clinch *v* river; décider
cling *iv* se cramponner
clinic *n* clinique
clip *v* accrocher
clipping *n* coupure
cloak *n* cape
clock *n* horloge
clog *v* engorger

cloister *n* cloître
clone *v* cloner
cloning *n* clonage
close *v* fermer
close *adj* proche
close to *pre* proche de
closed *adj* fermé
closely *adv* de près
closet *n* placard
closure *n* fermerutre
clot *n* caillot
cloth *n* tissu
clothe *v* vêtir
clothes *n* vêtements
clothing *n* vêtements
cloud *n* nuage
cloudy *adj* nuageux
clown *n* clown
club *n* club; discothèque
club *v* matraquer
clue *n* indice
clumsiness *n* maladresse
clumsy *adj* maladroit
cluster *n* grappe
clutch *n* embrayage
coach *v* entrainer; assister
coach *n* entraineur
coaching *n* entraînement
coagulate *v* coaguler
coagulation *n* coagulation
coal *n* charbon
coalition *n* coalition

coarse *adj* grossier; épais
coast *n* côte
coastal *adj* côtier
coastline *n* littoral
coat *n* manteau; couche
coax *v* cajoler
cob *n* cygne
cobblestone *n* pavé
cobweb *n* toile d'araignée
cocaine *n* cocaïne
cock *n* coq
cockpit *n* cockpit
cockroach *n* cafard
cocktail *n* cocktail
cocky *adj* impudent
cocoa *n* cacao
coconut *n* noix de coco
cod *n* morue
code *n* code; indicatif
codify *v* codifier
coefficient *n* coéfficient
coerce *v* forcer
coercion *n* coercition
coexist *v* coexister
coffee *n* café
coffin *n* cerceuil
cohabit *v* cohabiter
coherent *adj* cohérent
cohesion *n* cohésion
coin *n* monnaie
coincide *v* coincider
coincidence *n* coincidence

coincidental *adj* fortuit
cold *adj* froid
coldness *n* froideur
colic *n* colique
collaborate *v* collaborer
collaboration *n* collaboration
collaborator *n* collaborateur
collapse *v* collapser
collapse *n* effondrement
collar *n* col
collarbone *n* clavicule
collateral *adj* collatéral
colleague *n* collègue
collect *v* collectioner
collection *n* collection
collector *n* collecteur
college *n* université
collide *v* se heurter
collision *n* collision
cologne *n* eau-de-cologne
colon *n* côlon; deux-points
colonel *n* colonel
colonial *adj* colonial
colonization *n* colonisation
colonize *v* coloniser
colony *n* colonie
color *n* couleur
color *v* colorier; teinter
colorful *adj* coloré
colossal *adj* colossal
colt *n* poulain
column *n* colonne

coma *n* coma
comb *n* peigne
comb *v* peigner
combat *n* combat
combat *v* combattre
combatant *n* combatant
combination *n* combinaison
combine *v* combiner
combustible *n* combustible
combustion *n* combustion
come *iv* venir
come about *v* arriver
come across *v* passer
come apart *v* se casser
come back *v* revenir
come down *v* dscendre
come forward *v* s'avancer
come from *v* provenir
come in *v* entrer
come out *v* sortir
come over *v* passer
come up *v* soulever
comeback *n* come-back
comedian *n* comédien
comedy *n* comédie
comet *n* comète
comfort *n* confort
comfortable *adj* confortable
comforter *n* édredon
comical *adj* comique
coming *n* arrivée
coming *adj* porchain

comma *n* virgule
command *v* commander
commander *n* commandant
commandment *n* commandement
commemorate *v* commémorer
commence *v* commencer
commend *v* recommender
commendation *n* approbation
comment *v* commenter
comment *n* commentaire
commerce *n* commerce
commercial *adj* commercial
commission *n* commission
commit *v* commettre
commitment *n* engagement
committed *adj* engagé
committee *n* comité
common *adj* commun
commotion *n* vacarme
communicate *v* communiquer
communication *n* communication
communion *n* communion
communism *n* communisme
communist *adj* communiste
community *n* communauté
commute *v* échanger
compact *adj* compact
compact *v* comprimer
companion *n* companion
companionship *n* compagnie
company *n* compagnie
comparable *adj* comparable

C

comparative *adj* comparatif
compare *v* comparer
comparison *n* comparaison
compartment *n* compartiment
compass *n* boussole
compassion *n* compassion
compassionate *adj* compassioné
compatibility *n* compatibilité
compatible *adj* compatible
compatriot *n* compatriote
compel *v* obliger
compelling *adj* convaincant
compendium *n* recueil
compensate *v* compenser
compensation *n* compensation
compete *v* rivaliser
competence *n* compétence
competent *adj* compétent
competition *n* compétition
competitive *adj* compétitif
competitor *n* compétiteur
compile *v* établir
complain *v* se plaindre
complaint *n* plainte
complement *n* complément
complete *adj* complet
complete *v* complèter
completely *adv* complètement
completion *n* achèvement
complex *adj* compliqué
complexion *n* complexion
complexity *n* complexité

compliance *n* conformité
compliant *adj* conciliant
complicate *v* compliquer
complication *n* complication
complicity *n* complicité
compliment *n* compliment
complimentary *adj* flatteur; gratuit
comply *v* se conformer
component *n* composant
compose *v* composer
composed *adj* composé
composer *n* compositeur
composition *n* composition
compost *n* compost
composure *n* calme
compound *n* enceinte
compound *v* combiner
comprehend *v* comprendre
comprehensive *adj* compréhensif
compress *v* comprimer
compression *n* compression
comprise *v* comprendre
compromise *n* compromis
compromise *v* compromettre
compulsion *n* compulsion
compulsive *adj* compulsif
compulsory *adj* obligatoire
compute *v* calculer
computer *n* ordinateur
comrade *n* camarade
con man *n* escroc

conceal v dissimuler
concede v avouer
conceited adj fier
conceive v concevoir
concentrate v concentrer
concentration n concentration
concentric adj concentrique
concept n concept
conception n conception
concern v concerner
concern n inquiétude
concerning pre concernant
concert n concert
concession n concession
conciliate v concilier
conciliate adj conciliant
concise adj concis
conclude v conclure
conclusion n fin; conclusion
conclusive adj concluant
concoct v concocter
concoction n concoction
concrete n béton
concrete adj concret
concur v etre d'accord
concurrent adj concomitant
condemn v condamner
condemnation n condamnation
condensation n condensation
condense v condenser
condescend v daigner
condiment n condiment

condition n condition
conditional adj conditionel
conditioner n démêlant
condo n copropriété
condolences n condoléances
condone v tolérer
conducive adj favorable
conduct n conduite
conduct v conduire; mener
conductor n conducteur
cone n cone
confer v conférer
conference n conférence
confess v confesser
confession n confession
confessional n confessionnal
confessor n confesseur
confidant n confident
confide v confier
confidence n confiance
confident adj sûr; confiant
confidential adj confidentiel
confine v enfermer
confinement n détention
confirm v confirmer
confirmation n confirmation
confiscate v confiscate
confiscation n exploit
conflict n conflit
conflicting adj contradictoire
conform v conformer
conformist adj conformiste**

conformity *n* conformité
confound *v* confondre
confront *v* confronter
confrontation *n* confrontation
confuse *v* confondre
confusing *adj* déroutant
confusion *n* confusion
congenial *adj* congenial
congested *adj* congestionné
congestion *n* congestion
congratulate *v* féliciter
congratulations *n* félicitations
congregate *v* se rassembler
congregation *n* congrégation
congress *n* congrès
conjecture *n* spéculation
conjugal *adj* conjugal
conjugate *v* conjuger
conjunction *n* conjonction
conjure up *v* évoquer
connect *v* connecter
connection *n* connection
connote *v* connoter
conquer *v* conquérir
conqueror *n* conquérant
conquest *n* conquête
conscience *n* conscience
conscious *adj* consciencieux
consciousness *n* conscience
conscript *n* conscrit
consecrate *v* consacrer
consecration *n* consécration

consecutive *adj* consécutif
consensus *n* consensus
consent *v* consentir
consent *n* consentement
consequence *n* conséquence
consequent *adj* conséquent
conservation *n* conservation
conservative *adj* conservateur
conserve *v* conserver
conserve *n* confiture
consider *v* considérer
considerable *adj* considérable
considerate *adj* considér
consideration *n* attention
consignment *n* livraison
consist *v* consister
consistency *n* consistance
consistent *adj* régulier; conforme
consolation *n* consolation
console *v* consoler
consolidate *v* consolider
consonant *n* consomne
conspicuous *adj* flagrant
conspiracy *n* conspiration
conspirator *n* conspirateur
conspire *v* conspirer
constancy *n* constance
constant *adj* constancy
constellation *n* constellation
consternation *n* consternation
constipate *v* constiper
constipated *adj* constipé**

constipation n constipation
constitute v constituer
constitution n constitution
constrain v contraindre
constraint n contrainte
construct v construire
construction n construction
constructive adj constructif
consul n consul
consulate n consulat
consult v consulter
consultation n consultation
consume v consommer
consumer n consommateur
consumption n consommation
contact v contacter
contact n contact
contagious adj contagieux
contain v contenir
container n récipient
contaminate v contaminer
contamination n contamination
contemplate v contempler
contemporary adj contemporain
contempt n mépris
contend v disputer; soutenir
contender n concurrent
content adj satisfait
content v contenter
contentious adj conflictuel
contents n contenu
contest n concours; lutte

contestant n concurrent
context n contexte
continent n continent
continental adj continental
contingency n contingence
contingent adj contigent
continuation n continuation
continue v continuer
continuity n continuité
continuous adj continu
contour n contour
contraband n contrebande
contract v contracter
contract n contrat
contraction n contraction
contradict v contredire
contradiction n contradiction
contrary adj contraire
contrast v contraster
contrast n contraste
contribute v contribuer
contribution n contribution
contributor n contribuable
contrition n contrition
control n contrôle
control v contrôler
controversial adj controversé
controversy n controverse
convalescent adj convalescent
convene v convenir
convenience n commodité
convenient adj commode

C

convent *n* couvent
convention *n* convention
conventional *adj* conventionnel
converge *v* converger
conversation *n* conversation
converse *v* converser
conversely *adv* inversement
conversion *n* conversion
convert *v* convertir
convert *n* converti
convey *v* transmettre
conviction *n* conviction
convince *v* convaincre
convincing *adj* convainquant
convoluted *adj* tortueux
convoy *n* convoi
convulse *v* convulser
convulsion *n* convulsion
cook *v* cuisiner
cook *n* cuisinier
cookie *n* gateau sec
cooking *n* cuisine
cool *adj* cool; frais
cool *v* rafraîchir
cool down *v* refroidir
cooling *adj* refroidissement
coolness *n* fraîcheur
cooperate *v* coopérer
cooperation *n* collaboration
cooperative *adj* coopérative
coordinate *v* coordiner
coordination *n* coordination

coordinator *n* coordinateur
cop *n* policier
cope *v* surmonter
copier *n* photocopieuse
copper *n* cuivre
copy *v* copier
copy *n* copie
copyright *n* droit d'auteur
cord *n* corde; fil
cordial *adj* cordial
cordless *adj* sans fil
cordon *n* cordon
cordon off *v* boucler
core *n* centre
cork *n* liège
corn *n* maïs
corner *n* coin; virage
cornerstone *n* base
cornet *n* cornet
corollary *n* corollaire
coronary *adj* coronaire
coronation *n* couronnement
corporal *adj* corporel
corporal *n* caporal
corporation *n* société
corpse *n* cadavre
corpulent *adj* corpulent
corpuscle *n* corpuscle
correct *v* corriger
correct *adj* correct
correction *n* correction
correlate *v* corréler

correspond *v* correspondre
correspondent *n* correspondant
corresponding *adj* correspondant
corridor *n* corridor
corroborate *v* corroborer
corrode *v* corroder
corrupt *v* corrompre
corrupt *adj* corrompu
corruption *n* corruption
cosmetic *n* cosmétique
cosmic *adj* cosmique
cosmonaut *n* cosmonaute
cost *iv* couter
cost *n* cout
costly *adj* couteux
costume *n* costume
cottage *n* villa
cotton *n* coton
couch *n* canapé
cough *n* toux
cough *v* tousser
council *n* comité; conseil
counsel *v* conseiller
counsel *n* avocat; conseil
counselor *n* conseiller
count *v* compter
count *n* compte; total
countdown *n* décompte
countenance *n* contenance
counter *n* comptoir
counter *v* parer; riposter
counteract *v* contrecarrer

counterfeit *v* contrefaire
counterfeit *adj* contredfait
counterpart *n* homologue
countess *n* comtesse
countless *adj* incalculable
country *n* pays; campagne
countryman *n* compatriote
countryside *n* campagne
county *n* comté
coup *n* coup
couple *n* couple; deux
coupon *n* coupon
courage *n* courage
courageous *adj* courageux
courier *n* coursier
course *n* cours; plat
court *n* tribunal; cour
court *v* coutiser
courteous *adj* courtois
courtesy *n* coutoisie
courthouse *n* cour
courtship *n* cour
courtyard *n* cour
cousin *n* cousin
cove *n* avise
covenant *n* alliance
cover *n* couverture
cover *v* couvrir; fermer
cover up *v* dissimuler
coverage *n* couverture
covert *adj* secret
covet *v* lorgner

C

cow *n* vache
coward *n* lâche
cowardice *n* lâcheté
cowardly *adv* pereux
cowboy *n* cowboy
cozy *adj* douillet
crab *n* crabe
crack *n* fissure
crack *v* craquer; fendre
cradle *n* berceau
craft *n* artisanat; art
craftsman *n* artisan
cram *v* entasser
cramp *n* crampe
cramped *adj* exigu
crane *n* crane
crank *n* manivelle
cranky *adj* grincheux
crap *n* foutaises; merde
crappy *adj* minable
crash *n* fracas; accident
crash *v* s'écraser
crass *adj* grossier
crater *n* cratère
craving *n* envie
crawl *v* ramper
crayon *n* crayon
craziness *n* folie
crazy *adj* fou
creak *v* grincer
creak *n* grincement
cream *n* crème

creamy *adj* crèmeux
crease *n* pli; ride
crease *v* froisser
create *v* créer
creation *n* création
creative *adj* créatif
creativity *n* créativité
creator *n* créateur
creature *n* créature
credibility *n* crédibilité
credible *adj* crédible
credit *n* crédit
creditor *n* créditeur
creed *n* foi
creek *n* crique
creep *v* se glisser
creepy *adj* flippant
cremate *v* incinérer
crematorium *n* crématorium
crest *n* crête
crevice *n* fissure
crew *n* équipage
crib *n* berceau
cricket *n* grillon; cricket
crime *n* crime
criminal *adj* criminel
cripple *v* estropier
crisis *n* crise
crisp *adj* croustillant
crispy *adj* croustillant
criss-cross *v* croiser
criterion *n* critère**

critical *adj* crucial; critique
criticism *n* critique
criticize *v* critiquer
critique *n* critique
crockery *n* vaisselle
crocodile *n* crocodile
crony *n* copain
crook *n* escroc
crooked *adj* malhonnête
crop *n* récolte
cross *n* croix
cross *adj* opposé
cross *v* traverser
cross out *v* rayer
crossfire *n* feu croisé
crossing *n* traverse
crossroads *n* carrefour
crosswalk *n* passage couté
crossword *n* mots croisés
crouch *v* s'accroupir
crow *n* corneille
crow *v* exulter
crowbar *n* pied-de-biche
crowd *n* foule
crowd *v* entasser
crowded *adj* bondé
crown *n* courronne
crown *v* courronner
crowning *n* courronnement
crucial *adj* crucial
crucifix *n* crucifix
crucifixion *n* crucifixion

crucify *v* crucifier
crude *adj* vulgaire
cruel *adj* cruel
cruelty *n* cruauté
cruise *v* rouler
crumb *n* miette
crumble *v* émietter
crunchy *adj* croquant
crusade *n* croisade
crusader *n* croisé
crush *v* écraser
crushing *adj* écrasant
crust *n* croûte; culot
crusty *adj* craquant
crutch *n* béquille
cry *n* cri
cry *v* pleurer
cry out *v* s'écrier
crying *n* pleurs
crystal *n* cristal
cub *n* ourson
cube *n* cube
cubic *adj* cubique
cucumber *n* concombre
cuddle *v* câliner
cuff *n* menotte; revers
cuisine *n* cuisine
culminate *v* culminer
culpability *n* culpabilité
culprit *n* coupable
cult *n* culte
cultivate *v* cultiver

C

C

cultivation *n* culture
cultural *adj* culturel
culture *n* culture
cumbersome *adj* encombrant
cunning *adj* rusé
cup *n* tasse
cupboard *n* placard
curable *adj* curable
curator *n* conservateur
curb *v* courber
curb *n* trottoir
curdle *v* cailler
cure *v* guérir
cure *n* cure
curfew *n* couvre-feu
curiosity *n* curiosité
curious *adj* curieux
curl *v* boucler
curl *n* boucle
curly *adj* bouclé
currency *n* monnaie
current *adj* actuel
currently *adv* actuellement
curse *v* maudire
curtail *v* comprimer
curtain *n* rideau
curve *n* courbe
curve *v* courber
cushion *n* coussin
cushion *v* amortir
cuss *v* jurer
custodian *n* gardien

custody *n* détention
custom *n* coutume
customary *adj* habituel
customer *n* client
custom-made *adj* sur mesure
customs *n* douane
cut *n* coupure
cut *iv* couper
cut back *v* diminuer
cut down *v* réduire
cut off *v* couper
cut out *v* découper
cute *adj* mignon
cutlery *n* couverts
cutter *n* cutter
cyanide *n* cyanure
cycle *n* cycle
cyclist *n* cycliste
cyclone *n* cyclone
cylinder *n* cylindre
cynic *adj* cynique
cynicism *n* cynicisme
cypress *n* cyprès
cyst *n* kyste
czar *n* tsar

dad *n* papa
dagger *n* poignard
daily *adv* quotidien
daisy *n* marguerite
dam *n* barrage
damage *n* dégâts
damage *v* endommager
damaging *adj* nuisible
damn *v* maudire
damnation *n* damnation
damp *adj* humide
dampen *v* humecter; amortir
dance *n* danse
dance *v* danser
dancing *n* danse
dandruff *n* pellicules
danger *n* danger
dangerous *adj* dangereux
dangle *v* pendre
dare *v* défier
dare *n* défi
daring *adj* osé
dark *adj* foncé
darken *v* obscurcir
darkness *n* obscurité
darling *adj* chéri
darn *v* repriser
dart *n* fléchette
dash *v* se précipiter

dashing *adj* superbe
data *n* données
date *n* date; rendez-vous
date *v* sortir; dater
daughter *n* fille
daughter-in-law *n* belle-fille
daunt *v* décourager
daunting *adj* décourageant
dawn *n* aube
day *n* jour
daydream *v* rêvasser
daze *v* abasourdir
dazed *adj* abasourdi
dazzle *v* éblouir
dazzling *adj* éblouissant
de luxe *adj* luxurieux
deacon *n* diacre
dead *adj* mort
dead end *n* impasse
deaden *v* calmer
deadline *n* délai
deadly *adj* mortel
deaf *adj* sourd
deafen *v* assourdir
deafening *adj* assourdissant
deafness *n* surdité
deal *iv* traiter
deal *n* affaire
dealer *n* marchant
dealings *n* vente
dean *n* doyen
dear *adj* cher

death *n* mort
death toll *n* nombre de mort
deathbed *n* lit de mort
debase *v* profaner
debatable *adj* discutable
debate *v* débattre
debate *n* débat
debit *n* débit
debrief *v* débriefer
debris *n* débris
debt *n* dette
debtor *n* débiteur
debunk *v* déboulonner
debut *n* début
decade *n* décennie
decadence *n* décadence
decapitate *v* décapiter
decay *v* pourrir
decay *n* carie
deceased *adj* décédé
deceit *n* malhonnêteté
deceitful *adj* malhonnête
deceive *v* tromper
December *n* décembre
decency *n* politesse
decent *adj* convenable
deception *n* déception
deceptive *adj* trompeur
decide *v* décider
deciding *adj* décisif
decimal *adj* décimal
decimate *v* déciminer

decipher *v* déchiffrer
decision *n* décision
decisive *adj* décisif
deck *n* terrasse
declaration *n* déclaration
declare *v* déclarer
declension *n* déclinaison
decline *v* décliner
decline *n* clin
decompose *v* composer
décor *n* décor
decorate *v* décorer
decorative *adj* décoratif
decorum *n* décorum
decrease *v* diminuer
decrease *n* diminution
decree *n* décret
decree *v* décréter
decrepit *adj* décrépit
dedicate *v* dédicacer
dedication *n* dévouement
deduce *v* déduire
deduct *v* déduire
deductible *adj* déductible
deduction *n* déduction
deed *n* acte
deem *v* estimer; juger
deep *adj* profond
deepen *v* approfondir
deer *n* daim
deface *v* abîmer; enlaidir
defame *v* diffamer

defeat v battre
defeat n défaite
defect n défaut
defection n renonciation
defective adj défectueux
defend v défendre
defendant n accusé
defender n défenseur
defense n défense
defenseless adj sans défense
defer v remettre
defiant adj provocant
deficiency n insuffisance
deficient adj déficient
deficit n déficit
defile v tacher
define v définir
definite adj défini
definition n définition
definitive adj définitif
deflate v dégonfler
deform v déformer
deformity n déformité
defraud v arnaquer
defray v défrayer
defrost v décongeler
deft adj adroit
defuse v désamorcer
defy v défier
degenerate v dégénérer
degenerate adj dégénéré
degeneration n décadence

degradation n déchéance
degrade v dégrader
degrading adj dégradant
degree n degré; diplome
dehydrate v déshydrater
deign v daigner
deity n divinité
dejected adj découragé
delay v retarder
delay n délai
delegate v déléguer
delegate n délégué
delegation n délégation
delete v supprimer
deliberate v délibérer
deliberate adj délibéré
delicacy n gourmandise
delicate adj délicat
delicious adj délicieux
delight n plaisir
delight v ravir
delightful adj charmant
delinquency n délinquance
delinquent adj délinquant
deliver v livrer
delivery n livraison
delude v tromper
deluge n déluge
delusion n illusion
demand v demander
demand n demande
demanding adj exigeant

demean _v_ rabaisser
demeaning _adj_ humiliant
demeanor _n_ comportement
demented _adj_ dément
demise _n_ mort
democracy _n_ démocratie
democratic _adj_ démocratique
demolish _v_ démolir
demolition _n_ démolition
demon _n_ démon
demonstrate _v_ démontrer
demonstrative _adj_ démonstratif
demoralize _v_ démoraliser
demote _v_ rétrograder
den _n_ antre
denial _n_ dénégation
denigrate _v_ dénigrer
Denmark _n_ Danemark
denominator _n_ dénominateur
denote _v_ annoncer
denounce _v_ dénoncer
dense _adj_ dense; épais
density _n_ densité
dent _v_ cabosser
dent _n_ bosse
dental _adj_ dentaire
dentist _n_ dentiste
dentures _n_ dentier
deny _v_ démentir
deodorant _n_ déodorant
depart _v_ partir
department _n_ département

departure _n_ départ
depend _v_ dépendre
dependable _adj_ fiable
dependence _n_ dépendance
dependent _adj_ dépendant
depict _v_ représenter
deplete _v_ réduire
deplorable _adj_ déplorable
deplore _v_ déplorer
deploy _v_ déployer
deployment _n_ déploiement
deport _v_ déporter
deportation _n_ déportation
depose _v_ déposer
deposit _n_ dépôt
depot _n_ dépôt; gare
deprave _adj_ dépraver
depravity _n_ dépravation
depreciate _v_ déprécier
depreciation _n_ dépréciation
depress _v_ déprimer
depressing _adj_ déprimant
depression _n_ dépression
deprivation _n_ privation
deprive _v_ priver
deprived _adj_ privé
depth _n_ profondeur
derail _v_ dérailler
derailment _n_ déraillement
deranged _adj_ dérangé
derelict _adj_ délabré
derivative _adj_ dérivatif

derive _v_ dériver; provenir
derogatory _adj_ désobligeant
descend _v_ descendre
descendant _n_ descendant
descent _n_ origine
describe _v_ décrire
description _n_ description
descriptive _adj_ descriptif
desecrate _v_ profaner
desert _n_ désert
desert _v_ déserter
deserted _adj_ désert
deserter _n_ déserteur
deserve _v_ mériter
deserving _adj_ méritant
design _n_ motif; ébauche
designate _v_ désigner
desirable _adj_ désirable
desire _n_ désir
desire _v_ désirer
desist _v_ désister
desk _n_ bureau; réception
desolate _adj_ désoler
desolation _n_ désolation
despair _n_ désespoir
desperate _adj_ désespoir
despicable _adj_ désespéré
despise _v_ mépriser
despite _c_ malgré
despondent _adj_ abattu
despot _n_ despote
despotic _adj_ despotique

dessert _n_ dessert
destination _n_ destination
destiny _n_ destin
destitute _adj_ démuni
destroy _v_ détruire
destroyer _n_ croiseur
destruction _n_ destruction
destructive _adj_ destructif
detach _v_ détacher
detachable _adj_ détachable
detail _n_ détail
detail _v_ énumérer
detain _v_ retenir
detect _v_ détecter
detective _n_ détective
detector _n_ détecteur
detention _n_ détention
deter _v_ dissuader
detergent _n_ détergent
deteriorate _v_ détériorer
deterioration _n_ détérioration
determination _n_ détérmination
determine _v_ détérminer
deterrence _n_ dissuasion
detest _v_ détester
detestable _adj_ détestable
detonate _v_ exploser
detonation _n_ détonation
detonator _n_ détonateur
detour _n_ détour
detriment _n_ détriment
detrimental _adj_ nuisible

D

devaluation *n* dévaluation
devalue *v* dévaluer
devastate *v* dévaster
devastating *adj* ravageur
devastation *n* dévastation
develop *v* développer
development *n* développement
deviation *n* déviation
device *n* appareil
devil *n* diable
devious *adj* sournois
devise *v* concevoir
devoid *adj* vide
devote *v* consacrer
devotion *n* dévouement
devour *v* dévorer
devout *adj* pieux
dew *n* rosée
diabetes *n* diabète
diabetic *adj* diabètique
diabolical *adj* diabolique
diagnose *v* diagnostiquer
diagnosis *n* diagnostic
diagonal *adj* diagonal
diagram *n* diagramme
dial *n* cadran
dial *v* composer
dial tone *n* tonalité
dialect *n* dialecte
dialogue *n* dialogue
diameter *n* diamètre
diamond *n* diamant

diaper *n* couche
diarrhea *n* diarrhée
diary *n* journal intime
dice *n* dé
dictate *v* dicter
dictator *n* dictateur
dictatorial *adj* dictatorial
dictatorship *n* dictature
dictionary *n* dictionnaire
die *v* mourir
die out *v* disparaître
diet *n* régime
differ *v* différer
difference *n* différence
different *adj* différent
difficult *adj* difficile
difficulty *n* difficulté
diffuse *v* diffuser
dig *iv* creuser
digest *v* digérer
digestion *n* digestion
digestive *adj* digestif
digit *n* chiffre
dignify *v* dignifier
dignitary *n* dignitaire
dignity *n* dignité
digress *v* divaguer
dilapidated *adj* dilapidé
dilemma *n* dilemme
diligence *n* diligence
diligent *adj* diligent
dilute *v* diluer

dim *adj* sombre
dim *v* baisser
dime *n* piece de 10 cents
dimension *n* dimension
diminish *v* dimininuer
dine *v* dîner
diner *n* diner
dining room *n* salle à manger
dinner *n* dîner
dinosaur *n* dinosaure
diocese *n* diocèse
diploma *n* diplôme
diplomacy *n* diplomatie
diplomat *n* diplomate
diplomatic *adj* diplomatique
dire *adj* affreux
direct *adj* direct
direct *v* diriger
direction *n* direction
director *n* directeur
directory *n* annuaire
dirt *n* saleté
dirty *adj* sale
disability *n* infirmité
disabled *adj* infirme
disadvantage *n* désavantage
disagree *v* diverger
disagreeable *adj* désagréable
disagreement *n* désaccord
disappear *v* disparaître
disappearance *n* disparition
disappoint *v* décevoir

disappointing *adj* décevant
disappointment *n* déception
disapproval *n* désapprobation
disapprove *v* désapprouver
disarm *v* désarmer
disarmament *n* désarmement
disaster *n* désastre
disastrous *adj* désastreux
disband *v* dissoudre
disbelief *n* incrédulité
disburse *v* débourser
discard *v* jeter
discern *v* discerner
discharge *v* décharger
discharge *n* décharge
disciple *n* disciple
discipline *n* discipline
disclaim *v* nier
disclose *v* révéler
discomfort *n* gêne
disconnect *v* déconnecter
discontent *adj* mécontent
discontinue *v* discontinuer
discord *n* discorde
discordant *adj* discordant
discount *n* rabais
discount *v* solder
discourage *v* décourager
discouragement *n* découragement
discouraging *adj* décourageant
discover *v* découvrir
discovery *n* découverte

discredit v discréditer
discreet adj discret
discrepancy n divergence
discretion n discrétion
discriminate v discriminer
discrimination n discrimination
discuss v discuter
discussion n discussion
disdain n dédain
disease n maladie
disembark v débarquer
disenchanted adj désenchanté
disentangle v démêler
disfigure v défigurer
disgrace n disgrâce
disgrace v déshonorer
disgraceful adj honteux
disgruntled adj renfrogné
disguise v déguiser
disguise n déguisement
disgust n dégoût
disgusting adj dégoûtant
dish n plat
dishearten v démoraliser
dishonest adj maladie
dishonesty n malhonnêteté
dishonor n honte
dishonorable adj déshonorer
dishwasher n lave-vaisselle
disillusion n désillusion
disinfect v désinfecter
disinfectant n désinfectant

disintegrate v désintégrer
disintegration n désintégration
disinterested adj désintéressé
disk n disquette
dislike n aversion
dislocate v disloquer
dislodge v déplacer
disloyal adj déloyal
disloyalty n déloyauté
dismal adj lugubre
dismantle v démonter
dismay n consternation
dismay v consterner
dismiss v exclure
dismissal n exclusion
dismount v désarçonner
disobedience n désobéissance
disobedient adj désobéissan
disobey v désobéir
disorder n désordre
disorganized adj désorganisé
disoriented adj désorienté
disown v déshériter
disparity n disparité
dispatch v expédier
dispel v chasser
dispensation n dérogation
dispense v dispenser
dispersal n dispersion
disperse v disperser
displace v déplacer
display n étalage

display v exposer
displease v déplaire
displeasing adj déplaisant
displeasure n ennui
disposable adj jetable
disposal n poubelle
dispose v disposer
disprove v disprove
dispute n argument
dispute v argumenter
disqualify v disqualifier
disregard v négliger
disrepair n dégradation
disrespect n irrespect
disrespectful adj irrespectueux
disrupt v pertuber
disruption n perturbation
dissatisfied adj mécontent
disseminate v disséminer
dissident v dissidence
dissident adj dissident
dissimilar adj dissemblable
dissipate v dissiper
dissolute adj dissolu
dissolution n dissolution
dissolve v dissoudre
dissonant adj dissonant
dissuade v dissuader
distance n distance
distant adj distant
distaste n dégoût
distasteful adj dégoûtant

distill v distiller
distinct adj distinct
distinction n distinction
distinctive adj distinctif
distinguish v différencier
distort v déformer
distortion n déformation
distract v distraire
distraction n distraction
distraught adj éperdu
distress n détresse
distress v affliger
distressing adj affligeant
distribute v distribuer
distribution n distribution
district n district
distrust n méfiance
distrust v se méfier
distrustful adj méfiant
disturb v déranger
disturbance n perturbation
disturbing adj perturbant
disunity n désunion
disuse n désuétude
ditch n fossé
dive v plonger
diver n plongeur
diverse adj divers
diversify v diversifier
diversion n diversion
diversity n diversité
divert v détourner

divide *v* diviser

dividend *n* dividence

divine *adj* divin

diving *n* plongeon

divinity *n* divinité

divisible *adj* divisible

division *n* division

divorce *n* divorce

divorce *v* divorcer

divorcee *n* divorcée

divulge *v* divulger

dizziness *n* vertiges

dizzy *adj* étourdi

do *iv* faire

docile *adj* docile

docility *n* docilité

dock *n* appontement

dock *v* amarrer

doctor *n* docteur

doctrine *n* doctrine

document *n* document

dodge *v* éviter

dog *n* chien

dogmatic *adj* dogmatique

doll *n* poupée

dollar *n* dollar

dolphin *n* dauphin

dome *n* dome

domestic *adj* domestique

domesticate *v* domestiquer

dominate *v* dominer

domination *n* domination

domineering *adj* dominant

dominion *n* dominion

donate *v* léguer

donation *n* donation

donkey *n* âne

donor *n* donneur

doom *n* perte

doomed *adj* condamné

door *n* porte

doorbell *n* sonnette

doorstep *n* pas de porte

doorway *n* seuil

dope *n* drogue

dope *v* doper

dormitory *n* dortoire

dosage *n* dose

dossier *n* dossier

dot *n* point

double *adj* double

double *v* doubler

double-check *v* revérifier

double-cross *v* doubler

doubt *n* doute

doubt *v* douter

doubtful *adl* douteux

dough *n* pâte

dove *n* colombe

down *adv* en bas

downcast *adj* abattu

downfall *n* ruine

downhill *adv* descente

downpour *n* averse

downsize _v_ réduire
downstairs _adv_ en bas
down-to-earth _adj_ pratique
downtown _n_ centre-ville
downtrodden _adj_ tyrannisé
downturn _n_ déclin
dowry _n_ dot
doze _v_ assoupir
dozen _n_ douzaine
draft _n_ courant d'air
draft _v_ ébaucher
draftsman _n_ dessinateur
drag _v_ traîner
dragon _n_ dragon
drain _v_ égoutter
drainage _n_ égout
dramatic _adj_ dramatique
dramatize _v_ dramatiser
drape _n_ rideau
drastic _adj_ drastique
draw _n_ sort, attraction
draw _iv_ dessiner, attirer
drawback _n_ inconvénient
drawer _n_ tiroir
drawing _n_ dessin
dread _v_ redouter
dreaded _adj_ redoutable
dreadful _adj_ affreux
dream _iv_ rêver
dream _n_ rêve
dress _n_ robe
dress _v_ s'habiller

dresser _n_ commode
dressing _n_ dressing
dried _adj_ sec
drift _v_ dériver
drift apart _v_ se perdre de vue
drill _v_ percer; fraiser
drill _n_ foret; exercice
drink _iv_ boire
drink _n_ boisson
drinkable _adj_ buvable
drinker _n_ buveur
drip _v_ dégouliner
drip _n_ goutte
drive _n_ conduite; trajet
drive _iv_ conduire
drive at _v_ conduire
drive away _v_ chasser
driver _n_ conducteur
driveway _n_ allée de garage
drizzle _v_ bruiner
drizzle _n_ crachin
drop _n_ goutte; baisse
drop _v_ faire tomber
drop in _v_ passer
drop out _v_ abandonner
drought _n_ sécheresse
drown _v_ noyer
drowsy _adj_ endormi
drug _n_ drogue
drug _v_ droguer
drugstore _n_ pharmacie
drum _n_ tambour; baril

drunk *adj* soul
drunkenness *n* ivresse
dry *v* sécher
dry *adj* sec
dryclean *v* nettoyer à sec
dryer *n* séchoir
dual *adj* double
dubious *adj* douteux
duchess *n* duchesse
duck *n* canard
duck *v* baisser; plonger
duct *n* conduit
due *adj* dû
duel *n* duel
dues *n* cotisation
duke *n* duc
dull *adj* ennuyeux
duly *adv* dûment
dumb *adj* idiot; muet
dummy *n* mannequin
dummy *adj* idiot
dump *v* jeter
dump *n* décharge
dung *n* fumier
dungeon *n* donjon
dupe *v* duper
duplicate *v* reproduire
duplication *n* reproduction
durable *adj* durable
duration *n* durée
during *pre* pendant; durant
dusk *n* crépuscule

dust *n* poussière
dusty *adj* poussièreux
Dutch *adj* Néerlandais
duty *n* devoir
dwarf *n* nain
dwell *iv* habiter
dwelling *n* habitation
dwindle *v* diminuer
dye *v* teindre
dye *n* teinture
dying *adj* mourant
dynamic *adj* dynamique
dynamite *n* dynastie

each *adj* chaque
each other *adj* l'un l'autre
eager *adj* enthousiaste
eagerness *n* enthousiasme
eagle *n* aigle
ear *n* oreille; épis
earache *n* otite
eardrum *n* tambour
early *adv* tôt
earmark *v* désigner
earn *v* gagner
earnestly *adv* sérieusement

E

earnings *n* salaire
earphones *n* écouteurs
earring *n* boucle d'oreille.
earth *n* terre
earthquake *n* tremblement
earwax *n* cérumen
ease *v* faciliter
ease *n* facilité
easily *adv* facilement
east *n* est
eastbound *adj* direction est
Easter *n* Pâques
eastern *adj* de l'est
eastward *adv* vers l'est
easy *adj* facile
eat *iv* manger
eat away *v* ronger
eavesdrop *v* espionner
ebb *v* décliner, refluer
eccentric *adj* eccentrique
echo *n* écho
eclipse *n* éclipse
ecology *n* écologie
economical *adj* économique
economize *v* économiser
economy *n* économie
ecstasy *n* extase
ecstatic *adj* exalté
edge *n* bord
edgy *adj* énervé
edible *adj* comestible
edifice *n* édifice

edit *v* éditer
edition *n* édition
educate *v* éduquer
educational *adj* éducatif
eerie *adj* étrange
effect *n* effet
effective *adj* effective
effectiveness *n* efficacité
efficiency *n* efficacité
efficient *adj* efficace
effigy *n* effigie
effort *n* effort
effusive *adj* démonstratif
egg *n* oeuf
egg white *n* blanc d'oeuf
egoism *n* égoïsme
egoist *n* égoïste
eight *adj* huit
eighteen *adj* dix-huit
eighth *adj* huitième
eighty *adj* quantre-vingt
either *adj* chaque
either *adv* non plus
eject *v* éjecter
elapse *v* s'écouler
elastic *adj* élastique
elated *adj* jubilant
elbow *n* coude
elder *n* ancien
elderly *adj* âgé
elect *v* élir
election *n* élection

electric *adj* électrique
electrician *n* électricien
electricity *n* électricité
electrify *v* électrifier
electrocute *v* électrocuter
electronic *adj* électronique
elegance *n* élégance
elegant *adj* élégant
element *n* élément
elementary *adj* élémentaire
elephant *n* éléphant
elevate *v* élever
elevation *n* élévation
elevator *n* ascenceur
eleven *adj* onze
eleventh *adj* onzième
eligible *adj* éligible
eliminate *v* élimiter
elm *n* orme
eloquence *n* éloquence
else *adv* d'autre
elsewhere *adv* ailleurs
elude *v* éluder
elusive *adj* élusive
emaciated *adj* émacié
emanate *v* émaner
emancipate *v* émanciper
embalm *v* embaumer
embark *v* embarquer
embarrass *v* étreinte
embassy *n* embassade
embellish *v* embellir

embers *n* braises
embezzle *v* détourner
embitter *v* aigrir
emblem *n* emblème
embody *v* incarner
emboss *v* graufrer
embrace *v* étreindre
embrace *n* étreinte
embroider *v* broder
embroidery *n* broderie
embroil *v* mêler
embryo *n* embryon
emerald *n* émeraude
emerge *v* emerger
emergency *n* urgence
emigrant *n* émigrant
emigrate *v* émigrer
emission *n* émission
emit *v* émettre
emotion *n* émotion
emotional *adj* émotionel
emperor *n* empereur
emphasis *n* accent
emphasize *v* souligner
empire *n* empire
employ *v* employer
employee *n* employé
employer *n* employeur
employment *n* emploi
empress *n* impératrice
emptiness *n* vide
empty *adj* vide

empty *v* vider
enable *v* permettre
enchant *v* enchanter
enchanting *adj* enchanteur
encircle *v* encercler
enclave *n* enclave
enclosure *n* clôture
encompass *v* englober
encounter *v* rencontrer
encounter *n* rencontre
encourage *v* encourager
encroach *v* empiéter
encyclopedia *n* encyclopédie
end *n* fin
end *v* finir
end up *v* terminer
endanger *v* compromettre
endeavor *v* tenter
endeavor *n* tentative
ending *n* fin
endless *adj* sans fin
endorse *v* endosser
endorsement *n* endossement
endure *v* endurer
enemy *n* ennemi
energetic *adj* énergique
energy *n* énergie
enforce *v* appliquer, imposer
engage *v* engager
engaged *adj* engagé; fiancé
engagement *n* fiançailles
engine *n* moteur

engineer *n* ingénieur
England *n* Angleterre
English *adj* Anglais
engrave *v* graver
engraving *n* gravure
engrossed *adj* rédiger
engulf *v* engloutir; avaler
enhance *v* améliorer
enjoy *v* apprécier
enjoyable *adj* appréciable
enjoyment *n* plaisir
enlarge *v* élargir
enlargement *n* élargissement
enlighten *v* illuminer
enlist *v* engager
enormous *adj* énorme
enough *adv* assez
enrage *v* enrager
enrich *v* enrichir
enroll *v* s'inscrire
enrollment *n* inscription
ensure *v* assurer
entail *v* impliquer
entangle *v* enchevêtrer
enter *v* entrer
enterprise *n* enterprise
entertain *v* divertir
entertaining *adj* divertissant
entertainment *n* divertissement
enthrall *v* passionner
enthralling *adj* passionnant
enthuse *v* enthousiasmer

enthusiasm _n_ enthousiasme
entice _v_ attirer
enticement _n_ tentation
enticing _adj_ tentant
entire _adj_ entier
entirely _adv_ entièrement
entrance _n_ entrée
entreat _v_ requérir
entree _n_ plat principal
entrenched _adj_ établi
entrepreneur _n_ entrepreneur
entrust _v_ confier
entry _n_ entrée
enumerate _v_ enumérer
envelop _v_ envelopper
envelope _n_ enveloppe
envious _adj_ envieux
environment _n_ environnement
envisage _v_ envisager
envoy _n_ envoyé
envy _n_ envie
envy _v_ envier
epidemic _n_ épidémie
epilepsy _n_ épilepsie
episode _n_ épisode
epistle _n_ épître
epitaph _n_ épitaphe
epitomize _v_ incarner
epoch _n_ époque
equal _adj_ égal
equality _n_ égalité
equate _v_ assimiler

equation _n_ équation
equator _n_ équateur
equilibrium _n_ équilibre
equip _v_ équipe
equipment _n_ équipement
equivalent _adj_ équivalent
era _n_ ère
eradicate _v_ éradiquer
erase _v_ effacer
eraser _n_ effaceur
erect _v_ ériger
erect _adj_ droit
err _v_ se tromper
errand _n_ commission
erroneous _adj_ erroné
error _n_ erreur
erupt _v_ apparaître
eruption _n_ éruption
escalate _v_ escalader
escalator _n_ escalier roulant
escapade _n_ escapade
escape _v_ échapper
escape _n_ évasion
esophagus _n_ œsophage
especially _adv_ surtout
espionage _n_ espionage
essay _n_ essai
essence _n_ essence
essential _adj_ essentiel
establish _v_ établir
estate _n_ propriété
esteem _v_ estime

estimate *v* estimer
estimation *n* estimation
estranged *adj* séparé
estuary *n* estuaire
eternity *n* éternité
ethical *adj* ethique
ethics *n* moralité
etiquette *n* bienséance
euphoria *n* euphorie
Europe *n* Europe
European *adj* Européen
evacuate *v* évacuer
evade *v* évader
evaluate *v* évaluer
evaporate *v* évaporer
evasion *n* évasion
evasive *adj* évasif
eve *n* veil
even *adj* égal
even if *c* même si
even more *c* encore plus
evening *n* soirée
event *n* événement
eventuality *n* éventualité
eventually *adv* finalement
ever *adv* jamais
everlasting *adj* éternel
every *adj* chaque
everybody *pro* tout le monde
everyday *adj* tous les jours
everyone *pro* tout le monde
everything *pro* tout

evict *v* expulser
evidence *n* évidence
evil *n* mal
evil *adj* diabolique
evoke *v* évoquer
evolution *n* évolution
evolve *v* évoluer
exact *adj* exact
exaggerate *v* exagérer
exalt *v* exalter
examination *n* examination
examine *v* examiner
example *n* exemple
exasperate *v* exasperer
excavate *v* fouiller
exceed *v* surpasser
exceedingly *adv* extrêmement
excel *v* exceller
excellence *n* excellence
excellent *adj* excellent
except *pre* sauf
exception *n* exception
exceptional *adj* exceptionae
excerpt *n* extrait
excess *n* excès
excessive *adj* excessif
exchange *v* échanger
excite *v* exciter
excitement *n* excitation
exciting *adj* excitant
exclaim *v* exclamer
exclude *v* exclure**

E

excruciating *adj* atroce
excursion *n* excursion
excuse *v* excuser
excuse *n* excuse
execute *v* exécuter
executive *n* cadre
exemplary *adj* exemplaire
exemplify *v* exemplifier
exempt *adj* exempt
exemption *n* exemption
exercise *n* exercice
exercise *v* exercer
exert *v* exercer
exertion *n* effort
exhaust *v* épuiser
exhausting *adj* épuisant
exhaustion *n* épuisement
exhibit *v* exposer
exhibition *n* exposition
exhilarating *adj* exaltant
exhort *v* exhorter
exile *v* exiler
exile *n* exile
exist *v* exister
existence *n* existence
exit *n* sortie
exodus *n* exode
exonerate *v* exonérer
exorbitant *adj* exorbitant
exorcist *n* exorciste
exotic *adj* exotique
expand *v* étendre

expansion *n* expansion
expect *v* penser; attendre
expectancy *n* espérance
expectation *n* attente
expediency *n* opportunité
expedient *adj* expédient
expedition *n* expédition
expel *v* expulser
expenditure *n* dépense
expense *n* dépense
expensive *adj* cher
experience *n* expérience
experiment *n* expérience
expert *adj* expert
expiate *v* expier
expiation *n* expiation
expiration *n* expiration
expire *v* expirer
explain *v* expliquer
explicit *adj* explicite
explode *v* exploser
exploit *v* exploiter
exploit *n* exploit
explore *v* explorer
explorer *n* explorateur
explosion *n* explosion
explosive *adj* explosif
export *v* exporter
expose *v* exposer
exposed *adj* exposé
express *adj* rapide; exprès
express *v* exprimer

expression n expression
expressly adv expressément
expropriate v exproprier
expulsion n expulsion
exquisite adj exquis
extend v étendre
extension n extension
extent n étendue
extenuating adj atténuante
exterior adj extérieur
exterminate v exterminer
external adj externe
extinct adj disparu
extinguish v éteindre
extort v extorquer
extortion n extortion
extra adv extra
extract v extraire
extradite v extrader
extradition n extradition
extraneous adj étranger
extravagance n extravagance
extravagant adj extravagant
extreme adj extrême
extremist adj extrémiste
extremities n extrémités
extricate v se dépêtrer
extroverted adj extroverti
exude v exsuder
exult v exulter
eye n oeil
eyebrow n sourcil

eye-catching adj attrayant
eyeglasses n lunettes
eyelash n cil
eyelid n paupière
eyesight n vue
eyewitness n témoin oculaire

fable n fable
fabric n tissu
fabricate v fabriquer
fabulous adj fabuleux
face n visage
face up to v faire face
facet n facette; aspect
facilitate v faciliter
fact n fait
factor n facteur
factory n usine
factual adj factuel
faculty n faculté
fad n mode
fade v estomper
faded adj défraîchi
fail v échouer
failure n échec
faint v s'évanouir

faint *adj* faible
fair *n* foire
fair *adj* juste; pâle
fairness *n* équité
fairy *n* fée
faith *n* croyance
faithful *adj* fidèle
fake *v* falsifier
fake *adj* faux
fall *n* chute; automne
fall *iv* tomber
fall back *v* reculer
fall behind *v* être en retard
fall down *v* tomber
fall through *v* échouer
fallacy *n* erreur
fallout *n* retombées
falsehood *n* mensonge
falsify *v* falsifier
falter *v* défaillir
fame *n* renommée
familiar *adj* familier
family *n* famille
famine *n* famine
famous *adj* célèbre
fan *n* fan; ventilateur
fanatic *adj* fanatique
fancy *adj* sophistiqué
fang *n* crochet
fantastic *adj* fantastique
fantasy *n* fantasie
far *adv* loin

faraway *adj* lointain
farce *n* farce
fare *n* prix
farewell *n* adieu
farm *n* ferme
farmer *n* fermier
farming *n* exploitation
farmyard *n* cour de ferme
farther *adv* plus loin
fascinate *v* fasciner
fashion *n* mode
fashionable *adj* à la mode
fast *adj* rapide
fasten *v* attacher
fat *n* graisse
fat *adj* gros
fatal *adj* fatal
fate *n* sort
fateful *adj* fatidique
father *n* père
fatherhood *n* paternité
father-in-law *n* beau-père
fatherly *adj* paternel
fathom out *v* comprendre
fatigue *n* fatigue
fatten *v* engraisser
fatty *adj* graisseux
faucet *n* robinet
fault *n* faute
faulty *adj* défectueux
favor *n* service
favorable *adj* favorable

favorite *adj* favori
fear *n* peur
fearful *adj* craintif
feasible *adj* faisable
feast *n* fête
feat *n* exploitation
feather *n* plume
feature *n* caractéristique
February *n* février
fed up *adj* en avoir marre
federal *adj* fédéral
fee *n* frais
feeble *adj* faible
feed *iv* nourrir
feedback *n* évaluations
feel *iv* se sentir
feeling *n* sentiment
feelings *n* sentiments
feet *n* pied
feign *v* feindre
fellow *n* homme
felon *n* criminel
felony *n* crime
female *n* femelle; femme
feminine *adj* féminin
fence *n* clôture
fencing *n* escrime
fend *v* résister
fend off *v* repousser
fender *n* aile
ferment *v* fermenter
ferment *n* ferment

ferocious *adj* féroce
ferocity *n* férocité
ferry *n* ferry
fertile *adj* fertile
fertility *n* fertilité
fertilize *v* fertiliser
fervent *adj* fervent
fester *v* suppurer
festive *adj* festif
festivity *n* festivité
fetid *adj* fétide
fetus *n* foetus
feud *n* querelle
fever *n* fièvre
feverish *adj* fièvrieux
few *adj* quelque
fewer *adj* moins de
fiancé *n* fiancé
fiber *n* fibre
fickle *adj* inconstant
fiction *n* fiction
fictitious *adj* fictif
fiddle *n* violon
fidelity *n* fidélité
field *n* terrain
fierce *adj* féroce
fiery *adj* fougueux
fifteen *adj* quinze
fifth *adj* cinquième
fifty *adj* cinquante
fig *n* figue
fight *iv* se battre

F

fight _n_ bataille
fighter _n_ combattant
figure _n_ silhouette
figure out _v_ comprendre
file _v_ classer; limer
file _n_ lime; dossier
fill _v_ remplir
filling _n_ farce
film _n_ film
filter _n_ filtre
filter _v_ filtrer
filth _n_ crasse
filthy _adj_ crasseux
fin _n_ nageoire
final _adj_ final
finalize _v_ finaliser
finance _v_ finance
financial _adj_ financier
find _iv_ trouver
find out _v_ découvrir
fine _n_ amende
fine _adv_ bien
fine _adj_ fin
fine print _n_ petits caractères
finger _n_ doigt
fingernail _n_ ongle
fingerprint _n_ empreinte
fingertip _n_ bout du doigt
finish _v_ finir
Finland _n_ Finlande
Finnish _adj_ Finnois
fire _v_ allumer; licencier

fire _n_ feu
firearm _n_ arme à feu
firecracker _n_ pétard
firefighter _n_ pompier
fireman _n_ pompier
fireplace _n_ cheminée
firewood _n_ bois de chauffage
fireworks _n_ feu d'artifice
firm _adj_ ferme
firm _n_ entreprise
firmness _n_ fermeté
first _adj_ premier
fish _n_ poisson
fisherman _n_ pêcheur
fishy _adj_ suspect
fist _n_ poing
fit _n_ crise
fit _v_ tenir
fitness _n_ forme
fitting _adj_ adéquat
five _adj_ cinq
fix _v_ réparer
fjord _n_ fiord
flag _n_ drapeau
flagpole _n_ mât
flamboyant _adj_ flamboyant
flame _n_ flame
flammable _adj_ inflammable
flank _n_ flanc
flare _n_ balise
flare-up _v_ explosion
flash _n_ flash

flashlight _n_ lampe de poche
flashy _adj_ tape-à-l'œil
flat _n_ appartement
flat _adj_ plat
flatten _v_ aplatir
flatter _v_ flatter
flattery _n_ flatterie
flaunt _v_ étaler
flavor _n_ goût
flaw _n_ défaut
flawless _adj_ sans défaut
flea _n_ puce
flee _iv_ fuir
fleece _n_ toison
fleet _n_ flotte
fleeting _adj_ bref
flesh _n_ chair
flex _v_ fléchir
flexible _adj_ flexible
flicker _v_ clignoter
flier _n_ prospectus; pilote
flight _n_ vol; fuite
flimsy _adj_ léger
flip _v_ basculer
flirt _v_ flirter
float _v_ floter
flock _n_ troupeau
flog _v_ flageller
flood _v_ inonder
floodgate _n_ vanne
flooding _n_ inondation
floodlight _n_ projecteur

floor _n_ par terre
flop _n_ fiasco
floss _n_ fil dentaire
flour _n_ farine
flourish _v_ prospérer
flow _v_ couler
flow _n_ écoulement
flower _n_ fleur
flowerpot _n_ pot de fleur
flu _n_ grippe
fluctuate _v_ fluctuer
fluently _adv_ couramment
fluid _n_ fluide
flunk _v_ rater
flush _v_ rougir
flute _n_ flûte
flutter _v_ battre
fly _iv_ voler
fly _n_ vol
foam _n_ mousse
focus _n_ centre
focus on _v_ se concentrer
foe _n_ ennemi
fog _n_ brouillard
foggy _adj_ brumeux
foil _v_ papier d'aluminium
fold _v_ plier
folder _n_ chemise
folks _n_ parent
folksy _adj_ campagnard
follow _v_ suivre
follower _n_ disciple

F

folly *n* folie
fond *adj* affectueux; naïf
fondle *v* caresser
fondness *n* penchant
food *n* nourriture
foodstuff *n* denrée
fool *v* duper
fool *adj* idiot
foolproof *adj* infaillible
foot *n* pied
football *n* football
footprint *n* empreinte
footstep *n* pas
footwear *n* chaussures
for *pre* pour
forbid *iv* interdire
force *n* force
force *v* forcer
forceful *adj* ferme
forcibly *adv* fermement
forecast *iv* météo
forefront *n* avant
foreground *n* premier plan
forehead *n* front
foreign *adj* étranger, inconnu
foreigner *n* étranger
foreman *n* contremaître
foremost *adj* premier
foresee *iv* anticiper
foreshadow *v* prédire
foresight *n* prévoyance
forest *n* forêt

foretaste *n* avant-goût
foretell *v* prédire
forever *adv* toujours
forewarn *v* avertir
foreword *n* avant-propos
forfeit *v* déclarer forfait
forge *v* forger
forgery *n* falsification
forget *v* oublier
forgivable *adj* pardonnable
forgive *v* pardonner
forgiveness *n* pardon
fork *n* fouchette
form *n* forme
formal *adj* formel
formality *n* formalité
formalize *v* formaliser
formally *adv* formellement
format *n* format
formation *n* formation
former *adj* ex
formerly *adv* autrefois
formidable *adj* formidable
formula *n* formule
forsake *iv* abandonner
fort *n* fort
forthcoming *adj* futur
forthright *adj* direct
fortify *v* fortifier
fortitude *n* courage
fortress *n* forteresse
fortunate *adj* fortuné

fortune *n* fortune
forty *adj* quarante
forward *adv* avancer
fossil *n* fossile
foster *v* promouvoir
foul *adj* fétide
foundation *n* fondation
founder *n* fondateur
foundry *n* fonderie
fountain *n* fontaine
four *adj* quatre
fourteen *adj* quatorze
fourth *adj* quatrième
fox *n* renard
foxy *adj* sexy; rusé
fraction *n* fraction
fracture *n* fracture
fragile *adj* fragile
fragment *n* fragment
fragrance *n* parfum
fragrant *adj* odorant
frail *adj* fragile
frailty *n* fragilité
frame *n* cadre; corps
frame *v* encadrer
framework *n* structure; plan
France *n* France
franchise *n* chaine de magasin
frank *adj* franc
frankly *adv* franchement
frankness *n* franchise
frantic *adj* frénétique

fraternal *adj* fraternel
fraternity *n* fraternité
fraud *n* fraude
fraudulent *adj* fraudulent
freckle *n* tache de rousseur
free *v* libérer
free *adj* gratuit; libre
freedom *n* liberté
freeway *n* autoroute
freeze *iv* congeler
freezer *n* congélateur
freezing *adj* gelé
freight *n* transport
French *adj* français
frenetic *adj* frénétique
frenzied *adj* frénétique
frenzy *n* frénésie
frequency *n* fréquence
frequent *adj* fréquent
frequent *v* fréquenter
fresh *adj* frais
freshen *v* rafraîchir
freshness *n* fraîcheur
friar *n* moine
friction *n* friction
Friday *n* vendredi
fried *adj* fri
friend *n* ami
friendship *n* amitié
fries *n* frites
frigate *n* frégate
fright *n* peur

F

frighten *v* effrayer
frightening *adj* effrayant
frigid *adj* frigide
fringe *n* frange; périphérie
frivolous *adj* frivole
frog *n* grenouille
from *pre* de
front *n* devant; façade
front *adj* premier
frontage *n* devanture
frontier *n* frontière
frost *n* gel
frostbite *n* engelures
frostbitten *adj* gelé
frosty *adj* glacial
frown *v* froncer
frozen *adj* gelé
frugal *adj* frugal
frugality *n* frugalité
fruit *n* fruit
fruitful *adj* fructueux
fruity *adj* fruité
frustrate *v* frustrer
frustration *n* frustration
fry *v* fri
frying pan *n* poêle
fuel *n* carburant
fuel *v* alimenter
fugitive *n* fugitif
fulfill *v* accomlir
full *adj* rempli
fully *adv* entièrement

fumes *n* vapeurs
fumigate *v* fumer
fun *n* amusement
function *n* fonction
fund *n* fonds
fund *v* fonder
fundamental *adj* fondamental
funds *n* fonds
funeral *n* funérailles
fungus *n* champignon
funny *adj* drôle
fur *n* fourrure
furious *adj* furieux
furiously *adv* furieusement
furnace *n* fourneau
furnish *v* fournir
furnishings *n* meubles
furniture *n* meuble
furor *n* fureur
furrow *n* sillon
furry *adj* duveteux
further *adv* plus loin
furthermore *adv* de plus
fury *n* fureur
fuse *n* fusible
fusion *n* fusion
fuss *n* remue-ménage
fussy *adj* délicat
futile *adj* futile
futility *n* futilité
future *n* futur
fuzzy *adj* crépu

G

gadget *n* gadget

gag *n* blague; bâillon

gag *v* bâilloner

gage *v* mesurer

gain *v* gagner

gain *n* gain

gal *n* fille

galaxy *n* galaxie

gale *n* tempête

gall bladder *n* vésicule biliaire

gallant *adj* gallant

gallery *n* galerie

gallon *n* galon

gallop *v* galop

gallows *n* gibet

galvanize *v* galvaniser

gamble *v* parier

game *n* jeu

gang *n* bande

gangrene *n* gangrène

gangster *n* gangster

gap *n* trou; silence

garage *n* garage

garbage *n* poubelle

garden *n* jardin

gardener *n* jardinier

gargle *v* gargariser

garland *n* guirlande

garlic *n* ail

garment *n* vêtement

garnish *v* garnir

garnish *n* garniture

garrison *n* garnison

garrulous *adj* bavard

garter *n* jarretière

gas *n* essence; gaz

gash *n* entaille

gasoline *n* essence

gasp *v* haleter

gastric *adj* gastrique

gate *n* porte

gather *v* se réunir

gathering *n* réunion

gauge *v* calibrer

gauze *n* gaze

gaze *v* fixer

gear *n* matériel

gem *n* pierre précieuse

gender *n* genre

gene *n* gène

general *n* général

generalize *v* généraliser

generate *v* générer

generation *n* génération

generator *n* générateur

generic *adj* générique

generosity *n* générosité

genetic *adj* génétique

genial *adj* génial

genius *n* génie

genocide *n* génocide

G

genteel *adj* cultivé
gentle *adj* doux
gentleman *n* gentleman
gentleness *n* douceur
genuine *adj* authentique
geography *n* géographie
geology *n* géologie
geometry *n* géométrie
germ *n* germe
German *adj* allemand
Germany *n* Allemagne
germinate *v* germer
gerund *n* gérondif
gestation *n* gestation
gesticulate *v* gesticuler
gesture *n* geste
get *iv* devenir
get along *v* bien s'entendre
get away *v* s'échapper
get back *v* rentrer
get by *v* passer
get down *v* descendre
get down to *v* descendre
get in *v* entrer
get off *v* descendre
get out *v* sortir
get over *v* traverser
get together *v* se réunir
get up *v* se lever
geyser *n* geyser
ghastly *adj* horrible
ghost *n* fantôme

giant *n* géant
gift *n* cadeau
gifted *adj* doué
gigantic *adj* gigantesque
giggle *v* ricaner
gimmick *n* truc
ginger *n* gingembre
gingerly *adv* délicat
giraffe *n* girafe
girl *n* fille
girlfriend *n* petite amie
give *iv* donner
give away *v* donner
give back *v* redonner
give in *v* céder
give out *v* s'épuiser
give up *v* renoncer
glacier *n* glacier
glad *adj* content
gladiator *n* gladiateur
glamorous *adj* fascinant
glance *v* jeter un coup d'oeil
glance *n* coup d'oeil
gland *n* glande
glare *n* éclat
glass *n* verre
glasses *n* lunettes
gleam *n* lueur
gleam *v* luire
glide *v* planer
glimmer *n* lueur
glimpse *n* coup d'oeil

G

glimpse *v* entrevoir
glitter *v* paillette
globe *n* globe
globule *n* globule
gloom *n* morosité
gloomy *adj* morose
glorify *v* glorifier
glorious *adj* glorieux
glory *n* gloire
gloss *n* lustre
glossary *n* glossaire
glossy *adj* brillant
glove *n* gant
glow *v* luire; rayonner
glucose *n* glucose
glue *n* colle
glue *v* coller
glut *n* excès
glutton *n* glouton
gnaw *v* ronger
go *iv* aller
go ahead *v* commencer
go away *v* partir
go back *v* retourner
go down *v* descendre
go in *v* entrer
go on *v* continuer
go out *v* sortir
go over *v* aller; vérifier
go through *v* réaliser
go under *v* couler
go up *v* monter

goad *v* aiguillonner
goal *n* but; objectif
goalkeeper *n* gardien
goat *n* chèvre
gobble *v* engloutir
God *n* Dieu
goddess *n* déesse
godless *adj* impie
goggles *n* jumelles
gold *n* or
golden *adj* doré
good *adj* bon
good-looking *adj* beau
goodness *n* bonté
goods *n* biens
goodwill *n* bonne volonté
goof *v* gaffer
goof *n* gaffe
goose *n* oie
gorge *n* gorge
gorgeous *adj* superbe
gorilla *n* gorille
gory *adj* sanglant
gospel *n* gospel
gossip *v* ragoter
gossip *n* ragot
gout *n* goutte
govern *v* gouverner
government *n* gouvernement
governor *n* gouverneur
gown *n* robe de soirée
grab *v* saisir

G

grace *n* grâce
graceful *adj* gracieux
gracious *adj* bienveillant
grade *n* note
gradual *adj* graduel
graduate *n* diplômé
graduation *n* remise des diplômes
graft *v* greffer
graft *n* greffe
grain *n* grain
gram *n* gramme
grammar *n* grammaire
grand *adj* grandiose
grandchild *n* petit-enfant
granddad *n* grand-papa
grandfather *n* grand-père
grandmother *n* grand-mère
grandparents *n* grand-parents
grandson *n* petit-fils
grandstand *n* tribune
granite *n* granite
granny *n* mémé
grant *v* accorder
grant *n* bourse
grape *n* raisin
grapefruit *n* pamplemousse
grapevine *n* feuille de vigne
graphic *adj* graphique
grasp *n* maîtrise ; prise
grasp *v* saisir; comprendre
grass *n* herbe

grassroots *adj* populaire
grateful *adj* reconnaissant
gratify *v* gratifier
gratifying *adj* gratifiant
gratitude *n* gratitude
gratuity *n* pourboire
grave *n* sérieux
gravel *n* gravier
gravely *adv* sérieux
gravestone *adj* tombe
gravestone *n* tombe
graveyard *n* cimetière
gravitate *v* graviter
gravity *n* gravité
gravy *n* sauce
gray *adj* gris
grayish *adj* grisâtre
graze *v* picorer; effleurer
graze *n* écorchure
grease *v* graisser
grease *n* graisse
greasy *adj* graisseux
great *adj* super
greatness *n* grandeur
Greece *n* Grèce
greed *n* avidité
greedy *adj* avare
Greek *adj* grecque
green *adj* vert
green bean *n* haricot vert
greenhouse *n* serre
Greenland *n* Groenland

greet v saluer

greetings n salutations

gregarious adj grégaire

grenade n grenade

greyhound n lévrier

grief n chagrin

grievance n doléance

grieve v peiner

grill v griller

grill n gril

grim adj morose

grimace n grimace

grime n crasse

grind iv grincer

grip v agripper

grip n prise

gripe n plainte

grisly adj sinistre

groan v geindre

groan n gémissement

groceries n courses

groin n aine

groom n marié

groove n rainure

gross adj grossier; brut

grossly adv grossièrement

grotesque adj grotesque

grotto n grotte

grouch v râler

grouchy adj ronchon

ground n sol

groundless adj infondé

group n groupe

grow iv grandir

grow up v grandir

growl v grondement

grown-up n adulte

growth n croissance

grudge n rancune

grudgingly adv à contrecœur

gruelling adj ardu

gruesome adj effroyable

grumble v râler

grumpy adj râleur

guarantee v garantir

guarantee n garantie

guarantor n garant

guard n garde

guardian n gardien

guerrilla n guérillero

guess v deviner

guess n hypothèse

guest n invité

guidance n conseils

guide v guider

guide n guide

guidebook n guide

guidelines n directive

guild n guilde

guile n fourberie

guillotine n guillotine

guilt n culpabilité

guilty adj coupable

guitar n guitare

G

gulf *n* golf
gull *n* mouette
gullible *adj* crédule
gulp *v* engloutir
gulp *n* goulée
gulp down *v* avaler d'un coup
gum *n* gencive; gomme
gun *n* arme à feu
gun down *v* abattre
gunfire *n* fusillade
gunman *n* tireur
gunpowder *n* poudre
gunshot *n* coup de feu
gust *n* rafale
gusto *n* engouement
gusty *adj* venteux
gut *n* bide
guts *n* entrailles
gutter *n* gouttière; caniveau
guy *n* mec
guzzle *v* engloutir
gymnasium *n* gymnase
gynecology *n* gynécologie
gypsy *n* gitan

habit *n* habitude
habitable *adj* habitable
habitual *adj* habituel
hack *v* couper
haggle *v* marchander
hail *n* grêle
hail *v* grêler
hair *n* cheveux
hairbrush *n* brosse
haircut *n* coupe
hairdo *n* coiffure
hairdresser *n* coiffeur
hairpiece *n* postiche
hairy *adj* poilu
half *n* moitié
half *adj* partiel
hall *n* hall
hallucinate *v* halluciner
hallway *n* couloir
halt *v* arrêter
halve *v* partager en deux
ham *n* jambon
hamburger *n* hamburger
hamlet *n* hameau
hammer *n* marteau
hammock *n* hamac
hand *n* main
hand down *v* transmettre
hand in *v* remettre

hand out *v* distribuer
hand over *v* céder
handbag *n* sac à main
handbook *n* manuel
handcuffs *n* menotte
handful *n* poignée
handgun *n* arme de poing
handicap *n* handicap
handkerchief *n* mouchoir
handle *v* manipuler
handle *n* poignée
handmade *adj* fait main
handout *n* polycopié
handrail *n* rampe
handshake *n* poignée de main
handsome *adj* bel homme
handwriting *n* écriture
handy *adj* utile
hang *iv* pendre
hang around *v* attendre
hang on *v* garder
hang up *v* raccrocher
hanger *n* ceintre
hangup *n* complexe
happen *v* arriver
happening *n* événement
happiness *n* bonheur
happy *adj* heureux
harass *v* harceler
harassment *n* harcèlement
harbor *n* port
hard *adj* dur; difficile

harden *v* endurcir
hardly *adv* presque
hardness *n* dureté
hardship *n* épreuve
hardware *n* quincaillerie
hardy *adj* robuste
hare *n* lièvre
harm *v* nuire
harm *n* mal
harmful *adj* nuisible
harmless *adj* inoffensif
harmonize *v* harmoniser
harmony *n* harmonie
harp *n* harpe
harpoon *n* harpon
harrowing *adj* douloureux
harsh *adj* dur
harshly *adv* durement
harshness *n* dureté
harvest *n* récolte
harvest *v* récolter
hashish *n* hashish
hassle *v* harceler
hassle *n* complication
haste *n* hâte
hasten *v* hâter
hastily *adv* à la hâte
hasty *adj* hâtif
hat *n* chapeau
hatchet *n* hachette
hate *v* haïr
hateful *adj* haineux

H

hatred *n* haine
haughty *adj* hautain
haul *v* tirer
haunt *v* hanter
have *iv* avoir
have to *v* devoir
haven *n* refuge
havoc *n* grabuge
hawk *n* faucon
hay *n* foin
haystack *n* meule de foin
hazard *n* hasard; danger
hazardous *adj* dangereux
haze *n* brouillard
hazelnut *n* noisette
hazy *adj* brumeux
he *pro* il
head *n* tête
head for *v* se diriger vers
headache *n* mal de tête
heading *n* en-tête
head-on *adv* frontal
headphones *n* écouteurs
headway *n* progres
heal *v* guérir
healer *n* guérisseur
health *n* santé
healthy *adj* en bonne santé
heap *n* tas
heap *v* empiler
hear *iv* entendre
hearing *n* audition

hearsay *n* on-dit
hearse *n* corbillard
heart *n* coeur
heartbeat *n* battement
heartburn *n* brûlures
hearten *v* encourager
heartfelt *adj* sincère
hearth *n* foyer
heartless *adj* cruel
hearty *adj* copieux; cordial
heat *v* chauffer
heat *n* chaleur
heater *n* radiateur
heathen *n* païen
heating *n* chauffage
heatstroke *n* coup de chaleur
heatwave *n* vague de chaleur
heaven *n* paradis
heavenly *adj* paradisiaque
heaviness *n* lourdeur
heavy *adj* lourd
heckle *v* chahuter
hectic *adj* intense
heed *v* écouter
heel *n* talon
height *n* taille; hauteur
heighten *v* accroître
heinous *adj* abominable
heir *n* héritier
heiress *n* héritière
heist *n* cambriolage
helicopter *n* hélicoptère**

H

hell *n* enfer
hello *e* bonjour
helm *n* barre
helmet *n* casque
help *v* aider
help *n* aide
helper *n* assistant
helpful *adj* utile
helpless *adj* sans défense
hem *n* ourlet
hemisphere *n* hémisphère
hemorrhage *n* hémorragie
hen *n* poule
hence *adv* donc
henchman *n* acolyte
her *adj* son; sa; ses
herald *v* annoncer
herald *n* héraut
herb *n* herbe
here *adv* ici
hereafter *adv* ci-après
hereby *adv* donc
hereditary *adj* héréditaire
heresy *n* hérésie
heretic *adj* hérétique
heritage *n* héritage
hermetic *adj* hermétique
hermit *n* ermite
hernia *n* hernie
hero *n* héros
heroic *adj* héroïque
heroin *n* héroïne

heroism *n* héroïsme
hers *pro* à elle
herself *pro* elle-même
hesitant *adj* hésitant
hesitate *v* hésiter
hesitation *n* hésitation
heyday *n* âge d'or
hiccup *n* hoquet
hidden *adj* caché
hide *iv* se cacher
hideaway *n* retraite
hideous *adj* hideux
hierarchy *n* hiérarchie
high *adj* haut
highlight *n* mèche
highly *adv* hautement
Highness *n* Altesse
highway *n* autoroute
hijack *v* détourner
hijack *n* détournement
hijacker *n* pirate de l'air
hike *v* marcher
hike *n* randonnée
hilarious *adj* hilarant
hill *n* colline
hillside *n* versant
hilltop *n* sommet
hilly *adj* vallonné
hilt *n* garde; crosse
hinder *v* entraver
hindrance *n* entrave
hinge *n* charnière**

H

hint *n* indice
hint *v* faire allusion
hip *n* hanche
hire *v* engager; louer
his *adj* son; sa; ses
his *pro* à lui
Hispanic *adj* hispanique
hiss *v* siffler
historian *n* historien
history *n* histoire
hit *n* coup; succès
hit *iv* frapper
hitch *n* problème
hitch up *v* remonter
hitherto *adv* jusqu'ici
hive *n* ruche
hoard *v* trésor
hoarse *adj* rauque
hoax *n* canular
hobby *n* loisir
hog *n* porc verrat
hoist *v* hisser
hoist *n* palan
hold *iv* tenir; résister
hold back *v* se retenir
hold on to *v* s'accrocher à
hold out *v* tenir bon
hold up *v* soutenir; lever
holdup *n* holdup
hole *n* trou
holiday *n* vacances
holiness *n* sainteté

Holland *n* Hollande
hollow *adj* creu
holocaust *n* holocauste
holy *adj* saint
homage *n* hommage
home *n* maison
homeland *n* patrie
homeless *adj* sans-abri
homely *adj* simple
homemade *adj* fait maison
hometown *n* ville natale
homework *n* devoirs
homicide *n* homicide
homily *n* homélie
honest *adj* honnête
honesty *n* honnêteté
honey *n* miel
honeymoon *n* lune de miel
honk *v* klaxonner
honor *n* honneur
hood *n* capuchon
hoodlum *n* truand
hoof *n* sabot
hook *n* crochet; hameçon
hooligan *n* hooligan
hop *v* sautiller
hope *n* espoir
hopeful *adj* optimiste
hopefully *adv* pourvu que
hopeless *adj* désespéré
horizon *n* horizon
horizontal *adj* horizontal

hormone *n* hormone
horn *n* klaxon; corne
horrendous *adj* épouvantable
horrible *adj* horrible
horrify *v* horrifier
horror *n* horreur
horse *n* cheval
hose *n* tuyau
hospital *n* hôpital
hospitality *n* hôspitalité
hospitalize *v* hôspitaliser
host *n* hôte
hostage *n* otage
hostess *n* hôtesse
hostile *adj* hostile
hostility *n* hostilité
hot *adj* chaud
hotel *n* hôtel
hound *n* chien de chasse
hour *n* heure
house *n* maison
household *n* ménage
housekeeper *n* femme de ménage
housewife *n* femme au foyer
housework *n* ménage
hover *v* susprendre
how *adv* comment
however *c* cependant
howl *v* hurler
howl *n* hurlement
hub *n* centre

huddle *v* se blottir
hug *v* étreindre
hug *n* étreinte
huge *adj* immense
hull *n* coque
hum *v* fredonner
human *adj* humain
human being *n* être humain
humanities *n* humanités
humankind *n* humanité
humble *adj* humble
humbly *adv* humblement
humid *adj* humide
humidity *n* humidité
humiliate *v* humilier
humility *n* humilité
humor *n* humour
humorous *adj* humoristique
hump *n* bosse
hunch *n* intuition
hunchback *n* bossu
hunched *adj* bossu
hundred *adj* cent
hundredth *adj* centième
hunger *n* faim
hungry *adj* avoir faim
hunt *v* chasser
hunter *n* chasseur
hunting *n* chasse
hurdle *n* haie
hurl *v* lancer
hurricane *n* ouragan

H

hurriedly *adv* précipitamment
hurry *v* hâter
hurry up *v* se dépêcher
hurt *iv* souffrir
hurt *adj* blessé
hurtful *adj* blessant
husband *n* mari
hush *n* silence
hush up *v* étouffer
husky *adj* rauque; costaud
hustle *n* agitation
hut *n* hutte
hydraulic *adj* hydraulique
hydrogen *n* hydrogène
hyena *n* hyène
hygiene *n* hygiène
hymn *n* hymne
hyphen *n* trait d'union
hypnosis *n* hypnose
hypnotize *v* hypnotiser
hypocrisy *n* hypocrisie
hypocrite *adj* hypocrite
hypothesis *n* hypothèse
hysteria *n* hystérie
hysterical *adj* hystérique

I *pro* je
ice *n* glace
ice cream *n* glace
ice cube *n* glaçon
ice skate *v* patiner
iceberg *n* iceberg
icebox *n* freezer
ice-cold *adj* glacé
icon *n* icône
icy *adj* glacé
idea *n* idée
ideal *adj* idéal
identical *adj* identique
identify *v* identifier
identity *n* identité
ideology *n* idéologie
idiom *n* idiome
idiot *n* idiot
idiotic *adj* bête
idle *adj* paresseux
idol *n* idole
idolatry *n* idolatrie
if *c* si
ignite *v* allumer
ignorance *n* ignorance
ignorant *adj* ignorant
ignore *v* ignorer
ill *adj* malade
illegal *adj* illégal

illegible *adj* illisible
illegitimate *adj* illégitime
illicit *adj* illicite
illiterate *adj* analphabète
illness *n* maladie
illogical *adj* illogique
illuminate *v* illuminer
illusion *n* illusion
illustrate *v* illustrer
illustration *n* illustration
illustrious *adj* illustre
image *n* image
imagination *n* imagination
imagine *v* imaginer
imbalance *n* déséquilibre
imitate *v* imiter
imitation *n* imitation
immaculate *adj* immaculer
immature *adj* immature
immaturity *n* immaturité
immediately *adv* immédiatement
immense *adj* immense
immensity *n* immensité
immerse *v* immerger
immersion *n* immersion
immigrant *n* immigrant
immigrate *v* immigrer
immigration *n* immigration
imminent *adj* imminent
immobile *adj* immobile
immobilize *v* immobiliser
immoral *adj* immoral

immorality *n* immoralité
immortal *adj* immortel
immortality *n* immortalité
immune *adj* immunisé
immunity *n* immunité
immunize *v* immuniser
immutable *adj* immuable
impact *n* impact
impact *v* impacter
impair *v* détériorer
impartial *adj* impartiel
impatience *n* impatience
impatient *adj* impatient
impeccable *adj* impeccable
impediment *n* obstacle
impending *adj* imminent
imperfection *n* imperfection
imperial *adj* impérial
imperialism *n* impérialisme
impersonal *adj* impersonnel
impertinence *n* impertinence
impertinent *adj* impertinent
impetuous *adj* impétueux
implacable *adj* implacable
implant *v* implanter
implement *v* implémenter
implicate *v* impliquer
implication *n* implication
implicit *adj* implicite
implore *v* implorer
imply *v* impliquer
impolite *adj* mal poli

import *v* importer
importance *n* importance
importation *n* importation
impose *v* imposer
imposing *adj* imposant
imposition *n* imposition
impossibility *n* impossibilité
impossible *adj* impossible
impotent *adj* impotent
impound *v* confisquer
impoverished *adj* appauvri
imprecise *adj* imprécis
impress *v* impressionner
impressive *adj* impressionnant
imprison *v* emprisonner
improbable *adj* improbable
impromptu *adv* impromptu
improper *adj* impropre
improve *v* améliorer
improvement *n* amélioration
improvise *v* improviser
impulse *n* impulse
impulsive *adj* impulsif
impunity *n* impunité
impure *adj* impure
in *pre* dans
in depth *adv* en profondeur
inability *n* inabilité
inaccessible *adj* inaccessible
inaccurate *adj* inexact
inadequate *adj* insuffisant
inadmissible *adj* intolerable

inappropriate *adj* inadapté
inaugurate *v* inaugurer
inauguration *n* inauguration
incalculable *adj* incalculable
incapable *adj* incapable
incapacitate *v* incapaciter
incarcerate *v* incarcerer
incense *n* encens
incentive *n* avantage
inception *n* origine
incessant *adj* incessant
inch *n* pouce
incident *n* incident
incidentally *adv* incidemment
incision *n* incision
incite *v* inciter
incitement *n* excitation
inclination *n* inclination
incline *v* incliner
include *v* inclure
inclusive *adv* inclus
incoherent *adj* incohérent
income *n* salaire
incompatible *adj* incompatible
incompetence *n* incompétence
incompetent *adj* incompétent
incomplete *adj* incomplet
inconsistent *adj* inconsistent
incontinence *n* incontinence
inconvenient *adj* inconvénient
incorporate *v* incorporer
incorrect *adj* incorrect

incorrigible *adj* incorrigible
increase *v* augmenter
increase *n* augmentation
increasing *adj* croissant
incredible *adj* incroyable
increment *n* incrément
incriminate *v* incriminer
incur *v* obtenir
incurable *adj* incurable
indecency *n* indécence
indecision *n* indécision
indecisive *adj* indéssif
indeed *adv* en effet
indefinite *adj* indéfini
indemnify *v* indemniser
indemnity *n* indémnité
independence *n* indépendence
independent *adj* indépendent
index *n* index
indicate *v* indiquer
indication *n* indication
indict *v* inculper
indifference *n* indifférence
indifferent *adj* indifférent
indigent *adj* indigent
indigestion *n* indigestion
indirect *adj* indirect
indiscreet *adj* indiscret
indiscretion *n* indiscretion
indispensable *adj* indispensable
indisposed *adj* indisposé
indisputable *adj* indisputable

indivisible *adj* indivisible
indoctrinate *v* indoctriner
indoor *adv* à l'intérieur
induce *v* provoquer
indulge *v* céder
indulgent *adj* indulgent
industrious *adj* studieux
industry *n* industrie
ineffective *adj* inefficace
inefficient *adj* incompétent
inept *adj* incompétent
inequality *n* inégalité
inevitable *adj* inévitable
inexcusable *adj* inexcusable
inexpensive *adj* bon marché
inexperienced *adj* inexperienced
inexplicable *adj* inexplicable
infallible *adj* infallible
infamous *adj* infâme
infancy *n* petite enfance
infant *n* nourrisson
infantry *n* infanterie
infect *v* infecter
infection *n* infection
infectious *adj* infectieux
infer *v* inférer
inferior *adj* inférieur
infertile *adj* stérile
infested *adj* infesté
infidelity *n* infidélité
infiltrate *v* infiltrer
infiltration *n* infiltration

I

infinite *adj* infini
infirmary *n* infirmerie
inflammation *n* inflammation
inflate *v* gonfler
inflation *n* inflation
inflexible *adj* inflexible
inflict *v* infliger
influence *n* influence
influential *adj* influent
influenza *n* grippe
influx *n* afflux
inform *v* informer
informal *adj* informel
informant *n* informateur
information *n* information
informer *n* indicateur
infraction *n* infraction
infrequent *adj* rare
infuriate *v* rendre furieux
infusion *n* infusion
ingenuity *n* ingéniosité
ingest *v* ingester
ingot *n* lingot
ingrained *adj* enraciné
ingratitude *n* ingratitude
ingredient *n* ingrédient
inhabit *v* habiter
inhabitable *adj* inhabitable
inhabitant *n* habitant
inhale *v* inhaler
inherit *v* hériter
inheritance *n* héritage

inhibit *v* inhiber
inhuman *adj* inhumain
initial *adj* initiale
initially *adv* initialement
initials *n* initiales
initiate *v* initier
initiative *n* initiative
inject *v* injecter
injection *n* injection
injure *v* injurier
injurious *adj* nuisible
injury *n* blessure
injustice *n* injustice
ink *n* encre
inkling *n* soupçon
inlaid *adj* incrusté
inland *adv* intérieur
in-laws *n* beaux-parents
inmate *n* détenu
inn *n* auberge
innate *adj* inné
inner *adj* intérieur
innocence *n* innocence
innocent *adj* innocent
innovation *n* innovation
innuendo *n* insinuations
innumerable *adj* innumérable
input *n* apport
inquest *n* enquête
inquire *v* s'enquérir
inquiry *n* demande
inquisition *n* inquisition

insane *adj* dément
insanity *n* insanité
insatiable *adj* insatiable
inscription *n* inscription
insect *n* insecte
insecurity *n* insécurité
insensitive *adj* indélicat
inseparable *adj* insélparable
insert *v* insérer
insertion *n* insertion
inside *adj* intérieur
inside *pre* à l'intérieur de
inside out *adv* à l'envers
insignificant *adj* insignifiant
insincere *adj* hypocrite
insincerity *n* hypocrisie
insinuate *v* insinuer
insinuation *n* insinuation
insipid *adj* insipide
insist *v* insister
insistence *n* insistance
insolent *adj* insolent
insoluble *adj* insoluble
insomnia *n* insomnie
inspect *v* inspecter
inspection *n* inspection
inspector *n* inspecteur
inspiration *n* inspiration
inspire *v* inspirer
instability *n* instabilité
install *v* installer
installation *n* installation

installment *n* versement
instance *n* cas
instant *n* instant
instantly *adv* instantanément
instead *adv* au lieu de
instigate *v* provoquer
instil *v* instiller
instinct *n* instinct
institute *v* institut
institution *n* institution
instruct *v* instruire
instructor *n* instructeur
insufficient *adj* insuffisant
insulate *v* isoler
insulation *n* isolement
insult *v* insulter
insult *n* insulte
insurance *n* assurance
insure *v* assurer
insurgency *n* insurrection
insurrection *n* insurrection
intact *adj* intact
intake *n* consommation
integrate *v* intégrer
integration *n* intégration
integrity *n* intégrité
intelligent *adj* intélligent
intend *v* avoir l'intention
intense *adj* intense
intensify *v* intensifier
intensity *n* intensité
intensive *adj* intensif

I

intention *n* intention
intercede *v* intercéder
intercept *v* intercepter
intercession *n* intercession
interchange *v* échanger
interchange *n* échangeur
interest *n* intérêt
interested *adj* intéressé
interesting *adj* intéressant
interfere *v* s'interposer
interference *n* interférence
interior *adj* intérieur
interlude *n* intervalle
intermediary *n* intermédiaire
intern *v* interner
interpret *v* interpréter
interpretation *n* interprétation
interpreter *n* interprétateur
interrogate *v* interroger
interrupt *v* interrompre
interruption *n* interruption
intersect *v* croiser
intertwine *v* enlacer
interval *n* intervalle
intervene *v* intervenir
intervention *n* intervention
interview *n* interview
intestine *n* intestin
intimacy *n* intimité
intimate *adj* intime
intimidate *v* intimider
intolerable *adj* intolérable

intolerance *n* intolérance
intoxicated *adj* intoxiqué
intravenous *adj* intraveineux
intrepid *adj* intrépide
intricate *adj* compliqué
intrigue *n* intrigue
intriguing *adj* intriguant
intrinsic *adj* intrinsèque
introduce *v* introduire
introduction *n* introduction
introvert *adj* introverti
intrude *v* s'imposer
intruder *n* intrus
intrusion *n* intrusion
intuition *n* intuition
inundate *v* inonder
invade *v* envahir
invader *n* envahisseur
invalid *n* infirme
invalidate *v* invalider
invaluable *adj* insetimable
invasion *n* invasion
invent *v* inventer
invention *n* invention
inventory *n* inventaire
invest *v* investir
investigate *v* enquêter
investigation *n* investigation
investment *n* investissement
investor *n* investisseur
invincible *adj* invincible
invisible *adj* invisible

invitation *n* invitation
invite *v* inviter
invoice *n* facture
invoke *v* invoquer
involve *v* impliquer
involved *v* impliqué
involvement *n* participation
iodine *n* iode
irate *adj* furieux
Ireland *n* Irelande
Irish *adj* irelandais
iron *n* fer
iron *v* repasser
ironic *adj* ironique
irony *n* ironie
irrational *adj* irrationnal
irrefutable *adj* irrefutable
irregular *adj* irrégulier
irrelevant *adj* sans rapport
irreparable *adj* irréparable
irresistible *adj* irrésistible
irreversible *adj* irréversible
irrevocable *adj* irrévocable
irrigate *v* irriguer
irrigation *n* irrigation
irritate *v* irriter
irritating *adj* irritant
Islamic *adj* Islamique
island *n* île
isle *n* île
isolate *v* isoler
isolation *n* isolation

issue *n* problème
Italian *adj* Italien
italics *adj* italique
Italy *n* Italie
itch *v* démanger
itchiness *n* démangeaison
item *n* objet
itemize *v* énumérer
itinerary *n* itinéraire
ivory *n* ivoire

J

jackal *n* chacal
jacket *n* veste
jackpot *n* jackpot
jaguar *n* jaguar
jail *n* prison
jail *v* incarcérer
jailer *n* geôlier
jam *n* confiture; blocage
janitor *n* concierge
January *n* janvier
Japan *n* Japon
Japanese *adj* Japonais
jar *n* bocal
jasmine *n* jasmin
jaw *n* mâchoire

jealous *adj* jaloux
jealousy *n* jalousie
jeans *n* jeans
jeopardize *v* menacer
jerk *v* secouer
jerk *n* idiot; secousse
jersey *n* maillot
Jew *n* Juif
jewel *n* bijou
jeweler *n* bijoutier
jewelry store *n* bijouterie
Jewish *adj* Juif
jigsaw *n* scie sauteuse
job *n* travail
jobless *adj* sans emploi
join *v* joindre
joint *n* articulation; joint
jointly *adv* conjointement
joke *n* blague
joke *v* blaguer
jokingly *adv* en plaisantant
jolly *adj* jovial
jolt *v* sursauter
jolt *n* sursaut
journal *n* journal; revue
journalist *n* journaliste
journey *n* voyage
jovial *adj* jovial
joy *n* joie
joyful *adj* joyeux
joyfully *adv* joyeusement
jubilant *adj* exultant

Judaism *n* judaïsme
judge *n* juge
judgment *n* jugement
judicious *adj* judicieux
jug *n* cruche
juggler *n* jongleur
juice *n* jus
juicy *adj* juteux
July *n* juillet
jump *v* sauter
jump *n* saut
jumpy *adj* nerveux
junction *n* jonction
June *n* juin
jungle *n* jungle
junk *n* camelote
jury *n* jury
just *adj* juste
justice *n* justice
justify *v* justifier
justly *adv* justement
juvenile *n* jeune
juvenile *adj* juvénile

J

K

kangaroo *n* kangarou
karate *n* karaté
keep *iv* continuer; garder
keep on *v* continuer
keep up *v* suivre; soutenir
keg *n* fût
kennel *n* niche; chenil
kettle *n* bouilloire
key *n* clé; touche
key ring *n* porte-clés
keyboard *n* clavier
kick *v* frapper
kickoff *n* démarrage
kid *n* enfant; chevreau
kidnap *v* kidnapper
kidnapper *n* kidnappeur
kidnapping *n* kidnapping
kidney *n* rein
kidney bean *n* haricot rouge
kill *v* tuer
killer *n* tueur
killing *n* meurtre
kilogram *n* kilogramme
kilometer *n* kilomètre
kilowatt *n* kilowatt
kind *adj* aimable
kindle *v* allumer
kindly *adv* gentiment
kindness *n* bonté

king *n* roi
kingdom *n* royaume
kinship *n* parenté
kiosk *n* kiosque
kiss *v* embrasser
kiss *n* bisous
kitchen *n* cuisine
kite *n* cerf-volant
kitten *n* chaton
knee *n* genou
kneecap *n* rotule
kneel *iv* s'agenouiller
knife *n* couteau
knight *n* chevalier
knit *v* tricoter
knob *n* poignée
knock *v* cogner
knot *n* noeud
know *iv* savoir; connaitre
know-how *n* savoir-faire
knowingly *adv* siemment
knowledge *n* connaissance

L

lab *n* labo
label *n* étiquette
labor *n* travail
laborer *n* travailleur
labyrinth *n* labyrinthe
lace *n* dentelle
lack *v* manquer
lack *n* manque
lad *n* gars
ladder *n* échelle
laden *adj* plein
lady *n* dame
ladylike *adj* distingué
lagoon *n* lagune
lake *n* lac
lamb *n* agneau
lame *adj* boiteux; faible
lament *v* plaindre
lament *n* complainte
lamp *n* lampe
lamppost *n* réverbère
lampshade *n* abat-jour
land *n* terrain
land *v* aterrir
landfill *n* décharge
landing *n* aterrissage
landlady *n* propriétaire
landlord *n* propriétaire
landscape *n* paysage
lane *n* file
language *n* langage
languish *v* languir
lantern *n* lanterne
lap *n* genoux; piste
lapse *n* défaillance; pause
lapse *v* sombrer
larceny *n* vol
lard *n* lard
large *adj* large
larynx *n* larynx
laser *n* laser
lash *n* cil; fouet
lash *v* fouetter
lash out *v* frapper
last *v* durer
last *adj* dernier
last name *n* nom de famille
last night *adv* hier soir
lasting *adj* durable
lastly *adv* enfin
latch *n* loquet
late *adv* tard
lately *adv* dernièrement
later *adv* plus tard
later *adj* ultérieur
lateral *adj* latéral
latest *adj* dernier
lather *n* mousse
latitude *n* latitude
latter *adj* dernier
laugh *v* rire

laugh *n* rire
laughable *adj* risible
laughing stock *n* risée
laughter *n* rire
launch *n* lancement
launch *v* lancer
laundry *n* laverie
lavatory *n* toilette
lavish *adj* somptueux
lavish *v* prodiguer
law *n* loi
law-abiding *adj* respectueux
lawful *adj* légal
lawmaker *n* législateur
lawn *n* pelouse
lawsuit *n* poursuite
lawyer *n* avocat
lax *adj* relâché
laxative *adj* laxative
lay *n* disposition
lay *iv* mposer; pondre
lay off *v* licensier
layer *n* couche
layman *n* profane
lay-out *n* étalage
laziness *n* paresse
lazy *adj* presseux
lead *iv* mener
lead *n* avance; direction
leaded *adj* plombé
leader *n* dirigeant
leadership *n* direction

leading *adj* principal
leaf *n* feuille
leaflet *n* dépliant
league *n* ligue
leak *v* fuir
leak *n* fuite
leakage *n* fuite
lean *adj* mince; difficile
lean *iv* pencher
lean on *v* s'appuyer
leaning *n* penchant
leap *iv* bondir
leap *n* saut
leap year *n* année bissextile
learn *iv* apprendre
learned *adj* appris
learner *n* apprenant
learning *n* connaissance
lease *v* louer
lease *n* location
leash *n* laisse
least *adj* minimum
leather *n* cuir
leave *iv* partir
leave out *v* exclure
lectern *n* pupitre
lecture *n* conférence
leech *n* sangsue
leftovers *n* restes
leg *n* jambe
legacy *n* héritage
legal *adj* légal

L

legality *n* légalité

legalize *v* légaliserl

legend *n* légende

legible *adj* lisible

legion *n* légion

legislate *v* légiférer

legislation *n* législation

legislature *n* législature

legitimate *adj* légitime

leisure *n* loisir

lemon *n* citron

lemonade *n* limonade

lend *iv* prêter

length *n* longueur

lengthen *v* allonger

lengthy *adj* long

leniency *n* complaisance

lenient *adj* complaisant

lense *n* lentille

Lent *n* carême

lentil *n* lentille

leopard *n* léopard

leper *n* lépreux

leprosy *n* lépre

less *adj* moins

lessee *n* locataire

lessen *v* amoindrir

lesser *adj* moindre

lesson *n* leçon

lessor *n* bailleur

let *iv* laisser

let down *v* dénouer

let go *v* lâcher

lethal *adj* mortel

letter *n* lettre

lettuce *n* laitue

leukemia *n* leucémie

level *v* niveler

level *n* niveau; taux

lever *n* levier

leverage *n* avantage; poids

levy *v* prélever

lewd *adj* obscène

liability *n* responsabilité

liable *adj* responsible

liaison *n* liaison

liar *adj* menteur

libel *n* diffamation

liberate *v* libérer

liberation *n* libération

liberty *n* liberté

librarian *n* bibliothécaire

library *n* bibliothéque

lice *n* pou

licence *n* licence

license *v* autoriser

lick *v* lécher

lid *n* couvercle

lie *iv* s'allonger

lie *v* mentir

lie *n* mensonge

lieu *n* place

lieutenant *n* lieutenant

life *n* vie

lifeguard *n* maître nageur
lifeless *adj* sans vie
lifestyle *n* mode de vie
lifetime *adj* existence
lift *v* soulever
lift off *v* décoller
lift-off *n* décollage
ligament *n* ligament
light *iv* éclairer
light *adj* clair
light *n* lumière
lighter *n* briquet
lighthouse *n* phare
lighting *n* éclairage
lightly *adv* légèrement
lightning *n* éclair
lightweight *n* poids plume
likable *adj* aimable
like *pre* comme
like *v* adorer
likelihood *n* probabilité
likely *adv* probable
likeness *n* ressemblance
likewise *adv* pareillement
liking *n* goût
limb *n* membre
lime *n* citron vert
limestone *n* calcaire
limit *n* limite; frontière
limit *v* limiter
limitation *n* limitation
limp *v* boiter

linchpin *n* esse
line *n* ligne
line up *v* aligner
linen *n* linge; lin
linger *v* attarder
lingerie *n* lingerie
lingering *adj* persistant
lining *n* doublure
link *v* relier
link *n* maillon
lion *n* lion
lioness *n* lionne
lip *n* lèvre
liqueur *n* liqueur
liquid *n* liquide
liquidate *v* liquider
liquidation *n* liquidation
liquor *n* liqueur
list *v* énumérer
list *n* liste
listen *v* écouter
listener *n* auditeur
litany *n* litanie
liter *n* litre
literal *adj* littéral
literally *adv* littéralement
literate *adj* lettré
literature *n* littérature
litigate *v* poursuivre
litigation *n* litiges
litre *n* litre
litter *n* litière

L

little *adj* petit
little bit *n* un peu
little by little *adv* petit à petit
liturgy *n* liturgie
live *adj* vivant; en direct
live *v* habiter; vivre
livelihood *n* gagne-pain
lively *adj* animé
liver *n* foie
livestock *n* bétail
livid *adj* livide
living room *n* salle de séjour
lizard *n* lézard
load *v* charger
load *n* charge
loaded *adj* chargé; riche
loaf *n* pain
loan *v* prêter
loan *n* prêt
loathe *v* détester
loathing *n* haine
lobby *n* lobby; hall
lobster *n* homard
local *adj* local
localize *v* localiser
locate *v* situer
located *adj* situé
location *n* location
lock *v* vérouiller
lock *n* vérou
lock up *v* fermer
locker room *n* vestiaire

locksmith *n* serrurier
locust *n* criquet
lodge *v* pavillon
lodging *n* logement
lofty *adj* noble
log *n* bûche
log *v* noter
log in *v* se connecter
log off *v* se déconnecter
logic *n* logique
logical *adj* logique
loin *n* filet
loiter *v* loiter
loneliness *n* solitude
lonely *adv* seul
loner *n* solitaire
lonesome *adj* solitaire
long *adj* long
long for *v* attendre
longing *n* nostalgie
longitude *n* longitude
long-term *adj* long- erme
look *n* coup d'œil; style
look *v* regarder; vérifier
look after *v* s'occuper
look at *v* regarder
look for *v* chercher
look forward *v* attendre
look into *v* examiner
look out *v* guetter
look over *v* contrôler
look through *v* parcourir

looking glass *n* miroir

looks *n* apparence

loom *n* métier à tisser

loom *v* apparaître

loophole *n* lacune

loose *v* relâcher

loose *adj* ample; relâché

loosen *v* desserrer

loot *v* piller

loot *n* butin

lord *n* seigneur

lordship *n* seigneurie

lose *iv* predre

loser *n* perdant

loss *n* perte

lot *adv* beaucoup

lotion *n* lotion

lots *adj* beaucoup

lottery *n* lotterie

loud *adj* bruyant

loudly *adv* bruyamment

loudspeaker *n* haut-parleur

lounge *n* salon

louse *n* reclure

lousy *adj* minable

lovable *adj* aimable

love *v* aimer

love *n* amour

lovely *adj* charmant

lover *n* amant

loving *adj* tendre

low *adj* bas

lower *adj* inférieur

lowkey *adj* discret

lowly *adj* humble

loyal *adj* loyal

loyalty *n* loyauté

lubricate *v* lubrifier

lubrication *n* lubrication

lucid *adj* lucide

luck *n* chance

lucky *adj* chanceux

lucrative *adj* lucratif

ludicrous *adj* absurde

luggage *n* valise

lukewarm *adj* tiède

lull *n* accalmie

lumber *n* bois

luminous *adj* lumineux

lump *n* grumeau

lunacy *n* folie

lunatic *adj* lunatique

lunch *n* déjeuner

lung *n* poumon

lure *v* appâter

lurid *adj* criard

lurk *v* traîner

lush *adj* luxuriant

lust *v* désirer

lust *n* désir

lustful *adj* lascif

luxurious *adj* luxurieux

luxury *n* luxe

lynch *v* lyncher

L

lynx *n* lynx
lyrics *n* paroles

M

machine *n* machine
machine gun *n* miraillette
mad *adj* en colère
madam *n* madame
madden *v* choquer
madly *adv* éperdument
madman *n* fou
madness *n* folie
magazine *n* magazine
magic *n* magie
magical *adj* magique
magician *n* magicien
magistrate *n* magistrat
magnet *n* aimant
magnetic *adj* magnétique
magnetism *n* magnétisme
magnificent *adj* magnifique
magnify *v* agrandir
magnitude *n* grandeur
maid *n* femme de ménage
maiden *n* jeune fille
mail *v* poster
mail *n* courrier

mailbox *n* boîte aux lettres
mailman *n* postier
maim *v* estropier
main *adj* principal
mainly *adv* principalement
maintain *v* maintenir
maintenance *n* entretien
majestic *adj* majestueux
majesty *n* majesté
major *n* majeur
major *adj* important
major in *v* se spécialiser
majority *n* majorité
make *n* marque
make *iv* faire
make up *v* inventer
make up for *v* se rattraper
maker *n* fabricant
makeup *n* maquillage
malaria *n* paludisme
male *n* mâle
malevolent *adj* malveillant
malfunction *v* défaillir
malfunction *n* défaillance
malice *n* malice
malign *v* calomnier
malignancy *n* malignité
malignant *adj* cancéreux
malnutrition *n* malnutrition
mammal *n* mammifère
mammoth *n* mammouth
man *n* homme

manage *v* gérer
manageable *adj* maniable
management *n* direction
manager *n* directeur
mandate *n* mandat
mandatory *adj* obligatoire
maneuver *n* manœuvre
manger *n* mangeoire
mangle *v* mutiler
manhandle *v* malmener
manhunt *n* chasse à l'homme
maniac *adj* maniaque
manifest *v* manifester
manipulate *v* manipuler
mankind *n* humanité
manliness *n* virilité
manly *adj* virile
manner *n* manière
mannerism *n* manie
manners *n* manières
manpower *n* main-d'œuvre
mansion *n* manoir
manslaughter *n* homicide
manual *n* manuel
manual *adj* manuel
manufacture *v* fabriquer
manure *n* fumier
manuscript *n* manuscrit
many *adj* beaucoup
map *n* plan
marble *n* marbre
march *v* marcher

march *n* marche
March *n* mars
mare *n* jument
margin *n* marge
marginal *adj* marginal
marinate *v* mariner
marine *adj* marine
marital *adj* marital
mark *n* marque
mark *v* marquer
mark down *v* dévaloriser
marker *n* feutre
market *n* marché
marksman *n* tireur d'élite
marmalade *n* marmelade
marriage *n* mariage
married *adj* marié
marrow *n* moelle
marry *v* marier
Mars *n* Mars
marshal *n* maréchal
martyr *n* martyre
martyrdom *n* martyre
marvel *n* merveille
marvelous *adj* merveilleux
marxist *adj* marxiste
masculine *adj* masculin
mash *v* écraser
mask *n* masque
masochism *n* masochisme
mason *n* maçon
mass *n* masse; foule

M

massacre *n* massacre
massage *n* massage
massage *v* masser
masseur *n* masseur
masseuse *n* masseuse
massive *adj* massif
mast *n* mât
master *n* maître
master *v* maîtriser
mastermind *n* cerveau
mastermind *v* organiser
masterpiece *n* chef-d'œuvre
mastery *n* maîtrise
mat *n* tapis
match *n* match; allumette
match *v* assortir
mate *n* camarade
material *n* matière; étoffe
materialism *n* matérialisme
maternal *adj* maternel
maternity *n* maternité
math *n* maths
matriculate *v* immatriculer
matrimony *n* matrimonie
matter *n* affaire; problème
mattress *n* matelas
mature *adj* mûr
maturity *n* maturité
maul *v* molester
maxim *n* maxime
maximum *adj* maximum
May *n* mai

may *iv* pouvoir
may-be *adv* peut-être
mayhem *n* désordre
mayor *n* maire
maze *n* labyrinthe
meadow *n* pré
meager *adj* maigre
meal *n* repas
mean *iv* signifier
mean *adj* méchant
meaning *n* signification
meaningful *adj* significatif
meaningless *adj* insensé
meanness *n* méchanceté
means *n* moyen
meantime *adv* entre-temps
meanwhile *adv* pendant ce temps
measles *n* rougeole
measure *v* mesurer
measurement *n* dimension
meat *n* viande
meatball *n* boulette
mechanic *n* garagiste
mechanism *n* mécanisme
mechanize *v* mécaniser
medal *n* médaille
medallion *n* médaillon
meddle *v* mêler
mediate *v* négocier
mediator *n* médiateur
medication *n* médicament
medicinal *adj* médicinal

medicine *n* médecine
medieval *adj* médiéval
mediocre *adj* médiocre
mediocrity *n* médiocrité
meditate *v* méditer
meditation *n* méditation
medium *adj* moyen
meek *adj* docile
meekness *n* soumission
meet *iv* rencontrer
meeting *n* rencontre
melancholy *n* mélancolie
mellow *adj* calme
mellow *v* adoucir
melodic *adj* mélodieux
melody *n* mélodie
melon *n* melon
melt *v* fondre
member *n* membre
membership *n* adhésion
membrane *n* membrane
memento *n* souvenir
memo *n* note
memoirs *n* mémoires
memorable *adj* mémorable
memorize *v* mémoriser
memory *n* mémoire
men *n* hommes
menace *n* menace
mend *v* racommoder
meningitis *n* méningite
menopause *n* ménopause

menstruation *n* menstruation
mental *adj* mental
mentality *n* mentalité
mentally *adv* mentalement
mention *v* mentionner
mention *n* mention
menu *n* menu
merchandise *n* marchandise
merchant *n* marchant
merciful *adj* miséricordieux
merciless *adj* sans merci
mercury *n* mercure
mercy *n* pitié
merely *adv* simplement
merge *v* fusionner
merger *n* fusion
merit *n* mérite
merit *v* mériter
mermaid *n* sirène
merry *adj* joyeux
mesh *n* grillage
mesmerize *v* hypnotiser
mess *n* désordre
mess around *v* embêter
message *n* message
messenger *n* messager
Messiah *n* Messie
messy *adj* désordonné
metal *n* métal
metallic *adj* métallique
metaphor *n* métaphore
meteor *n* météore

M

meter *n* mètre
method *n* méthode
methodical *adj* méthodique
meticulous *adj* méticuleux
metric *adj* mètrique
metropolis *n* métropole
Mexican *adj* mexicain
mice *n* souris
microbe *n* microbe
microphone *n* microphone
microscope *n* microscope
microwave *n* micro-onde
midair *n* en plein ciel
midday *n* mi-journée
middle *n* milieu
middleman *n* intermédiaire
midget *n* nain
midnight *n* minuit
midwife *n* sage-femme
mighty *adj* puissant
migraine *n* migraine
migrant *n* migrant
migrate *v* émigrer
mild *adj* léger
mildew *n* moisissure
mile *n* mile
mileage *n* kilométrage
militant *adj* militant
milk *n* lait
milky *adj* laiteux
mill *n* moulin
millennium *n* millénaire

milligram *n* milligramme
millimeter *n* millimètre
million *n* million
millionaire *n* millionaire
mime *v* mimer
mince *v* hacher
mincemeat *n* viande hachée
mind *v* surveiller; déranger
mind *n* esprit
mind-boggling *adj* stupéfiant
mindful *adj* conscient
mindless *adj* abrutissant
mine *n* mine
mine *v* extraire
mine *pro* le mien
minefield *n* champ de mines
miner *n* mineur
mineral *n* minéral
mingle *v* se confondre
miniature *n* miniature
minimize *v* minimiser
minimum *n* minimum
miniskirt *n* mini-jupe
minister *n* ministre; pasteur
ministry *n* ministère
minor *adj* mineur
minority *n* minorité
mint *n* menthe
mint *v* frapper; forger
minus *adj* moins
minute *n* minute
miracle *n* miracle

M

miraculous *adj* miraculeux
mirage *n* mirage
mirror *n* miroir
misbehave *v* se dissiper
miscalculate *v* mal calculer
miscarriage *n* fausse-couche
mischief *n* espièglerie
mischievous *adj* espiègle
misdemeanor *n* délit
miser *n* avare
miserable *adj* misérable
misery *n* souffrance
misfit *adj* marginal
misfortune *n* malchance
misgiving *n* appréhension
misguided *adj* erroné
mislead *v* fourvoyer
misleading *adj* trompeur
misplace *v* égarer
misprint *n* coquille
miss *v* manquer
miss *n* manque
missile *n* missile
missing *adj* manquante
mission *n* mission
missionary *n* missionaire
mist *n* brume
mistake *iv* se tromper
mistake *n* erreur
mistaken *adj* erroné
mister *n* monsieur
mistreat *v* malmener

mistreatment *n* maltraitance
mistress *n* maîtresse
mistrust *n* méfiance
mistrust *v* se méfier
misty *adj* brumeux
mitigate *v* mitiger
mix *v* mélanger
mixed-up *adj* impliqué
mixer *n* mixeur
mixture *n* mixture
mix-up *n* confusion
moan *v* gémir
moan *n* gémissement
mob *v* asaillir
mob *n* foule
mobile *adj* mobile
mobilize *v* mobiliser
mobster *n* bandit
mock *v* moquer
mockery *n* moquerie
mode *n* mode
model *n* modèle
moderate *adj* modérer
moderation *n* modération
modern *adj* moderne
modernize *v* moderniser
modest *adj* modeste
modesty *n* modestie
modify *v* modifier
module *n* module
moisten *v* humecter
moisture *n* humidité

M

molar n molaire
mold v mouler
mold n moule
moldy adj moisi
mole n taupe
molecule n molécule
molest v molester
mom n maman
moment n moment
momentous adj essentiel
monarch n monarque
monarchy n monarchie
monastery n monastère
monastic adj monastique
Monday n Lundi
money n argent
money order n mandat postal
monitor v surveiller
monk n moine
monkey n singe
monogamy n monogamie
monologue n monologue
monopolize v monopoliser
monopoly n monopolie
monotonous adj monotone
monotony n monotonie
monster n monstre
monstrous adj monstrueux
month n mois
monthly adv mensuel
monument n monument
monumental adj monumental

mood n humeur
moody adj instable
moon n lune
moor v mouiller
mop v nettoyer
moral adj moral
moral n moral
morality n moralité
more adj plus
moreover adv de plus
morning n matin
moron adj crétin
morphine n morphine
morsel n morceau
mortal adj mortel
mortality n mortalité
mortar n mortier
mortgage n emprunt
mortification n mortification
mortify v mortifier
mortuary n mortuaire
mosaic n mosaïque
mosque n mosquée
mosquito n moustique
moss n mousse
most adj la plupart
mostly adv surtout
motel n motel
moth n mite
mother n mère
motherhood n maternité
mother-in-law n belle-mère

M

motion *n* mouvement
motionless *adj* immobile
motivate *v* miotiver
motive *n* motif
motor *n* moteur
motorcycle *n* moto
motto *n* devise
mouldy *adj* moisi
mount *n* mont
mount *v* monter
mountain *n* montagne
mountainous *adj* montagneux
mourn *v* pleurer
mourning *n* deuil
mouse *n* souris
mouth *n* bouche
move *n* mouvement
move *v* déménager
move back *v* retourner
move forward *v* avancer
move out *v* déménager
movement *n* mouvement
movie *n* film
mow *v* tondre
much *adv* beaucoup
mucus *n* mucus
mud *n* boue
muddle *n* pagaille
muddy *adj* boueux
muffle *v* assourdir
muffler *n* silencieux
mug *n* tasse

mug *v* agresser
mugging *n* agression
mule *n* mulet
multiple *adj* multiple
multiplication *n* multiplication
multiply *v* multiplier
multitude *n* multitude
mumble *v* marmonner
mummy *n* momie
mumps *n* oreillons
munch *v* mâcher
munitions *n* munitions
murder *n* meurtre
murderer *n* meurtrier
murky *adj* trouble
murmur *v* murmurer
murmur *n* murmure
muscle *n* muscle
museum *n* musée
mushroom *n* champignon
music *n* musique
musician *n* musicien
Muslim *adj* musulman
must *iv* devoir
mustache *n* moustache
mustard *n* moutarde
muster *v* rallier
mutate *v* muter
mute *adj* muet
mutilate *v* mutiler
mutiny *n* mutinerie
mutually *adv* mutuellement

M

muzzle *v* museler
muzzle *n* muselière
my *adj* mon; ma
myopic *adj* myope
myself *pro* moi-même
mysterious *adj* mystérieux
mystery *n* mystère
mystic *adj* mystique
mystify *v* mystifier
myth *n* mythe

M
N

nag *v* embêter
nagging *adj* tenace
nail *n* ongle
naive *adj* naïf
naked *adj* nu
name *n* nom
namely *adv* c'est-à-dire
nanny *n* nourrice
nap *n* sieste
napkin *n* serviette
narcotic *n* narcotique
narrate *v* narrer
narrow *adj* étroit
narrowly *adv* étroitement
nasty *adj* désagréable

nation *n* nation
national *adj* national
nationality *n* nationalité
nationalize *v* nationaliser
native *adj* natif
natural *adj* naturel
naturally *adv* naturellement
nature *n* nature
naughty *adj* désobéissant
nausea *n* nausée
nave *n* nef
navel *n* nombril
navigate *v* naviguer
navigation *n* navigation
navy *n* marrine
navy blue *adj* bleu marrine
near *pre* près
nearby *adj* proche
nearly *adv* presque
nearsighted *adj* myope
neat *adj* ordonné; cool
neatly *adv* soigneusement
necessary *adj* nécessaire
necessitate *v* nécessiter
necessity *n* nécessité
neck *n* cou
necklace *n* colier
necktie *n* cravate
need *v* devoir; manquer
need *n* besoin
needle *n* aiguille
needless *adj* inutile

needy *adj* nécessiteux
negative *adj* négatif
neglect *v* négliger
neglect *n* négligence
negligence *n* négligence
negligent *adj* négligent
negotiate *v* négocier
negotiation *n* négotiation
neighbor *n* voisin
neighborhood *n* voisinage
neither *adj* aucun
neither *adv* non plus
nephew *n* neveu
nerve *n* nerf
nervous *adj* nerveux
nest *n* nid
net *n* filet
Netherlands *n* Pays-Bas
network *n* réseau
neurotic *adj* névrosé
neutral *adj* neutre
neutralize *v* neutraliser
never *adv* jamais
nevertheless *adv* néanmoins
new *adj* nouveau
newborn *n* nouveau-né
newcomer *n* arrivant
newly *adv* nouvelement
newlywed *adj* jeunes mariés
news *n* informations
newsletter *n* bulletin
newspaper *n* journal

newsstand *n* kiosque
next *adj* suivant
next door *adj* à côté
nibble *v* grignoter
nice *adj* sympa
nicely *adv* gentiment
nickel *n* nickel
nickname *n* surnom
nicotine *n* nicotine
niece *n* nièce
night *n* nuit
nightfall *n* tombée de la nuit
nightgown *n* robe de nuit
nightingale *n* rossignol
nightmare *n* cauchemar
nine *adj* neuf
nineteen *adj* dix-neuf
ninety *adj* qutre-vingt-dix
ninth *adj* neuvième
nip *n* pincement
nip *v* pincer
nipple *n* mamelon
nitpicking *adj* pinailleur
nitrogen *n* azote
no one *pro* personne
nobility *n* noblesse
noble *adj* noble
nobleman *n* noble
nobody *pro* personne
nocturnal *adj* nocturne
nod *v* hocher; saluer
noise *n* bruit

N

noisily *adv* bruyamment
noisy *adj* bruyant
nominate *v* niminer
none *pre* aucun
nonetheless *c* pourtant
nonsense *n* baliverne
nonsmoker *n* non-fumeur
nonstop *adv* sans arrêt
noon *n* midi
noose *n* noeud coulant
nor *c* non plus
norm *n* norme
normal *adj* normal
normalize *v* normaliser
normally *adv* normalement
north *n* nord
northeast *n* nord-est
northern *adj* nordique
Norway *n* Norvège
Norwegian *adj* Norvègien
nose *n* nez
nostalgia *n* nostalgie
nostril *n* narine
nosy *adj* curieux
not *adv* ne...pas
notable *adj* notable
notably *adv* notablement
notary *n* notaire
notation *n* notation
note *v* noter
notebook *n* cahier
noteworthy *adj* notable

nothing *n* rien
notice *v* remarquer
notice *n* notification
noticeable *adj* apparent
notification *n* notification
notify *v* notifier
notion *n* notion
notorious *adj* notorieux
noun *n* nom
nourish *v* nourrir
nourishment *n* nourriture
novel *n* roman
novelist *n* romancier
novelty *n* nouveauté
November *n* novembre
novice *n* débutant
now *adv* maintenant
nowadays *adv* de nos jours
nowhere *adv* nulpart
noxious *adj* nocif
nozzle *n* embout
nuance *n* nuance
nuclear *adj* nucléaire
nude *adj* nu
nudism *n* nudisme
nudist *n* nudiste
nudity *n* nudité
nuisance *n* nuisance
null *adj* nul
nullify *v* annuler
numb *adj* engourdi
number *n* nombre

N

numerous *adj* nombreux
nun *n* religieuse
nurse *n* infirmier
nurse *v* soigner; allaiter
nursery *n* crèche; pépinière
nurture *v* élever
nut *n* noix; fou
nutrition *n* nutrition
nutritious *adj* nourrissant
nut-shell *n* coquille de noix
nutty *adj* dingue

oak *n* chêne
oar *n* rame
oasis *n* oasis
oath *n* serment
oatmeal *n* avoine
obedience *n* obéissance
obedient *adj* obéissant
obese *adj* obese
obey *v* obéir
object *v* protester
object *n* objet
objection *n* objection
objective *n* objectif
obligate *v* obliger

obligation *n* obligation
obligatory *adj* obligatoire
oblige *v* obliger
obliged *adj* obligé
oblique *adj* oblique
obliterate *v* obliterer
oblivion *n* oubli
oblivious *adj* inconscient
oblong *adj* oblongue
obnoxious *adj* odieux
obscene *adj* obscène
obscenity *n* obscènité
obscure *adj* obscure
obscurity *n* obscurité
observation *n* observation
observatory *n* observatoire
observe *v* observer
obsess *v* obséder
obsession *n* obsession
obsolete *adj* obsolète
obstacle *n* obstacle
obstinacy *n* opiniâtreté
obstinate *adj* obstiner
obstruct *v* bloquer
obstruction *n* obstruction
obtain *v* obtenir
obvious *adj* évident
obviously *adv* évidemment
occasion *n* occasion
occult *adj* occulte
occupant *n* occupant
occupation *n* occupation

N
O

occupy *v* occuper
occur survenir
occurrence *n* événement
ocean *n* océan
October *n* octobre
octopus *n* pieuvre
odd *adj* impair; curieux
oddity *n* curiosité
odds *n* chances
odious *adj* odieux
odometer *n* odomètre
odor *n* odeur
odyssey *n* odyssée
of *pre* de
offend *v* offenser
offense *n* offense
offensive *adj* offensif
offer *v* offrir
offer *n* offre
offering *n* offrande
office *n* bureau
officer *n* officier
official *adj* officiel
offset *v* compenser
offspring *n* progéniture
off-the-record *adj* confidentiel
often *adv* souvent
oil *n* pétrole; huile
ointment *n* pommade
okay *adv* d'accord
old *adj* vieux
old age *n* vieillesse

old-fashioned *adj* vieux jeu
olive *n* olive
olympics *n* jeux olympiques
omelette *n* omelette
omen *n* présage
ominous *adj* fatidique
omission *n* omission
omit *v* omettre
on *pre* sur
once *adv* une fois
once *c* dès que
one *adj* un
oneself *pre* soi-même
ongoing *adj* continuel
onion *n* oignon
onlooker *n* spectateur
only *adv* seulement
onset *n* début
onslaught *n* attaque
onwards *adv* en avant
opaque *adj* opaque
open *v* ouvrir
open *adj* ouvert
open up *v* ouvrir
opening *n* ouverture
open-minded *adj* ouvert d'esprit
openness *n* franchise
opera *n* opéra
operate *v* opérer
operation *n* opération
opinion *n* opinion
opinionated *adj* obstiné

opium *n* opium
opponent *n* adversaire
opportune *adj* opportun
opportunity *n* opportunité
oppose *v* opposer
opposite *adj* opposé
opposite *adv* en face
opposite *n* contraire
opposition *n* opposition
oppress *v* opprimer
oppression *n* oppression
opt for *v* opter
optical *adj* optique
optician *n* opticien
optimism *n* optimisme
optimistic *adj* optimiste
option *n* option
optional *adj* optionel
opulence *n* opulence
or *c* ou
oracle *n* oracle
orally *adv* oralement
orange *n* orange
orangutan *n* orang-outang
orbit *n* orbite
orchard *n* verger
orchestra *n* orchestre
ordain *v* ordonner
ordeal *n* épreuve
order *n* commande
ordinarily *adv* ordinairement
ordinary *adj* ordinaire

ordination *n* ordination
ore *n* minerai
organ *n* organe
organism *n* organisme
organist *n* organiste
organization *n* organisation
organize *v* organiser
orient *n* orient
oriental *adj* oriental
orientation *n* orientation
oriented *adj* orienté
origin *n* origine
original *adj* original
originally *adv* à l'original
originate *v* commencer
ornament *n* ornement
ornamental *adj* ornemental
orphan *n* orphelin
orphanage *n* orphelinat
orthodox *adj* orthodoxe
ostentatious *adj* ostentatoire
ostrich *n* autruche
other *adj* autre
otherwise *adv* autrement
otter *n* loutre
ought to *iv* devoir
ounce *n* once
our *adj* notre/nos
ours *pro* nôtre
ourselves *pro* nous-mêmes
oust *v* remplacer
out *adv* dehors

O

outbreak *n* irruption

outburst *n* explosion

outcast *adj* exclu

outcome *n* résultat

outcry *n* huées

outdated *adj* dépassé

outdo *v* surpasser

outdoor *adv* extérieur

outdoors *adv* plein air

outer *adj* extérieur

outfit *n* ensemble

outgoing *adj* sociable

outing *n* sortie

outlast *v* durer

outlaw *v* défendre

outlet *n* sortie; prise

outline *n* plan; contour

outline *v* ébaucher

outlive *v* survivre

outlook *n* perspectives

outmoded *adj* suranné

outperform *v* surpasser

outpouring *n* épanchement

output *n* rendement

outrage *n* outrage

outrageous *adj* outrageant

outright *adj* absolu

outrun *v* distancier

outset *n* début

outshine *v* éclipser

outside *adv* extérieur

outsider *n* étranger

outskirts *n* périphérie

outspoken *adj* franc

outstanding *adj* remarquable

outstretched *adj* tendu

outward *adj* extérieur

oval *adj* oval

ovary *n* ovaire

ovation *n* ovation

oven *n* four

over *pre* par-dessus

overall *adv* globalement

overbearing *adj* dominateur

overboard *adv* par-dessus bord

overcast *adj* couvert

overcharge *v* surcharger

overcoat *n* pardessus

overcome *v* triompher

overcrowded *adj* surpeuplé

overdo *v* exagérer

overdone *adj* exagéré

overdose *n* overdose

overdue *adj* en retard

overestimate *v* surestimer

overflow *v* inonder

overhaul *v* moderniser

overlap *v* chevaucher

overlook *v* négliger

overpower *v* vaincre

override *v* outrepasser

overrule *v* rejeter

overrun *v* envahir

overseas *adv* outre-mer

oversee *v* gérer
overshadow *v* éclipser
oversight *n* inadvertance
overstate *v* grandir
overstep *v* transgresser
overtake *v* doubler
overthrow *v* renverser
overthrow *n* renversement
overturn *v* culbuter
overview *n* vue d'ensemble
overweight *adj* corpulent
overwhelm *v* submerger
owe *v* devoir
owing to *adv* à cause de
owl *n* hibou
own *v* posséder
own *adj* propre
owner *n* propriétaire
ownership *n* propriété
ox *n* bœuf
oxygen *n* oxygène
oyster *n* huître

pace *n* pass
pacify *v* pacifier
pack *v* emballer
package *n* paquet
pact *n* pacte
pad *v* rembourrer
padding *n* rembourrage
paddle *v* pagayer
padlock *n* cadenas
pagan *adj* païen
page *n* page; passage
pail *n* seau
pain *n* douleur
painful *adj* douloureux
painkiller *n* analgésique
painless *adj* indolore
paint *v* peindre
paint *n* peinture
paintbrush *n* pinceau
painter *n* peintre
painting *n* tableau; peinture
pair *n* pair
pajamas *n* pyjama
pal *n* copain
palace *n* palace
palate *n* palais
pale *adj* pâle
paleness *n* pâleur
palm *n* paume

O
P

palpable *adj* palpable
paltry *adj* paltry
pamper *v* choyer
pamphlet *n* brochure
pan *n* casserole
pancreas *n* pancréas
pander *v* flatter
pang *n* crampe
panic *n* panique
panorama *n* panorama
panther *n* panthère
pantry *n* garde-manger
pants *n* pantalon
pantyhose *n* collant
papacy *n* papauté
paper *n* papier
paperclip *n* trombonne
paperwork *n* paperasserie
parable *n* parabole
parachute *n* parachute
parade *n* parade
paradise *n* paradis
paradox *n* paradoxe
paragraph *n* paragraphe
parakeet *n* perroquet
parallel *n* parallèle
paralysis *n* paralysie
paralyze *v* paralyser
parameters *n* paramètre
paramount *adj* prédominant
paranoid *adj* paranoïde
parasite *n* parasite

paratrooper *n* parachutiste
parcel *n* paquet
parcel post *n* colis postaux
parch *v* dessécher
parchment *n* parchemin
pardon *v* pardonner
pardon *n* pardon
parenthesis *n* parenthèse
parents *n* parents
parish *n* parois
parishioner *n* paroissien
parity *n* parité
park *v* garer
park *n* parc
parking *n* parking
parliament *n* parlement
parrot *n* perroquet
parsley *n* persil
parsnip *n* panais
part *v* séparer
part *n* partie
partial *adj* partiel
partially *adv* partielement
participate *v* participer
participation *n* participation
participle *n* participe
particle *n* particule
particular *adj* particulier
particularly *adv* spécialement
parting *n* séparation
partisan *n* partisan
partition *n* partition**

partly *adv* en partie
partner *n* partenaire
partnership *n* partenariat
partridge *n* perdrix
party *n* soirée; partie
pass *n* passe
pass *v* passer
pass around *v* faire circuler
pass away *v* décéder
pass out *v* s'évanouir
passage *n* passage
passenger *n* passager
passer-by *n* passant
passion *n* passion
passionate *adj* passioné
passive *adj* passif
passport *n* passeport
password *n* mot de passe
past *adj* passé
paste *v* coller
paste *n* pâte
pasteurize *v* pasteuriser
pastime *n* passe-temps
pastor *n* pasteur
pastoral *adj* pastoral
pastry *n* pâtisserie
pasture *n* pâturage
pat *n* pate
patch *v* rapiécer
patch *n* piéce
patent *n* brevet
patent *adj* manifeste

paternity *n* paternité
path *n* chemin
pathetic *adj* pathétique
patience *n* patience
patient *adj* patient
patio *n* patio
patriarch *n* patriarche
patrimony *n* patrimoine
patriot *n* patriote
patriotic *adj* patriotique
patrol *n* patrouille
patron *n* patron; mécène
patronage *n* patronage
patronize *v* patronner
pattern *n* patron
pavement *n* chaussée
pavilion *n* pavillon
paw *n* patte
pawnbroker *n* prêteur sur gage
pay *n* salaire
pay *iv* payer
pay back *v* rembourser
payable *adj* payable
paycheck *n* paye
payee *n* bénéficiaire
payment *n* paiement
pea *n* pois
peace *n* paix
peaceful *adj* paisible
peach *n* pêche
peacock *n* paon
peak *n* pic

P

peanut *n* cacahuète
pear *n* poire
pearl *n* perle
peasant *n* paysan
pebble *n* galet
peck *v* picorer
peck *n* coup de bec
peculiar *adj* particulier
pedagogy *n* pédagogie
pedal *n* pédale
pedantic *adj* pédant
pedestrian *n* pédestrien
peel *v* perler
peel *n* pelure; peau
peer *n* pair
pelican *n* pélican
pellet *n* balle
pen *n* stylo
penalize *v* pénaliser
penalty *n* pénalité
penance *n* pénitence
penchant *n* penchant
pencil *n* crayon
pendant *n* pendantif
pending *adj* imminent
pendulum *n* pendule
penetrate *v* pénétrer
penguin *n* pingouin
penicillin *n* pénicilline
peninsula *n* péninsule
penitent *n* pénitent
penniless *adj* sans sou

penny *n* 1 cent
pension *n* pension
pentagon *n* pentagone
pent-up *adj* cloîtré
people *n* gens
pepper *n* poivre
per *pre* par
perceive *v* percevoir
percent *adv* pour cent
percentage *n* pourcentage
perception *n* perception
perennial *adj* pérenne
perfect *adj* parfait
perfection *n* perfection
perforate *v* perforer
perforation *n* perforation
perform *v* jouer; accomplir
performance *n* performance
perfume *n* parfum
perhaps *adv* peut-être
peril *n* péril
perilous *adj* périlleux
perimeter *n* périmètre
period *n* période
perish *v* périr
perishable *adj* périssable
perjury *n* parjure
permanent *adj* permanent
permeate *v* imprégner
permission *n* permission
permit *v* permettre
pernicious *adj* pernicieux

P

perpetrate *v* perpétrer
persecute *v* persécuter
persevere *v* persévérer
persist *v* persister
persistence *n* persistance
persistent *adj* persistant
person *n* personne
personal *adj* personnel
personality *n* personnalité
personify *v* personnifier
personnel *n* personnel
perspective *n* perspective
perspiration *n* transpiration
perspire *v* transprirer
persuade *v* persuader
persuasion *n* persuasion
persuasive *adj* persuasif
pertain *v* concerner
pertinent *adj* pertinent
perturb *v* perturber
perverse *adj* pervers
pervert *v* pervertir
pervert *adj* pervers
pessimism *n* pessimisme
pessimistic *adj* pessimiste
pest *n* peste
pester *v* harceler
pesticide *n* pesticide
petal *n* pétale
petite *adj* petite
petition *n* pétition
petrified *adj* pétrifié

petroleum *n* pétrole
pettiness *n* mesquinerie
petty *adj* mineur; mesquin
pew *n* banc d'église
phantom *n* fantôme
pharmacist *n* pharmacien
pharmacy *n* pharmacie
phase *n* phase
pheasant *n* faisan
phenomenon *n* phénomène
philosopher *n* philosophe
philosophy *n* philosophie
phobia *n* phobie
phone *n* téléphone
phone *v* téléphoner
phoney *adj* poseur
phosphorus *n* phosphore
photo *n* photo
photocopy *n* photocopie
photograph *v* photographier
photographer *n* photographe
photography *n* photographie
phrase *n* phrase
physically *adv* physiquement
physician *n* docteur
physics *n* physique
pianist *n* pianiste
piano *n* piano
pick *v* choisir; cueillir
pick up *v* ramasser
pickpocket *n* pickpocket
pickup *n* camionette

picture *n* photo; image
picture *v* imaginer
picturesque *adj* pitoresque
pie *n* tarte
piece *n* morceau
piecemeal *adv* petit à petit
pier *n* embarcadère
pierce *v* percer
piercing *n* piercing
piety *n* pitié
pig *n* cochon
pigeon *n* pigeon
piggy bank *n* tirelire
pile *v* empiler
pile *n* pile
pile up *v* s'accumuler
pilfer *v* marauder
pilgrim *n* pèlerin
pilgrimage *n* pèlerinage
pill *n* pilule
pillage *v* pillage
pillar *n* pilier
pillow *n* oreiller
pillowcase *n* taie d'oreiller
pilot *n* pilote
pimple *n* bouton
pin *n* épingle
pincers *n* tenailles
pinch *v* pincer
pinch *n* pincée; pincement
pine *n* pin
pineapple *n* ananas

pink *adj* rose
pinpoint *v* localiser
pint *n* pinte
pioneer *n* pionnier
pious *adj* pieux
pipe *n* pipe
pipeline *n* oléoduc
piracy *n* piraterie
pirate *n* pirate
pistol *n* pistolet
pit *n* fosse
pitchfork *n* fourche
pitfall *n* embûche; fraude
pitiful *adj* pitoyable
pity *n* pitié
placard *n* placard
placate *v* calmer
place *n* endroit
placid *adj* placide
plague *n* peste
plain *n* plaine
plain *adj* simple; uni
plainly *adv* sobrement
plaintiff *n* plaignant
plan *v* planifier
plan *n* plan
plane *n* avion
planet *n* planète
plant *v* planter
plant *n* plante
plaster *n* plâtre
plaster *v* plâtrer

P

plastic *n* plastique
plate *n* assiette
plateau *n* plateau
platform *n* plate-forme
platinum *n* platine
platoon *n* peloton
plausible *adj* plausible
play *v* jouer; mettre
play *n* jeu; partie
player *n* joueur
playful *adj* joueur
plea *n* supplication
plead *v* plaider; supplier
pleasant *adj* plaisant
please *v* satisfaire
pleasing *adj* plaisant
pleasure *n* plaisir
pleat *n* pli
pleated *adj* plié
pledge *v* promettre
pledge *n* promesse
plentiful *adj* abondant
plenty *n* abondance
pliable *adj* malléable
pliers *n* tenailles
plot *v* comploter
plot *n* complot
plow *v* labourer
ploy *n* stratagème
pluck *v* cueillir
plug *v* brancher
plug *n* prise; cheville

plum *n* prune
plumber *n* plombier
plumbing *n* plomberie
plummet *v* s'effondrer
plump *adj* potelé
plunder *v* piller
plunge *v* plonger; chuter
plunge *n* plongeon
plural *n* pluriel
plus *adj* plus
plush *adj* peluché
plutonium *n* plutonium
pneumonia *n* pneumonie
pocket *n* poche
poem *n* poème
poet *n* poète
poetry *n* poèsie
poignant *adj* poignant
point *n* pointe
point *v* diriger; indiquer
pointed *adj* pointu
pointless *adj* inutile
poise *n* sang-froid
poison *v* empoisoner
poison *n* poison
poisoning *n* empoisonant
poisonous *adj* vénéneux
Poland *n* Polande
polar *adj* polaire
pole *n* pole
police *n* police
policeman *n* policier

P

policy *n* politique
Polish *adj* Polonais
polish *n* cire
polish *v* polir
polite *adj* poli
politeness *n* politesse
politician *n* politicien
politics *n* politique
poll *n* sondage
pollen *n* pollen
pollute *v* polluer
pollution *n* pollution
polygamist *adj* polygamiste
polygamy *n* polygamie
pomegranate *n* grenade
pomposity *n* emphase
pond *n* mare
ponder *v* délibérer
pontiff *n* pontife
pool *n* piscine; billard
poor *n* pauvre
poorly *adv* pauvrement
popcorn *n* popcorn
Pope *n* Pape
poppy *n* pavot
popular *adj* populaire
popularize *v* populariser
populate *v* résider
population *n* population
porcelain *n* porcelaine
porch *n* porche
porcupine *n* porc-épic

pore *n* pore
pork *n* porc
porous *adj* poreux
port *n* port
portable *adj* portable
portent *n* présage
porter *n* porteur
portion *n* portion
portrait *n* portrait
portray *v* décrire
Portugal *n* Portugal
Portuguese *adj* portugais
pose *v* poser; constituer
pose *n* pose
posh *adj* chic
position *n* position
positive *adj* positive
possess *v* posséder
possession *n* possession
possibility *n* possibilité
possible *adj* possible
post *n* poste; courrier
post office *n* poste
postage *n* affranchissement
postcard *n* carte postale
poster *n* poster
posterity *n* postérité
postman *n* facteur
postmark *n* cachet postal
postpone *v* ajourner
postponement *n* ajournement
pot *n* pot; canabis

P

potato *n* pomme de terre
potent *adj* puissant
potential *adj* potentiel
pothole *n* nid-de-poule
poultry *n* volaille
pound *v* marteler
pound *n* livre
pour *v* verser
poverty *n* pauvreté
powder *n* poudre
power *n* pouvoir
powerful *adj* puissant
powerless *adj* sans pouvoir
practical *adj* pratique
practice *n* entraînement
practise *v* s'entraîner
practising *adj* pratiquant
pragmatist *adj* pragmatique
prairie *n* prairie
praise *v* louer
praise *n* louange
praiseworthy *adj* louable
prank *n* farce
prawn *n* crevette
pray *v* prier
prayer *n* prière
preach *v* prêcher
preacher *n* pasteur
preaching *n* prédication
preamble *n* preamble
precarious *adj* précaire
precaution *n* précaution

precede *v* précéder
precedent *n* précédent
preceding *adj* précédent
precept *n* précepte
precious *adj* précieux
precipice *n* précipice
precipitate *v* précipiter
precise *adj* précis
precision *n* précision
precocious *adj* précoce
precursor *n* précurseur
predecessor *n* prédécesseur
predicament *n* prédicament
predict *v* prédir
prediction *n* prédiction
predilection *n* prédilection
predisposed *adj* prédisposé
predominate *v* prédominer
preempt *v* préempter
prefabricate *v* préfrabriquer
preface *n* préface
prefer *v* préférer
preference *n* préférence
prefix *n* préfixe
pregnancy *n* grossesse
pregnant *adj* enceinte
prehistoric *adj* préhistorique
prejudice *n* préjudice
preliminary *adj* préliminaire
prelude *n* prélude
premature *adj* prématuré
premeditate *v* prémédité

premeditation *n* préméditation

premier *adj* premier

premise *n* prémisse

premonition *n* prémonition

preoccupation *n* préoccupation

preoccupy *v* préoccuper

preparation *n* préparation

prepare *v* préparer

preposition *n* préposition

prerequisite *n* préalable

prerogative *n* prérogative

prescribe *v* prescrire

prescription *n* prescription

presence *n* présence

present *adj* présent

present *v* présenter

presentation *n* présentation

preserve *v* préserver

preside *v* présider

presidency *n* présidence

president *n* président

press *n* presse; pression

press *v* presser; pousser

pressing *adj* pressant

pressure *v* taire pression

pressure *n* pression

prestige *n* prestige

presume *v* présumer

presumption *n* présomption

presuppose *v* présupposer

presupposition *n* présupposition

pretend *v* prétendre

pretense *n* façade

pretension *n* prétention

pretty *adj* joli

prevail *v* prévaloir

prevalent *adj* répandu

prevent *v* empêcher

prevention *n* prévention

preventive *adj* préventif

preview *n* bande annonce

previous *adj* précédent

previously *adv* auparavant

prey *n* proie

price *n* prix

pricey *adj* cher

prick *v* piquer

pride *n* fierté

priest *n* prêtre

priestess *n* prêtresse

priesthood *n* prêtrise

primacy *n* primauté

primarily *adv* essentiellement

prime *adj* principal

primitive *adj* primitif

prince *n* prince

princess *n* princesse

principal *adj* principal

principle *n* principe

print *v* imprimer

print *n* empreinte

printer *n* imprimante

printing *n* impression

prior *adj* antérieur

priority n prioritaire
prism n prisme
prison n prison
prisoner n prisonier
privacy n vie privée
private adj privé
privilege n privilège
prize n prix
probability n probabilité
probable adj probable
probe v sonder
probing n probatoire
problem n problème
problematic adj problèmatique
procedure n procédure
proceed v procéder
proceedings n procédure
proceeds n recette
process v procéder
process n processus
procession n procession
proclaim v proclamer
proclamation n proclamation
procrastinate v procrastiner
procreate v procreate
procure v procurer
prod v inciter
prodigious adj prodigieux
prodigy n prodige
produce v produire
produce n produits
product n produit

production n production
productive adj productif
profane adj profane
profess v professer
profession n profession
professional adj professionel
professor n professeur
proficiency n compétence
proficient adj compétent
profile n profile
profit v profiter
profit n profit
profitable adj profitable
profound adj profond
program n programme
programmer n programmeur
progress v progresser
progress n progrès
progressive adj progressif
prohibit v interdire
prohibition n prohibition
project v projeter
project n projet
projectile n projectile
prologue n prologue
prolong v prolonger
promenade n promenade
prominent adj prominent
promise n promesse
promote v promouvoir
promotion n promotion
prompt adj rapide

prone *adj* prostré
pronoun *n* pronom
pronounce *v* prononcer
proof *n* preuve
propaganda *n* propagande
propagate *v* propager
propel *v* propulser
propensity *n* propension
proper *adj* correct
properly *adv* correctement
property *n* propriété
prophecy *n* prophétie
prophet *n* prophète
proportion *n* proportion
proposal *n* proposition
propose *v* proposer
proposition *n* proposition
prose *n* prose
prosecute *v* poursuivre
prosecutor *n* procureur
prospect *n* espoir
prosper *v* prospérer
prosperity *n* prospérité
prosperous *adj* prospère
prostate *n* prostate
prostrate *adj* prostré
protect *v* protéger
protection *n* protection
protein *n* protéine
protest *v* protester
protest *n* proteste
protocol *n* protocole

prototype *n* prototype
protract *v* prolonger
protracted *adj* prolongé
protrude *v* dépasser
proud *adj* fier
proudly *adv* fièrement
prove *v* prouver
proven *adj* prouvé
proverb *n* proverbe
provide *v* fournir
providence *n* providence
providing that *c* à condition que
province *n* province
provision *n* provision
provisional *adj* provisoire
provocation *n* provocation
provoke *v* provoquer
prow *n* proue
prowl *v* rôder
prowler *n* rôdeur
proximity *n* proximité
proxy *n* mandataire
prudence *n* prudence
prudent *adj* prudent
prune *v* tailler
prune *n* pruneau
prurient *adj* lubrique
pseudonym *n* pseudonyme
psychiatrist *n* psychiatre
psychiatry *n* psychiatrie
psychic *adj* psychique
psychology *n* psychologie**

P

psychopath *n* psychopathe
puberty *n* puberté
public *adj* publique
publication *n* publication
publicity *n* publicité
publicly *adv* publiquement
publish *v* publier
publisher *n* éditeur
pudding *n* pudding
puerile *adj* puéril
puff *n* bouffée
puffy *adj* bouffi
pull *v* tirer
pull down *v* décendre
pull out *v* déboîter
pulley *n* poulie
pulp *n* pulpe
pulpit *n* pupitre
pulsate *v* pulser
pulse *n* pulse
pulverize *v* pulvériser
pump *v* pomper
pump *n* pompe
pumpkin *n* citrouille
punch *v* cogner
punch *n* coup de poing
punctual *adj* ponctuel
puncture *n* crevaison
punish *v* punir
punishable *adj* punissable
punishment *n* punission
pupil *n* élève

puppet *n* marionnette
puppy *n* chiot
purchase *v* acheter
purchase *n* achat
pure *adj* pur
puree *n* purée
purgatory *n* purgatoire
purge *n* purge
purge *v* purger
purification *n* purification
purify *v* purifier
purity *n* pureté
purple *adj* violet
purpose *n* raison
purposely *adv* exprès
purse *n* sac à main
pursue *v* poursuivre
pursuit *n* poursuite
pus *n* pus
push *v* pousser
pushy *adj* arriviste
put *iv* prendre; mettre
put away *v* ranger
put off *v* effrayer
put out *v* éteindre
put up *v* opposer
put up with *v* supporter
putrid *adj* putride
puzzle *n* puzzle
puzzling *adj* déroutant
pyramid *n* pyramide
python *n* python

quagmire *n* bourbier
quail *n* caille
quake *v* trembler
qualify *v* qualifier
quality *n* qualité
qualm *n* nausée
quandery *n* dilemme
quantity *n* quantité
quarrel *v* se quereller
quarrel *n* querelle
quarrelsome *adj* querelleur
quarry *n* carrière
quarter *n* quart
quarterly *adj* trimestriel
quash *v* annuler; rejeter
queen *n* reine
queer *adj* singulier
quell *v* soulager
quench *v* étancher
quest *n* quête
question *v* questionner
question *n* question
questionable *adj* discutable
questionnaire *n* questionnaire
queue *n* queue
quick *adj* rapide
quicken *v* accélérer
quickly *adv* rapidement
quicksand *n* sable mouvant

quiet *adj* silencieux
quietness *n* silence
quilt *n* quilt
quit *iv* partir
quite *adv* complètement
quiver *v* tremblement
quiz *v* tester
quotation *n* guillemet
quote *v* citer
quotient *n* quotient

rabbi *n* rabbi
rabbit *n* lapin
rabies *n* rage
raccoon *n* raton laveur
race *n* course; race
racism *n* racisme
racist *adj* raciste
racket *n* raquette; raffut
racketeering *n* racket
radar *n* radar
radiation *n* radiation
radiator *n* radiateur
radical *adj* radical
radio *n* radio
radish *n* radis

radius *n* radius
raffle *n* tombola
raft *n* radeau
rag *n* chiffon
rage *n* rage
ragged *adj* déchiqueté
raid *n* razzia; raid
raider *n* pilleur
rail *n* rail; balustrade
railroad *n* chemin de fer
rain *n* pluie
rain *v* pleuvoir
rainbow *n* arc-en-ciel
raincoat *n* imperméable
rainfall *n* précipitations
rainy *adj* pluvieux
raise *n* augmentation
raise *v* augmenter
raisin *n* raisin sec
rake *n* râteau
rally *n* rassemblement
ram *n* bélier
ram *v* enfoncer
ramification *n* ramification
ramp *n* rampe
rampage *v* saccager
rampant *adj* rampant
ramson *n* rançon
ranch *n* ranch
rancor *n* rancœur
randomly *adv* au hasard
range *n* gamme

rank *n* rang; grade
rank *v* classer
ransack *v* fouiller
rape *v* violer
rape *n* viol
rapid *adj* rapide
rapist *n* violeur
rapport *n* rapport
rare *adj* rare
rarely *adv* rarement
rascal *n* coquin
rash *n* rougeurs
raspberry *n* framboise
rat *n* rat
rate *n* rythme; taux
rather *adv* plutôt
ratification *n* ratification
ratify *v* ratifier
ratio *n* ratio
ration *v* rationner
ration *n* ration
rational *adj* rationnel
rationalize *v* rationaliser
rattle *v* vibrer
ravage *v* ravager
ravage *n* ravage
rave *v* s'emballer
raven *n* corbeau
ravine *n* ravin
raw *adj* cru
ray *n* rayon
raze *v* raser

R

razor *n* rasoir
reach *v* atteindre
reach *n* compétence
react *v* réagir
reaction *n* réaction
read *iv* lire
reader *n* lecteur
readiness *n* préparation
reading *n* lecture
ready *adj* prêt
real *adj* réel
realism *n* réalisme
reality *n* réalité
realize *v* réaliser
really *adv* vraiment
realm *n* royaume
reap *v* moissonner
reappear *v* reparaître
rear *v* se cabrer
rear *n* arrière
rear *adj* arrière
reason *v* raisonner
reason *n* raison
reasonable *adj* raisonnable
reasoning *n* raisonnement
reassure *v* rassurer
rebate *n* rabais
rebel *v* se rebeller
rebel *n* rebelle
rebellion *n* rebellion
rebirth *n* renaissance
rebound *v* rebondir

rebuff *v* repousser; refuser
rebuff *n* rebuffade
rebuild *v* reconstruire
rebuke *v* réprimander
rebuke *n* réprimande
rebut *v* réfuter
recall *v* rapeller
recant *v* se rétracter
recap *v* récapituler
recapture *v* recapturer
recede *v* s'estomper
receipt *n* note
receive *v* recevoir
recent *adj* récent
reception *n* réception
receptionist *n* réceptioniste
receptive *adj* réceptif
recess *n* récréation
recession *n* récession
recharge *v* recharger
recipe *n* recette
reciprocal *adj* réciproque
recital *n* récital
recite *v* réciter
reckless *adj* imprudent
reckon *v* compter
reckon on *v* compter sur
reclaim *v* réclamer
recline *v* incliner
recluse *n* reclus
recognize *v* reconnaître
recollect *v* se souvenir

R

recollection *n* souvenir
recommend *v* recommander
recompense *v* récompenser
recompense *n* récompense
reconcile *v* réconcilier
reconsider *v* reconsidérer
reconstruct *v* reconstruire
record *v* enregistre
record *n* disque; registre
recorder *n* flûte
recording *n* enregistrement
recount *n* recomptage
recoup *v* récupérer
recourse *v* recourrir
recourse *n* recours
recover *v* recouvrir
recovery *n* rétablissement
recreate *v* recréer
recreation *n* récréation
recruit *v* recruter
recruit *n* recru
recruitment *n* recrutement
rectangle *n* rectangle
rectangular *adj* rectangulaire
rectify *v* rectifier
rector *n* pasteur
rectum *n* rectum
recuperate *v* récupérer
recur *v* réapparaître
recurrence *n* récurrence
recycle *v* recycler
red *adj* rouge

red tape *n* paperasserie
redden *v* rougir
redeem *v* retirer
redemption *n* rédemption
redo *v* refaire
redouble *v* redoubler
redress *v* réparation
reduce *v* réduire
redundant *adj* redondant
reed *n* roseau
reef *n* récif
reel *n* réel; moulinet
reelect *v* réélire
reenactment *n* reconstitution
reentry *n* rentrée
refer to *v* évoquer
referee *n* arbitre
reference *n* référence
referendum *n* référendum
refill *v* remplir
refine *v* raffiner
refinery *n* raffinerie
reflect *v* refléter
reflection *n* reflet
reflexive *adj* réfléchi
reform *v* réformer
reform *n* réforme
refrain *v* se retenir
refresh *v* rafraîchir
refreshing *adj* rafraîchissant
refrigerate *v* frigorifier
refuge *n* refuge

R

refugee _n_ réfugié
refund _v_ rembourser
refurbish _v_ rénover
refusal _n_ refus
refuse _v_ refuser
refuse _n_ refus
refute _v_ réfuter
regain _v_ retrouver
regal _adj_ royal
regard _v_ considérer
regarding _pre_ concernant
regardless _adv_ quoi qu'il en soit
regards _n_ amitiés
regeneration _n_ régénération
regent _n_ régent
regime _n_ régime
regiment _n_ régiment
region _n_ région
regional _adj_ régional
register _v_ registe
registration _n_ inscription
regret _v_ regretter
regret _n_ regret
regrettable _adj_ regrettable
regularity _n_ régularité
regularly _adv_ régulièrement
regulate _v_ réguler
regulation _n_ régulation
rehabilitate _v_ réhabiliter
rehearsal _n_ répétition
rehearse _v_ répéter
reign _v_ règner

reign _n_ règne
reimburse _v_ rembourser
rein _n_ rêne
reindeer _n_ renne
reinforce _v_ renforcer
reinforcements _n_ renfort
reiterate _v_ réitérer
reject _v_ refuser
rejection _n_ rejet
rejoice _v_ se réjouir
rejoin _v_ rejoindre
rejuvenate _v_ rajeunir
relapse _n_ rechute
related _adj_ apparenté
relationship _n_ rapports
relative _adj_ relatif
relative _n_ parent
relax _v_ se relaxer
relaxation _n_ relaxation
relaxing _adj_ relaxant
relay _v_ relayer
release _v_ lâcher; sortir
relegate _v_ reléguer
relent _v_ céder
relentless _adj_ acharné
relevant _adj_ pertinent
reliable _adj_ fiable
reliance _n_ confiance
relic _n_ relique
relief _n_ soulagement
relieve _v_ soulager; relever
religion _n_ religion

R

religious *adj* religieux
relinquish *v* abandonner
relish *v* s'avourer
relive *v* revivre
relocate *v* délocaliser
relocation *n* délocalisation
reluctant *adj* réticent
rely on *v* fier
remain *v* rester
remainder *n* reste
remaining *adj* restant
remains *n* restes
remake *v* refaire
remark *v* remarquer
remark *n* remarque
remarkable *adj* remarquable
remarry *v* se remarier
remedy *v* remèdier
remedy *n* remède
remember *v* se rappeller
remembrance *n* souvenir
remind *v* se rappeller
reminder *n* rappel
remission *n* rémission
remit *v* attibutions
remittance *n* versement
remnant *n* reste
remodel *v* remodeler
remorse *n* remords
remote *adj* isolé
removal *n* enlèvement
remove *v* enlever

remunerate *v* rémunérer
renew *v* renouveler
renewal *n* renouveau
renounce *v* renoncer
renovate *v* rénover
renovation *n* rénovation
renowned *adj* célèbre
rent *v* louer
rent *n* loyer
reorganize *v* réorganiser
repair *v* réparation
reparation *n* réparation
repatriate *v* rapatrier
repay *v* rembourser
repeal *v* abroger
repeal *n* abrogation
repeat *v* répéter
repel *v* repousser
repent *v* repentir
repentance *n* repentance
repetition *n* répétition
replace *v* remplacer
replenish *v* reconstituer
replete *adj* rempli
replica *n* réplique
replicate *v* répliquer
reply *v* répondre
reply *n* réponse
report *v* rapporter
report *n* rapport
reporter *n* reporter
repose *v* reposer

R

repose *n* repos
represent *v* représenter
repress *v* réprimer
repression *n* répression
reprieve *n* diminution
reprint *v* réimprimer
reprint *n* réimpression
reprisal *n* représailles
reproach *v* reprocher
reproach *n* reproche
reproduce *v* reproduire
reproduction *n* reproduction
reptile *n* reptile
republic *n* république
repudiate *v* répudier
repugnant *adj* répugnant
repulse *v* repousser
repulsive *adj* repoussant
reputation *n* réputation
reputedly *adv* apparemment
request *v* solliciter
request *n* demande
require *v* exiger
requirement *n* obligation
rescue *v* sauver
rescue *n* secours
research *v* rechercher
research *n* chercheur
resemblance *n* ressemblance
resemble *v* ressembler
resent *v* ne pas aimer
resentment *n* ressentiment

reservation *n* réserve
reserve *v* réserver
reservoir *n* réservoir
reside *v* résider
residence *n* résidence
residue *n* résidu
resign *v* démissionner
resignation *n* démission
resilient *adj* résilient
resist *v* résister
resistance *n* résistance
resolute *adj* résolu
resolution *n* résolution
resolve *v* résoudre
resort *v* recourir
resounding *adj* retentissant
resource *n* ressource
respect *v* respecter
respect *n* respect
respectful *adj* respectueux
respective *adj* respectif
respiration *n* respiration
respite *n* répit
respond *v* répondre
response *n* réponse
responsibility *n* responsabilité
responsible *adj* responsable
responsive *adj* réactif
rest *v* se reposer
rest *n* repos
rest room *n* toilettes
restaurant *n* restaurant

R

restful _adj_ reposant
restitution _n_ restitution
restless _adj_ agité
restoration _n_ restauration
restore _v_ rétablir
restrain _v_ retenir
restraint _n_ restriction
restrict _v_ restraindre
result _n_ résultat
resume _v_ résumer
resumption _n_ reprise
resurrection _n_ résurrection
resuscitate _v_ réanimer
retain _v_ retenir
retaliate _v_ réagir
retaliation _n_ représailles
retarded _adj_ retardé
retention _n_ rétention
retire _v_ retraiter; se retirer
retirement _n_ retraite
retract _v_ rétracter
retreat _v_ reculer
retreat _n_ retraite
retrieval _n_ récupération
retrieve _v_ récupérer
retroactive _adj_ rétroactif
return _v_ retourner
return _n_ retour
reunion _n_ réunion
reveal _v_ révéler
revealing _adj_ révélateur
revel _v_ se délecter

revelation _n_ révélation
revenge _v_ venger
revenge _n_ vengeance
revenue _n_ revenu
reverence _n_ révérence
reversal _n_ renversement
reverse _n_ inverse
reversible _adj_ réversible
revert _v_ retourner
review _v_ reconsidérer
review _n_ revue; rapport
revise _v_ réviser
revision _n_ révision
revive _v_ ranimer
revoke _v_ révoquer
revolt _v_ révolter
revolt _n_ révolte
revolting _adj_ révoltant
revolve _v_ tourner
revolver _v_ revolver
revue _n_ revue
revulsion _n_ dégoût
reward _v_ récompenser
reward _n_ récompense
rewarding _adj_ gratifiant
rheumatism _n_ rhumatisme
rhinoceros _n_ rhinocéros
rhyme _n_ rime
rhythm _n_ rythme
rib _n_ côte
ribbon _n_ ruban
rice _n_ riz

R

rich *adj* riche
rid of *iv* se débarrasser de
riddle *n* charade
ride *iv* monter
ridge *n* arête
ridicule *v* ridiculiser
ridicule *n* ridicule
ridiculous *adj* ridicule
rifle *n* fusil
rift *n* faille
right *adv* à droite
right *adj* droit; juste
right *n* droite
rigid *adj* rigide
rigor *n* rigeur
rim *n* bord; jante
ring *iv* sonner
ring *n* anneau; sonnerie
ringleader *n* meneur
rinse *v* rincer
riot *v* se mutiner
riot *n* émeute
rip *v* déchirer
rip off *v* arracher
ripe *adj* mûr
ripen *v* mûrir
ripple *n* ondulation
rise *iv* monter
risk *v* risquer
risk *n* risque
risky *adj* risqué
rite *n* rite

rival *n* rival
rivalry *n* rivalité
river *n* fleuve
rivet *v* riveter
riveting *adj* fascinant
road *n* route
roam *v* parcourir
roar *v* rugir
roar *n* rugissement
roast *v* rôtir
roast *n* rôti
rob *v* voler
robber *n* voleur
robbery *n* vol
robe *n* robe de chambre
robust *adj* robuste
rock *n* pierre
rocket *n* roquette
rocky *adj* rocheux
rod *n* tige
rodent *n* rongeur
roll *v* rouler
romance *n* romance
roof *n* toit
room *n* chambre; salle
roomy *adj* spacieux
rooster *n* coq
root *n* racine
rope *n* corde
rosary *n* rosaire
rose *n* rose
rosy *adj* rose

R

rot *v* pourrir
rot *n* pourriture
rotate *v* tourner
rotation *n* rotation
rotten *adj* pourri
rough *adj* rêche
round *adj* rond
rouse *v* soulever
rousing *adj* exaltant
route *n* route
routine *n* routine
row *v* ramer
row *n* rang
rowdy *adj* tapageur
royal *adj* royal
royalty *n* royauté
rub *v* frotter
rubber *n* caoutchouc
rubbish *n* déchets
rubble *n* décombres
ruby *n* rubis
rudder *n* gouvernail
rude *adj* rude
rudeness *n* insolence
rudimentary *adj* rudimentaire
rug *n* tapis
ruin *v* ruiner
ruin *n* ruine
rule *v* diriger
rule *n* règle
ruler *n* règle; dirigeant
rum *n* rhum

rumble *v* gronder
rumble *n* grondement
rumor *n* rumeur
run *iv* courir
run away *v* s'enfuir
run into *v* heurter
run out *v* s'épuiser
run over *v* écraser
run up *v* accumuler
runner *n* coureur
runway *n* piste
rupture *n* rupture
rupture *v* fracturer
rural *adj* rural
ruse *n* ruse
rush *v* se dépêcher
Russia *n* Russie
Russian *adj* russe
rust *v* rouiller
rust *n* rouille
rustic *adj* rustique
rust-proof *adj* antirouille
rusty *adj* rouillé
ruthless *adj* impitoyable
rye *n* seigle

R

S

sabotage *v* saboter
sabotage *n* sabotage
sack *v* piller; expulser
sack *n* sac; expulsion
sacrament *n* sacrement
sacred *adj* sacré
sacrifice *n* sacrifice
sacrilege *n* sacrilège
sad *adj* triste
sadden *v* attrister
saddle *n* selle
sadist *n* sadiste
sadness *n* tristesse
safe *adj* sauf
safeguard *n* garantie
safety *n* sécurité
sail *n* voile
sailboat *n* voilier
sailor *n* marin
saint *n* saint
salad *n* salade
salary *n* salaire
sale *n* vente
sale slip *n* reçu
salesman *n* vendeur
saliva *n* salive
salmon *n* saumon
saloon *n* saloon
salt *n* sel

salty *adj* salé
salvage *v* sauver
salvation *n* salut
same *adj* même
sample *n* échantillon
sanctify *v* sanctifier
sanction *v* sanctionner
sanction *n* sanction
sanctity *n* sainteté
sanctuary *n* sanctuaire
sand *n* sable
sandal *n* sandale
sandpaper *n* papier de verre
sandwich *n* sandwich
sane *adj* sain
sanity *n* santé mentale
sap *n* sève
sap *v* infirmer
saphire *n* saphire
sarcasm *n* sarcasme
sarcastic *adj* sarcastique
sardine *n* sardine
satanic *adj* satanique
satellite *n* satellite
satire *n* satire
satisfaction *n* satisfaction
satisfactory *adj* satisfaisant
satisfy *v* satisfaire
saturate *v* saturer
Saturday *n* samedi
sauce *n* sauce
saucepan *n* casserole

S

saucer *n* soucoupe
sausage *n* saucisse
savage *adj* sauvage
savagery *n* sauvagerie
save *v* sauver
savings *n* économies
savior *n* sauveur
savor *v* savourer
saw *iv* scier
saw *n* scie
say *iv* dire
saying *n* dicton
scaffolding *n* échafaudage
scald *v* ébouillanter
scale *v* escalader
scale *n* balance; écaille
scalp *n* cuir chevelu
scam *n* escroquerie
scan *v* scruter; scanner
scandal *n* scandale
scandalize *v* scandaliser
scapegoat *n* bouc émissaire
scar *n* cicatrice
scarce *adj* rare
scarcely *adv* rarement
scarcity *n* rareté
scare *v* effrayer
scare *n* peur
scare away *v* faire fuir
scarf *n* écharpe
scary *adj* effrayant
scatter *v* disperser

scenario *n* scénario
scene *n* scène; lieux
scenery *n* paysage
scenic *adj* scénique
scent *n* odeur
sceptic *adj* sceptique
schedule *v* programmer
schedule *n* horaire
scheme *n* combine; projet
schism *n* schisme
scholarship *n* bourse
school *n* école
science *n* science
scientific *adj* scientifique
scientist *n* scientifique
scissors *n* ciseaux
scoff *v* railler
scold *v* gronder
scolding *n* réprimande
scooter *n* scooter
scope *n* champ
scorch *v* brûler
score *n* score
score *v* marquer
scorn *v* mépris
scornful *adj* méprisant
scorpion *n* scorpion
scoundrel *n* fumier
scour *v* récurer
scourge *n* fouet
scout *n* scout
scramble *v* brouiller

S

scrambled *adj* brouillé

scrap *n* bout

scrap *v* se débarrasser

scrape *v* gratter

scratch *v* gratter

scratch *n* égratignure

scream *v* crier

scream *n* cri

screech *v* hurler

screen *n* écran; paravent

screen *v* contrôler; projeter

screw *v* visser; arnaquer

screw *n* vis

screwdriver *n* tourne-vis

scribble *v* gribouiller

script *n* script

scroll *n* rouleau

scrub *v* nettoyer

scruples *n* scrupule

scrupulous *adj* scrupuleux

scrutiny *n* examen

scuffle *n* bagarre

sculptor *n* sculpteur

sculpture *n* sculpture

sea *n* mer

seafood *n* fruits de mer

seagull *n* mouette

seal *v* sceller

seal *n* phoque; sceau

seal off *v* isoler

seam *n* couture

seamless *adj* continu

seamstress *n* couturière

search *v* rechercher

search *n* recherche

seashore *n* littoral

seaside *adj* bord de mer

season *n* saison

seasonal *adj* saisonnier

seasoning *n* épices

seat *n* siège

seated *adj* assis

secluded *adj* retiré

seclusion *n* isolement

second *n* second

secondary *adj* secondaire

secrecy *n* secret

secret *n* secret

secretary *n* secrétaire

secretly *adv* secrètement

sect *n* secte

section *n* section

sector *n* secteur

secure *v* securiser

secure *adj* stable

security *n* sécurité

sedation *n* sédation

seduce *v* séduire

seduction *n* séduction

see *iv* voir

seed *n* graine

seedy *adj* louche

seek *iv* chercher

seem *v* sembler

S

see-through *adj* transparant
segment *n* segment
segregate *v* séparer
segregation *n* séparation
seize *v* empoigner; saisir
seizure *n* attaque
seldom *adv* rarement
select *v* sélectionner
selection *n* sélection
self-esteem *n* amour-propre
self-evident *adj* évident
selfish *adj* égoïste
selfishness *n* égoïsme
self-respect *n* dignité
sell *iv* vendre
seller *n* vendeur
sellout *n* trahison
semblance *n* apparence
semester *n* semestre
seminary *n* séminaire
senate *n* sénat
senator *n* sénateur
send *iv* envoyer
sender *n* expéditeur
senile *adj* sénile
senior *adj* aîné
seniority *n* ancienneté
sensation *n* sensation
sense *v* deviner
sense *n* sens; intelligence
senseless *adj* absurde
sensible *adj* sensible

sensitive *adj* sensible
sensual *adj* sensuel
sentence *v* condomner
sentence *n* peine; phrase
sentiment *n* sentiment
sentimental *adj* sentimental
sentry *n* sentinelle
separate *v* séparer
separate *adj* séparé
separation *n* séparation
September *n* septembre
sequel *n* suite
sequence *n* séquence
serenade *n* sérénade
serene *adj* serein
serenity *n* sérénité
sergeant *n* sergent
series *n* série
serious *adj* sérieux; grave
seriousness *n* sérieux; gravité
sermon *n* sermon
serpent *n* serpent
serum *n* sérum
servant *n* serviteur
serve *v* servir; délivrer
service *n* service
service *v* entretenir
session *n* séance
set *n* jeu
set about *v* se mettre
set off *v* exploser
set out *v* exposer

S

set up v assembler
setback n contretemps
setting n monture
settle v installer; calmer
settle down v s'installer
settle for v se contenter
settlement n accord
settler n colon
setup n coup monté
seven adj sept
seventeen adj dix-sept
seventh adj septième
seventy adj soixante-dix
sever v sectionner
several adj plusieurs
severance n rupture
severe adj sévère; rigoureux
severity n sévérité
sew v coudre
sewer n égout
sewing n couture
sex n sexe
sexuality n sexualité
shabby adj défraîchi
shack n cabane
shackle n cadenas
shade n ombre; ton
shadow n ombre
shady adj ombragé
shake iv secouer
shaken adj choqué
shaky adj branlant

shallow adj peu profond
sham n imposteur
shambles n pagaille
shame v déshonorer
shame n honte
shameful adj honteux
shameless adj impudent
shape v former
shape n forme
share v partager
share n part; action
shareholder n actionnaire
shark n requin
sharp adj tranchant; vif
sharpen v aiguiser; tailler
sharpener n taille-crayon
shatter v briser
shattering adj bouleversant
shave v raser
she pro elle
shear iv tondre
shed iv verser
sheep n mouton
sheets n draps
shelf n étagère
shell n coquille
shellfish n coquillages
shelter v abriter
shelter n abri
shelves n rayonnage
shepherd n berger
sherry n sherry

S

shield _v_ protéger
shield _n_ bouclier
shift _n_ changement
shift _v_ refeter; bouger
shine _iv_ briller
shiny _adj_ brillant
ship _n_ bateau
shipment _n_ cargaison
shipwreck _n_ naufrage
shipyard _n_ chantier naval
shirk _v_ fuir
shirt _n_ chemise
shiver _v_ frissonner
shiver _n_ frisson
shock _v_ choquer
shock _n_ choc; souffle
shocking _adj_ choquant
shoe _n_ chaussure
shoelace _n_ lacet
shoepolish _n_ cirage
shoot _iv_ tirer; lancer
shoot down _v_ abattre
shop _v_ faire ses courses
shop _n_ magasin
shoplifting _n_ vol à l'étalage
shopping _n_ shopping
shore _n_ rive
short _adj_ court; petit
shortage _n_ pénurie
shortcoming _n_ défaut
shortcut _n_ raccourci
shorten _v_ abréger

shorthand _n_ sténographie
shortlived _adj_ de courte durée
shortly _adv_ bientôt
shorts _n_ short
shortsighted _adj_ myope
shot _n_ tir; pousse
shotgun _n_ fusil
shoulder _n_ épaule
shout _v_ crier
shout _n_ cri
shouting _n_ cris
shove _v_ pousser
shovel _n_ pelle
show _iv_ montrer
show off _v_ se vanter
show up _v_ se voir
showdown _n_ confrontation
shower _n_ douche
shrapnel _n_ éclats d'obus
shred _v_ déchiqueter
shred _n_ lambeau
shrewd _adj_ habile
shriek _v_ hurler
shriek _n_ hurlement
shrimp _n_ crevette
shrine _n_ sanctuaire
shrink _iv_ rétrécir
shroud _n_ linceul
shrouded _adj_ enveloppé
shrub _n_ arbuste
shudder _n_ frisson
shudder _v_ frissonner

S

shuffle *v* mélanger

shun *v* dédaigner

shut *iv* fermer

shut off *v* couper

shut up *v* se taire

shuttle *v* transporter

shy *adj* timide

shyness *n* timidité

sick *adj* malade

sicken *v* écœurer

sickening *adj* écœurant

sickle *n* faucille

sickness *n* maladie

side *n* côté

sideburns *n* pattes

sidestep *v* éviter

sidewalk *n* trottoir

sideways *adv* de côté

siege *n* siège

siege *v* assièger

sift *v* tamiser

sigh *n* soupir

sigh *v* soupirer

sight *n* vue

sightseeing *v* tourisme

sign *v* signer

sign *n* affiche; signe

signal *n* signal

signature *n* signature

significance *n* signification

significant *adj* considérable

signify *v* signifier

silence *n* silence

silence *v* taire

silent *adj* silencieux

silhouette *n* silhouette

silk *n* soie

silly *adj* loufoque

silver *n* argent

silversmith *n* orfèvre

silverware *n* argenterie

similar *adj* similaire

similarity *n* similarité

simmer *v* mijoter

simple *adj* simple

simplicity *n* simplicité

simplify *v* simplifier

simply *adv* simplement

simulate *v* simuler

simultaneous *adj* simultané

sin *v* péché

sin *n* pécher

since *c* depuis que

since *pre* depuis

since then *adv* depuis

sincere *adj* sincère

sincerity *n* sincèrité

sinful *adj* inique

sing *iv* chanter

singer *n* chanteur

single *n* célibataire

single *adj* célibataire

singlehanded *adj* non-assisté

singleminded *adj* résolu

S

singular *adj* singulier
sinister *adj* sinistre
sink *iv* couler
sink in *v* pénétrer
sinner *n* pécheur
sip *v* siroter
sip *n* gorgée
sir *n* Monsieur
siren *n* sirène
sirloin *n* filet
sissy *adj* efféminé
sister *n* soeur
sister-in-law *n* belle-soeur
sit *iv* s'asseoir
site *n* site
sitting *n* séance
situated *adj* situé
situation *n* situation
six *adj* six
sixteen *adj* seize
sixth *adj* sixième
sixty *adj* soixante
sizable *adj* ample
size *n* taille
size up *v* mesurer
skate *v* patiner
skate *n* patin
skeleton *n* squelette
skeptic *adj* sceptique
sketch *v* esquisser
sketch *n* esquisse
ski *v* skier

skill *n* talent
skillful *adj* talentueux
skim *v* écrémer
skin *v* écorcher
skin *n* peau
skinny *adj* maigre
skip *v* sauter
skip *n* bond
skirmish *n* échauffourée
skirt *n* jupe
skull *n* crâne
sky *n* ciel
skylight *n* lucarne
skyscraper *n* gratte-ciel
slab *n* dalle
slack *adj* détendu
slacken *v* se relâcher
slacks *n* pantalon
slam *v* claquer
slander *n* calomnie
slanted *adj* oblique
slap *n* claque
slap *v* gifler
slash *n* balafre
slash *v* couper
slate *n* ardoise
slaughter *v* abattre
slaughter *n* abattage
slave *n* esclave
slavery *n* esclavage
slay *iv* tuer
sleazy *adj* maillé

S

sleep *iv* dormir
sleep *n* sommeil
sleeve *n* manche
sleeveless *adj* sans manche
sleigh *n* luge
slender *adj* mince
slice *v* trancher
slice *n* tranche
slide *iv* glisser
slightly *adv* légèrement
slim *adj* fin; mince
slip *v* glisser
slip *n* erreur; reçu
slipper *n* pantoufle
slippery *adj* glissant
slit *iv* déchirer
slob *adj* flemmard
slogan *n* slogan
slope *n* pente
sloppy *adj* débraillé
slot *n* fente
slow *adj* lent
slow down *v* ralentir
slow motion *n* ralenti
slowly *adv* lentement
sluggish *adj* endormi
slum *n* bidonville
slump *v* décliner
slump *n* déclin
slur *v* insulter
sly *adj* sournois
smack *n* claque

smack *v* frapper
small *adj* petit
smallpox *n* variole
smart *adj* intelligent
smash *v* briser
smear *n* tache
smear *v* appliquer; étaler
smell *iv* sentir
smelly *adj* malodorant
smile *v* sourire
smile *n* sourire
smith *n* forgeron
smoke *v* fumer
smoked *adj* fumé
smoker *n* fumeur
smoking gun *n* fumée
smooth *v* lisser
smooth *adj* lisse
smoothly *adv* doucement
smoothness *n* douceur
smother *v* étouffer
smuggler *n* contrebandier
snail *n* escargot
snake *n* serpent
snapshot *n* photo
snare *v* piéger
snare *n* piège
snatch *v* attraper
sneeze *v* éternuer
sneeze *n* éternuement
sniff *v* renifler
sniper *n* sniper

S

snooze *v* sommeiller
snore *v* ronfler
snore *n* ronflement
snow *v* neiger
snow *n* neige
snowfall *n* chute de neige
snowflake *n* flocon de neige
snub *v* repousser
snub *n* affront
soak *v* tremper
soak in *v* pénétrer
soak up *v* absorber
soar *v* augmenter
sob *v* sangloter
sob *n* sanglot
sober *adj* sobre
so-called *adj* ainsi nommé
sociable *adj* sociable
socialism *n* socialisme
socialist *adj* socialiste
socialize *v* socialiser
society *n* société
sock *n* chaussette
sod *n* gazon
soda *n* soda
sofa *n* sofa
soft *adj* doux
soften *v* adoucir
softly *adv* doucement
softness *n* douceur
soggy *adj* détrempé
soil *v* salir

soil *n* sol
soiled *adj* sale
solace *n* soulagement
solar *adj* solaire
solder *v* souder
soldier *n* soldat
sold-out *adj* épuisé
sole *n* semelle
sole *adj* unique
solely *adv* seulement
solemn *adj* solennel
solicit *v* soliciter
solid *adj* solide
solidarity *n* solidarité
solitary *adj* solitaire
solitude *n* solitude
soluble *adj* soluble
solution *n* solution
solve *v* résoudre
solvent *adj* solvant
somber *adj* sombre
some *adj* quelques
somebody *pro* quelqu'un
someday *adv* un jour
somehow *adv* en quelque sorte
someone *pro* quelqu'un
something *pro* quelque chose
sometimes *adv* quelquefois
somewhat *adv* plutôt
son *n* fils
song *n* chanson
son-in-law *n* gendre**

S

soon *adv* bientôt

soothe *v* calmer

sorcerer *n* sorcier

sorcery *n* sorcellerie

sore *n* plaie

sore *adj* irrité

sorrow *n* chagrin

sorrowful *adj* affligé

sorry *adj* désolé

sort *n* sorte

sort out *v* régler

soul *n* âme

sound *n* son; bruit

sound *v* sembler; sonner

sound out *v* interroger

soup *n* soupe

sour *adj* aigre

source *n* source

south *n* sud

southeast *n* sudest

southern *adj* du sud

southerner *n* sudiste

southwest *n* sudouest

souvenir *n* souvenir

sovereign *adj* souverain

sovereignty *n* souveraineté

soviet *adj* soviétique

sow *iv* semer

spa *n* spa

space *n* espace

space out *v* espacer

spacious *adj* spacieux

spade *n* pique

Spain *n* Espagne

span *v* enjamber

span *n* durée; envergure

Spaniard *n* Espagnol

Spanish *adj* espagnol

spank *v* fesser

spanking *n* fessée

spare *v* épargner; éviter

spare *adj* de secours

spare part *n* pièce de rechange

sparingly *adv* avec parcimonie

spark *n* étincelle

spark off *v* déclencher

spark plug *n* bougie

sparkle *v* scintiller

sparrow *n* moineau

sparse *adj* clairsemé

spasm *n* spasme

speak *iv* parler

speaker *n* orateur; haut-parleur

spear *n* lance

spearhead *v* mener

special *adj* spécial

specialize *v* spécialiser

specialty *n* spécialité

species *n* races

specific *adj* précis

specimen *n* spécimen

speck *n* tache

spectacle *n* spectacle

spectator *n* spectateur

S

speculate *v* spéculer
speculation *n* spéculation
speech *n* speech
speechless *adj* coi
speed *iv* faire de la vitesse
speed *n* vitesse
speedily *adv* rapidement
speedy *adj* rapide
spell *iv* épeler
spell *n* sort
spelling *n* orthographe
spend *iv* dépenser
spending *n* dépense
sperm *n* sperme
sphere *n* sphère
spice *n* épice
spicy *adj* épicé
spider *n* araignée
spiderweb *n* toile d'araignée
spill *iv* renverser
spill *n* chute
spin *iv* filer; tourner
spine *n* colonne
spineless *adj* faible
spinster *n* fileuse
spirit *n* esprit
spiritual *adj* spirituel
spit *iv* saliver
spite *n* rancune
spiteful *adj* rancunier
splash *v* éclabousser
splendid *adj* splendide

splendor *n* splendeur
splint *n* attelle
splinter *n* écharde
splinter *v* fendre
split *n* fissure
split *iv* diviser
split up *v* diviser
spoil *v* gâcher
spoils *n* butin
sponge *n* éponge
sponsor *n* sponsor
spontaneity *n* spontanéité
spontaneous *adj* spontané
spooky *adj* sinistre
spool *n* bobine
spoon *n* cuillère
spoonful *n* cuillerée
sporadic *adj* sporadique
sport *n* sport
sportsman *n* sportif
sporty *adj* sportif
spot *v* repérer
spot *n* tache; endroit
spotless *adj* impeccable
spotlight *n* projecteur
spouse *n* époux
sprain *v* entorse
sprawl *v* étalement
spray *v* vaporiser
spread *iv* s'étaler; s'étendre
spring *iv* bondir; déclencher
spring *n* printemps; source

S

springboard *n* tremplin
sprinkle *v* arroser
sprout *v* germer
spruce up *v* astiquer
spur *v* éperonner
spur *n* éperon
spy *v* espionner
spy *n* espion
squalid *adj* sordide
squander *v* gaspiller
square *adj* carré
square *n* carré; place
squash *v* courge
squeak *v* grincement
squeaky *adj* grinçant
squeamish *adj* douillet
squeeze *v* serrer; percer
squeeze in *v* se glisser
squid *n* calmar
squirrel *n* écureuil
stab *v* poignarder
stab *n* coup de couteau
stability *n* stabilité
stable *adj* stable
stable *n* étable
stack *v* empiler
stack *n* pile
staff *n* personnel
stage *n* stade; scène
stage *v* simuler
stagger *v* stupéfier
staggering *adj* sidérant

stagnant *adj* stagnant
stagnate *v* stagner
stagnation *n* stagnation
stain *v* tacher
stain *n* tache
stair *n* escalier
staircase *n* escalier
stairs *n* escaliers
stake *n* enjeu; participation
stake *v* miser
stale *adj* rassis
stalemate *n* impasse
stalk *v* hanter
stalk *n* queue
stall *n* stand
stall *v* caler
stammer *v* bafouillage
stamp *v* tamponner
stamp *n* timbre
stamp out *v* réprimer
stampede *n* débandade
stand *iv* se lever
stand *n* support
stand for *v* représenter
stand out *v* briller
stand up *v* soutenir
standard *n* standard; norme
standardize *v* standardiser
standing *n* réputation
standpoint *n* point de vue
staple *v* agrafer
staple *n* agrafe**

S

stapler *n* agrafeuse

star *n* étoile

starch *n* féculents

stare *v* fixer

stark *adj* désolé

start *v* commencer

start *n* début

startle *v* sursauter

startled *adj* surpris

starvation *n* famine

starve *v* affamer

state *n* état; situation

state *v* déclarer

statement *n* déclaration

station *n* station

stationary *adj* fixe

stationery *n* papeterie

statistic *n* statistique

statue *n* statue

status *n* status social

statute *n* loi

staunch *adj* loyal

stay *v* rester

stay *n* séjour

steady *adj* constant; régulier

steak *n* steak

steal *iv* voler

stealthy *adj* furtif

steam *n* vapeur

steel *n* acier

steep *adj* raide

stem *n* tige

stem *v* découler

stench *n* puanteur

step *n* étape; pas

step down *v* se retirer

step out *v* sortir

step up *v* s'avancer

stepbrother *n* demi-frère

step-by-step *adv* étape par étape

stepdaughter *n* belle-fille

stepfather *n* beau-père

stepladder *n* escabeau

stepmother *n* belle-mère

stepsister *n* demi-soeur

stepson *n* beau-fils

sterile *adj* stérile

sterilize *v* stériliser

stern *n* poupe

stern *adj* sévère

sternly *adv* sévèrement

stew *n* ragoût

stewardess *n* hôtesse

stick *n* bâton

stick *iv* planter; coller

stick around *v* rester

stick out *v* sortir

stick to *v* coller a

sticker *n* autocollant

sticky *adj* adhésif

stiff *adj* raide

stiffen *v* se raidir

stiffness *n* raideur

stifle *v* étouffer; réprimer

S

stifling *adj* étouffant

still *adj* calme

still *adv* encore

stimulant *n* stimulant

stimulate *v* stimuler

stimulus *n* stimulus

sting *iv* piqûre

sting *n* piquer; cuire

stinging *adj* piquant

stingy *adj* radin

stink *iv* puer

stink *n* puanteur

stinking *adj* puant

stipulate *v* stipuler

stir *v* remuer; trembler

stir up *v* provoquer

stitch *v* coudre

stitch *n* maille

stock *n* stock; bétail

stocking *n* bas

stockpile *n* réserves

stockroom *n* réserve

stoic *adj* stoïque

stomach *n* estomac

stone *n* pierre

stool *n* tabouret

stop *v* arrêter

stop *n* arrêt

stop by *v* passer

stop over *v* faire escale

storage *n* entreposage

store *v* entreposer

store *n* magasin

stork *n* cigogne

storm *n* tempête

stormy *adj* orageux

story *n* histoire; étage

stove *n* cuisinière

straight *adj* droit

straighten out *v* redresser

strain *v* égoutter

strain *n* stress

strained *adj* tendu

strainer *n* passoire

strait *n* détroit

stranded *adj* isolé

strange *adj* étrange

stranger *n* étranger

strangle *v* étrangler

strap *n* bride

strategy *n* stratégie

straw *n* paille

strawberry *n* fraise

stray *adj* perdu

stray *v* s'égarer

stream *n* ruisseau; torrent

street *n* rue

streetcar *n* tram

streetlight *n* lampadaire

strength *n* force

strengthen *v* renfocer

strenuous *adj* ardu

stress *n* stress; accent

stressful *adj* stressant

S

stretch *n* étendue
stretch *v* étendre
stretcher *n* brancard
strict *adj* strict
stride *iv* parcourir
strife *n* discorde
strike *n* grève
strike *iv* frapper
strike back *v* riposter
strike out *v* frapper
strike up *v* commencer
striking *adj* frappant
string *n* ficelle; corde
stringent *adj* rigoureux
strip *n* piste
strip *v* se déshabiller
stripe *n* rayure
striped *adj* rayé
strive *iv* s'attacher
stroke *n* coup; attaque
stroll *v* se promener
strong *adj* fort
structure *n* structure
struggle *v* lutter
struggle *n* lutte
stub *n* talon
stubborn *adj* obstiné
student *n* étudiant
study *v* étudier
stuff *n* choses; affaires
stuff *v* rembourrer
stuffing *n* farce

stuffy *adj* étouffant
stumble *v* trébucher
stun *v* assommer
stunning *adj* éblouissant
stupendous *adj* prodigieux
stupid *adj* stupide
stupidity *n* stupidité
sturdy *adj* robuste
stutter *v* stutter
style *n* style
subdue *v* contenir
subdued *adj* discret
subject *v* exposer
subject *n* sujet; matière
sublime *adj* sublime
submerge *v* submerger
submissive *adj* soumis
submit *v* soumettre
subpoena *v* assigner
subpoena *n* citation
subscribe *v* souscrire
subscription *n* abonnement
subsequent *adj* subséquent
subsidiary *adj* subsidiaire
subsidize *v* subventionner
subsidy *n* subvention
subsist *v* subsister
substance *n* substance
substandard *adj* inférieur
substantial *adj* substantiel
substitute *v* substituer
substitute *n* substitu

S

subtitle *n* sous-titre
subtle *adj* subtile
subtract *v* soustraire
subtraction *n* soustraction
suburb *n* banlieue
subway *n* métro
succeed *v* réussir
success *n* réussite
successful *adj* réussi
successor *n* successeur
succulent *adj* succulent
succumb *v* succomber
such *adj* comme
suck *v* sucer
sudden *adj* soudain
sue *v* poursuivre
suffer *v* souffrir
suffer from *v* souffir de
suffering *n* souffrance
sufficient *adj* suffisamment
suffocate *v* suffoquer
sugar *n* sucre
suggest *v* suggérer
suggestion *n* suggestion
suggestive *adj* suggestif
suicide *n* suicide
suit *n* costume
suitable *adj* approprié
suitcase *n* valise
sullen *adj* sombre
sulphur *n* soufre
sum *n* somme

sum up *v* résumer
summarize *v* résumer
summary *n* résumé
summer *n* été
summit *n* sommet
summon *v* mander
sumptuous *adj* somptueux
sun *n* soleil
sunblock *n* écran solaire
sunburn *n* coup de soleil
Sunday *n* dimanche
sundown *n* crépuscule
sunglasses *n* lunettes de soleil
sunken *adj* immergé
sunny *adj* ensoleillé
sunrise *n* lever du soleil
sunset *n* coucher du soleil
superb *adj* superbe
superfluous *adj* superflu
superior *adj* supérieur
superiority *n* supériorité
supermarket *n* supermarché
superpower *n* superpuissance
supersede *v* remplacer
superstition *n* superstition
supervise *v* surveiller
supervision *n* supervision
supper *n* souper
supple *adj* souple
supplier *n* fournisseur
supplies *n* réserves
supply *v* fournir

S

support _v_ soutenir
supporter _n_ partisan
suppose _v_ supposer
supposing _c_ supposons que
supposition _n_ supposition
suppress _v_ supprimer
supremacy _n_ domination
supreme _adj_ suprême
surcharge _n_ surcharge
sure _adj_ sure
surely _adv_ surement
surf _v_ surfer
surface _n_ surface
surge _n_ hausse
surgeon _n_ chirurgien
surgical _adv_ chirurgical
surname _n_ surnom
surpass _v_ surpasser
surplus _n_ surplus
surprise _v_ surprendre
surprise _n_ surprise
surrender _v_ capituler
surrender _n_ capitulation
surround _v_ entourer
surroundings _n_ environs
surveillance _n_ surveillance
survey _n_ sondage
survival _n_ survie
survive _v_ survivre
survivor _n_ survivant
susceptible _adj_ sensible
suspect _v_ suspecter

suspect _n_ suspect
suspend _v_ suspendre
suspenders _n_ bretelles
suspense _n_ suspense
suspension _n_ suspension
suspicion _n_ suspicion
suspicious _adj_ suspicieux
sustain _v_ sustenter
sustenance _n_ nourriture
swallow _v_ avaler
swamp _n_ marais
swamped _adj_ submergé
swan _n_ cygne
swap _v_ échanger
swap _n_ échange
swarm _n_ essaim
sway _v_ chanceler
swear _iv_ jurer
sweat _n_ transpiration
sweat _v_ transpirer
sweater _n_ sweat
Sweden _n_ Suède
Sweedish _adj_ suèdois
sweep _iv_ balayer
sweet _adj_ doux; sucré
sweeten _v_ sucrer
sweetheart _n_ chéri
sweetness _n_ douceur
sweets _n_ sucreries
swell _iv_ enfler
swelling _n_ enflure
swift _adj_ rapide

S

swim *iv* nager
swimmer *n* nageur
swimming *n* natation
swindle *v* escroquer
swindle *n* escroquerie
swindler *n* escroc
swing *iv* se balancer
swing *n* balançoire
Swiss *adj* suisse
switch *v* intervertir
switch *n* interrupteur
switch off *v* éteindre
switch on *v* allumer
Switzerland *n* Suisse
swivel *v* pivoter
swollen *adj* enflé
sword *n* épée
swordfish *n* espadon
syllable *n* syllabe
symbol *n* symbole
symbolic *adj* symbolique
symmetry *n* symétrie
sympathize *v* compatir
sympathy *n* sympathie
symphony *n* symphonie
symptom *n* symptome
synagogue *n* synagogue
synchronize *v* synchroniser
synod *n* synode
synonym *n* synonyme
synthesis *n* synthèse
syphilis *n* syphilis

syringe *n* seringue
syrup *n* sirop
system *n* système
systematic *adj* systèmatique

table *n* table
tablecloth *n* nappe
tablespoon *n* cuillère à soupe
tablet *n* comprimé; tablette
tack *n* clou
tackle *v* plaquer
tact *n* tact
tactful *adj* discret
tactical *adj* tactique
tactics *n* tactique
tag *n* étiquette
tail *n* queue
tail *v* suivre
tailor *n* tailleur
tainted *adj* avarié
take *iv* prendre
take apart *v* démonter
take away *v* s'emparer
take back *v* reprendre
take in *v* rentrer; duper
take off *v* décoller

take out _v_ sortir
take over _v_ s'emparer
tale _n_ conte
talent _n_ talent
talk _v_ parler
talkative _adj_ bavard
tall _adj_ grand
tame _v_ apprivoiser
tangent _n_ tangente
tangerine _n_ mandarine
tangible _adj_ tangible
tangle _n_ enchevêtrement
tank _n_ réservoir
tanned _adj_ bronzé
tantamount to _adj_ équivalent
tantrum _n_ caprice
tap _n_ robinet
tape _n_ cassette
tape recorder _n_ magnétophone
tapestry _n_ tapisserie
tar _n_ goudron
tarantula _n_ tarentule
tardy _adv_ tardif
target _n_ cible; objectif
tariff _n_ tarif
tarnish _v_ tarnir
tart _n_ tarte
tartar _n_ tartare
task _n_ tâche
taste _v_ goûter; sentir
taste _n_ goût
tasteful _adj_ de bon goût

tasteless _adj_ de mauvais goût
tasty _adj_ savoureux
tavern _n_ taverne
tax _n_ taxe
tea _n_ thé
teach _iv_ enseigner
teacher _n_ enseignant
team _n_ équipe
teapot _n_ théière
tear _iv_ se déchirer
tear _n_ larme
tearful _adj_ larmoyant
tease _v_ tourmenter
teaspoon _n_ cuillère à café
technical _adj_ technique
technicality _n_ technicité
technician _n_ technicien
technique _n_ technique
technology _n_ technologie
tedious _adj_ ennuyeux
tedium _n_ ennui
teenager _n_ adolescent
teeth _n_ dents
telegram _n_ télégramme
telepathy _n_ télépathie
telephone _n_ téléphone
telescope _n_ téléscope
televise _v_ téléviser
television _n_ télévision
tell _iv_ raconter
teller _n_ conteur
telling _adj_ révélateur

temper *n* tempérament
temperature *n* température
tempest *n* tempête
temple *n* temple
temporary *adj* temporaire
tempt *v* tenter
temptation *n* tentation
tempting *adj* tentant
ten *adj* dix
tenacity *n* tenacité
tenant *n* locataire
tendency *n* tendance
tender *adj* tendre; sensible
tenderness *n* tendresse
tennis *n* tennis
tenor *n* ténor
tense *adj* tendu
tension *n* tension
tent *n* tente
tentacle *n* tentacule
tentative *adj* tentative
tenth *n* dixième
tenuous *adj* mince
tepid *adj* tiède
term *n* terme
terminate *v* terminer
terminology *n* terminologie
termite *n* termite
terms *n* termes
terrace *n* terrasse
terrain *n* terrain
terrestrial *adj* terrestre

terrible *adj* terrible
terrific *adj* terrible
terrify *v* terrifier
terrifying *adj* terrifiant
territory *n* territoire
terror *n* terreur
terrorism *n* terrorisme
terrorist *n* terroriste
terrorize *v* terroriser
terse *adj* court
test *v* tester
test *n* test
testament *n* testament
testify *v* testifier
testimony *n* témoignage
text *n* texte
textbook *n* livre
texture *n* texture
thank *v* remercier
thankful *adj* reconnaissant
thanks *n* remerciements
that *adj* que
thaw *v* décongeler
thaw *n* dégel
theater *n* théâtre
theft *n* vol
theme *n* thème
themselves *pro* eux-mêmes
then *adv* alors
theologian *n* théologien
theology *n* théologie
theory *n* théorie

T

therapy *n* thérapie
there *adv* il y a
therefore *adv* donc
thermometer *n* thermomètre
thermostat *n* thermostat
these *adj* ces
thesis *n* thèse
they *pro* ils; elles
thick *adj* épais; stupide
thicken *v* épaissir
thickness *n* épaisseur
thief *n* voleur
thigh *n* cuisse
thin *adj* mince; fin
thing *n* chose
think *iv* penser
third *adj* troisième
thirst *v* avoir soif
thirsty *adj* assoiffé
thirteen *adj* treize
thirty *adj* trente
this *adj* ce; cette
thorn *n* épine
thorny *adj* épineux
thorough *adj* minutieux
those *adj* ceux-là; ces
though *c* bien que
thought *n* idée
thoughtful *adj* attentionné
thousand *adj* mille
thread *v* enfiler
thread *n* fil

threat *n* menace
threaten *v* menacer
three *adj* trois
thresh *v* battre
threshold *n* orée; seuil
thrifty *adj* économe
thrill *v* emballer
thrive *v* prospérer
throat *n* gorge
throb *n* battement
throb *v* battre
thrombosis *n* thrombose
throne *n* trône
throng *n* foule
through *pre* à travers
throw *iv* lancer
throw away *v* jeter
throw up *v* vomir
thug *n* voyou
thumb *n* pouce
thumbtack *n* punaise
thunder *n* tonnerre
thunderbolt *n* foudre
thunderstorm *n* orage
Thursday *n* jeudi
thus *adv* ainsi
thwart *v* contrarier
thyroid *n* thyroïde
tickle *v* chatouiller
tickle *n* chatouillement
ticklish *adj* chatouilleux
tidal wave *n* raz-de-marée

T

tide *n* marée
tidy *adj* soigné
tie *v* nouer; égaliser
tie *n* lien; match nul
tiger *n* tigre
tight *adj* serré
tighten *v* serrer
tile *n* carreau; tuile
till *adv* jusqu'à
till *v* labourer
tilt *v* incliner
timber *n* bois
time *n* temps
time *v* chronométrer
timeless *adj* intemporel
timely *adj* opportun
times *n* temps
timetable *n* horaire
timid *adj* timide
timidity *n* timidité
tin *n* étain
tiny *adj* minuscule
tip *n* pointe; pourboire
tired *adj* fatigué
tiredness *n* fatigue
tireless *adj* infatigable
tiresome *adj* infatigant
tissue *n* mouchoir
title *n* titre
to *pre* chez; vers
toad *n* crapaud
toast *v* griller

toast *n* toast
toaster *n* grille-pain
tobacco *n* tabac
today *adv* aujourd'hui
toddler *n* mambin
toe *n* doigt de pied
toenail *n* ongle de pied
together *adv* ensemble
toil *v* travailler
toilet *n* toilettes
token *n* jeton
tolerable *adj* tolérable
tolerance *n* tolérance
tolerate *v* tolérer
toll *n* péage; glas
toll *v* sonner
tomato *n* tomate
tomb *n* tombe
tombstone *n* pierre tombale
tomorrow *adv* demain
ton *n* tonne
tone *n* ton
tongs *n* pinces
tongue *n* langue
tonic *n* tonique
tonight *adv* ce soir
tonsil *n* amygdale
too *adv* aussi
tool *n* outil
tooth *n* dent
toothache *n* rage de dent
toothpick *n* cure-dents

top *n* dessus
topic *n* sujet
topple *v* basculer
torch *n* torche
torment *v* tourmenter
torment *n* tourment
torrent *n* torrent
torrid *adj* torride
torso *n* torse
tortoise *n* tortue
torture *v* torturer
torture *n* torture
toss *v* jeter
total *adj* total
totalitarian *adj* totalitaire
totality *n* totalité
touch *n* contact; touche
touch *v* toucher
touch on *v* évoquer
touch up *v* retoucher
touching *adj* touchant
tough *adj* coriace
toughen *v* durcir
tour *n* tour
tourism *n* tourisme
tourist *n* touriste
tournament *n* tournois
tow *v* remorquer
tow truck *n* dépanneuse
towards *pre* vers
towel *n* serviette
tower *n* tour

towering *adj* imposant
town *n* ville
town hall *n* mairie
toxic *adj* toxique
toxin *n* toxine
toy *n* jouet
trace *v* tracer
track *n* traces
track *v* retrouver
traction *n* extension
tractor *n* tracteur
trade *n* commerce
trade *v* échanger
trademark *n* marque déposée
trader *n* commerçant
tradition *n* tradition
traffic *n* circulation; trafic
traffic *v* trafiquer
tragedy *n* tragédie
tragic *adj* tragique
trail *v* traîner
trail *n* piste
trailer *n* remorque
train *n* train
train *v* former
trainee *n* stagiaire
trainer *n* entraîneur
training *n* stage
trait *n* trait
traitor *n* traître
trajectory *n* trajectoire
tram *n* tram

trample *v* piétiner
trance *n* trance
tranquility *n* tranquilité
transaction *n* transaction
transcend *v* transcender
transcribe *v* transcire
transfer *v* transférer
transfer *n* transfert
transform *v* transformer
transformation *n* transformation
transfusion *n* transfusion
transient *adj* transitoire
transit *n* transit
transition *n* transition
translate *v* traduire
translator *n* traducteur
transmit *v* transmettre
transparent *adj* transparent
transplant *v* transplanter
transport *v* transport
trap *n* piège
trash *n* poubelle
trash can *n* poubelle
traumatic *adj* traumatique
traumatize *v* traumatiser
travel *v* voyager
traveler *n* voyageur
tray *n* plateau
treacherous *adj* traître
treachery *n* tricherie
tread *iv* marcher
treason *n* trahison

treasure *n* trésor
treasurer *n* trésorier
treat *v* traiter
treat *n* gâterie
treatment *n* traitement; soins
treaty *n* traité
tree *n* arbre
tremble *v* trembler
tremendous *adj* immense
tremor *n* secousse
trench *n* tranchée
trend *n* trendance
trendy *adj* branché
trial *n* procès; essai
triangle *n* triangle
tribe *n* tribu
tribunal *n* tribunal
tribute *n* hommage
trick *v* duper
trick *n* combine; tour
trickle *v* dégouliner
trigger *v* déclencher
trigger *n* gâchette
trim *v* tailler
trimester *n* trimestre
trimmings *n* passementerie
trip *n* voyage; chute
trip *v* trébucher
triple *adj* triple
tripod *n* tripode
triumph *n* triomphe
triumphant *adj* triomphant

trivial *adj* banal
trivialize *v* banaliser
trolley *n* trolley
troop *n* troupe
trophy *n* trophée
tropic *n* tropique
tropical *adj* tropical
trouble *n* ennuis
trouble *v* troubler
troublesome *adj* gênant
trousers *n* pantalon
trout *n* truite
truce *n* trêve
truck *n* camion
trucker *n* routier
trumped-up *adj* forgé
trumpet *n* trompette
trunk *n* coffre; trompe
trust *v* faire confiance
trust *n* confiance
truth *n* vérité
truthful *adj* vrai
try *v* essayer
tub *n* baignoire
tuberculosis *n* tuberculose
Tuesday *n* mardi
tuition *n* frais de scolarité
tulip *n* tulipe
tumble *v* tomber
tummy *n* estomac
tumor *n* tumeur
tumult *n* tumulte

tumultuous *adj* tumultueux
tuna *n* thon
tune *n* air
tune *v* accorder
tune up *v* accorder
tunic *n* tunique
tunnel *n* tunnel
turbine *n* turbine
turbulence *n* turbulence
turf *n* gazon
Turk *adj* turque
Turkey *n* Turquie
turmoil *n* tourment
turn *n* tour
turn *v* tourner
turn back *v* retourner
turn down *v* minimiser
turn in *v* rendre
turn off *v* éteindre
turn on *v* allumer
turn over *v* retouner
turn up *v* arriver
turret *n* tourelle
turtle *n* tortue
tusk *n* défense
tutor *n* tuteur
tweezers *n* pincette
twelfth *adj* douzième
twelve *adj* douze
twentieth *adj* vingtième
twenty *adj* vingt
twice *adv* deux fois

T

twilight *n* crépuscule
twin *n* jumeau
twinkle *v* scintiller
twist *v* tordre
twist *n* torsade; foulure
twisted *adj* tordu
twister *n* tornade
two *adj* deux
tycoon *n* magnat
type *n* type; caractères
type *v* taper
typical *adj* typique
tyranny *n* tyrannie
tyrant *n* tyran

U

ugliness *n* laideur
ugly *adj* laid
ulcer *n* ulcère
ultimate *adj* ultime
ultimatum *n* ultimatum
ultrasound *n* ultrasons
umbrella *n* parapluie
umpire *n* arbitre
unable *adj* incapable
unanimity *n* unanimité
unassuming *adj* modeste

unattached *adj* détaché
unavoidable *adj* inévitable
unaware *adj* méconnaissant
unbearable *adj* insupportable
unbeatable *adj* imbattable
unbelievable *adj* incroyable
unbiased *adj* impartial
unbroken *adj* intact
unbutton *v* déboutonner
uncertain *adj* incertain
uncle *n* oncle
uncomfortable *adj* inconfortable
uncommon *adj* rare
unconscious *adj* inconscient
uncover *v* découvrir
undecided *adj* indécis
undeniable *adj* indéniable
under *pre* sous
underdog *n* opprimé
undergo *v* subir
underground *adj* sous-terrain
underline *v* souligner
underlying *adj* sous-jacent
undermine *v* saper
underneath *pre* dessous
understand *v* comprendre
undertake *v* rentreprendre
underwear *n* sous-vêtements
underwrite *v* couvrir
undeserved *adj* immérité
undesirable *adj* undésirable
undisputed *adj* incontesté

undo *v* défaire
undress *v* déshabiller
undue *adj* excessif
unearth *v* dénicher
uneasiness *n* appréhension
uneasy *adj* anxieux
uneducated *adj* inculte
unemployed *adj* chômeur
unemployment *n* chômage
unending *adj* éternel
unequal *adj* inégal
uneven *adj* inégal
uneventful *adj* ordinaire
unexpected *adj* imprévu
unfailing *adj* indéfectible
unfair *adj* injuste
unfairly *adv* injustement
unfairness *n* injustice
unfaithful *adj* infidèle
unfamiliar *adj* inconnu
unfasten *v* défaire
unfavorable *adj* défavorable
unfit *adj* inadéquat
unfold *v* déplier
unforeseen *adj* imprévu
unforgettable *adj* inoubliable
unfriendly *adj* inhospitalier
ungrateful *adj* ingrat
unhappiness *n* tristesse
unhappy *adj* triste
unharmed *adj* intact
unhealthy *adj* maladif

unhurt *adj* idemne
unification *n* unification
uniform *n* uniforme
uniformity *n* uniformité
unify *v* unifier
unilateral *adj* unilatéral
union *n* union
unique *adj* unique
unit *n* unité
unite *v* unir
unity *n* unité
universal *adj* universel
universe *n* univers
university *n* université
unjust *adj* injuste
unjustified *adj* injustifié
unknown *adj* inconnu
unlawful *adj* illégal
unleaded *adj* sans plomb
unleash *v* déchaîner
unless *c* à moins que
unlike *adj* contrairement à
unlikely *adj* improbable
unlimited *adj* illimité
unload *v* décharger
unlock *v* ouvrir
unlucky *adj* malchanceux
unmarried *adj* unmarried
unmask *v* démasquer
unmistakable *adj* incontestable
unnecessary *adj* inutile
unnoticed *adj* inaperçu

unoccupied *adj* inoccupé
unofficially *adv* officieusement
unpack *v* déballer
unpleasant *adj* désagréable
unplug *v* débrancher
unpopular *adj* impopulaire
unpredictable *adj* imprévisible
unravel *v* démêler
unreal *adj* irréel
unrealistic *adj* irréaliste
unreasonable *adj* déraisonnable
unrelated *adj* sans rapport
unreliable *adj* peu fiable
unrest *n* malaise
unsafe *adj* malsain
unselfish *adj* désintéressé
unspeakable *adj* inexprimable
unstable *adj* instable
unsteady *adj* instable
unsuccessful *adj* infructueux
unsuitable *adj* inopportun
unsuspecting *adj* crédule
unthinkable *adj* impensable
untie *v* dénouer
until *pre* jusqu'à
untimely *adj* inopportun
untouchable *adj* intouchable
untrue *adj* faux
unusual *adj* original
unveil *v* dévoiler
unwind *v* dévider
unwise *adj* imprudent

unwrap *v* déballer
upbringing *n* éducation
upcoming *adj* prochain
update *v* actualiser
upgrade *v* améliorer
uphill *adv* uphill
uphold *v* maintenir
upholstery *n* revêtement
upkeep *n* entretien
upon *pre* sur
upper *adj* supérieur
upright *adj* debout
uprising *n* soulèvement
uproar *n* tumulte
uproot *v* déraciner
upset *v* bouleverser
upside-down *adv* inversé
upstairs *adv* en haut
uptight *adj* coincé
up-to-date *adj* moderne
upturn *n* remontée
urban *adj* urbain
urge *n* envie
urge *v* presser
urgency *n* urgence
urgent *adj* urgent
urinate *v* uriner
urine *n* urine
urn *n* urne
us *pro* nous
usage *n* usage
use *v* utiliser

use *n* usage
used to *adj* être habitué à
useful *adj* utile
usefulness *n* utilité
useless *adj* inutile
user *n* utilisateur
usher *n* ouvreuse
usual *adj* habituel
usurp *v* usurper
utensil *n* ustensile
uterus *n* utérus
utilize *v* utiliser
utmost *adj* extrême
utter *v* prononcer

vacancy *n* vacance
vacant *adj* vacant
vacate *v* quitter
vacation *n* vacances
vaccinate *v* vacciner
vaccine *n* vaccin
vacillate *v* vaciller
vagrant *n* vagabond
vague *adj* vague
vain *adj* vaniteux
vainly *adv* en vain

valiant *adj* vaillant
valid *adj* valide
validate *v* valider
validity *n* validité
valley *n* vallée
valuable *adj* de valeur
value *n* valeur
valve *n* valve
vampire *n* vampire
van *n* van
vandal *n* vandale
vandalism *n* vandalisme
vandalize *v* vandaliser
vanguard *n* avant-garde
vanish *v* disparaître
vanity *n* vanité
vanquish *v* vaincre
vaporize *v* vaporiser
variable *adj* variable
varied *adj* varié; divers
variety *n* variété
various *adj* divers
varnish *v* vernir
varnish *n* verni
vary *v* varier
vase *n* vase
vast *adj* vaste
veal *n* veau
veer *v* virer
vegetable *n* légume
vegetarian *v* végétarien
vegetation *n* végétation

vehicle *n* véhicule
veil *n* voile
vein *n* veine
velocity *n* vélocité
velvet *n* velours
venerate *v* vénérer
vengeance *n* vengeance
venison *n* chevreuil
venom *n* venin
vent *n* bouche d'aération
ventilate *v* ventiler
ventilation *n* ventilation
venture *v* s'aventurer
venture *n* aventure
verb *n* verbe
verbally *adv* verbalement
verbatim *adv* mot pour mot
verdict *n* verdict
verge *n* verge
verification *n* verification
verify *v* vérifier
versatile *adj* versatile
verse *n* vers
versed *adj* versé
version *n* version
versus *pre* contre
vertebra *n* vertèbre
very *adv* très
vessel *n* vaisseau
vest *n* veston
vestige *n* vestige
veteran *n* vétéran

veterinarian *n* vétérinaire
viaduct *n* viaduc
vibrant *adj* éclatant
vibrate *v* vibrer
vibration *n* vibration
vice *n* vice
vicinity *n* voisinage
vicious *adj* vicieux
victim *n* victime
victimize *v* victimiser
victor *n* vainqueur
victorious *adj* victorieux
victory *n* victoire
view *n* vue
view *v* voir
viewpoint *n* point de vue
vigil *n* veille; veilleur
village *n* village
villager *n* villageois
villain *n* méchant
vindicate *v* justifier
vindictive *adj* vindicatif
vine *n* vigne
vinegar *n* vinaigre
vineyard *n* vignoble
violate *v* violer
violence *n* violence
violent *adj* violent
violet *n* violette
violin *n* violon
violinist *n* violoniste
viper *n* vipère

virgin *n* vièrge
virginity *n* virginité
virile *adj* viril
virility *n* virilité
virtually *adv* virtuellement
virtue *n* vertu
virtuous *adj* vertueux
virulent *adj* virulent
virus *n* virus
visibility *n* visibilité
visible *adj* visible
vision *n* vision
visit *n* visite
visit *v* visiter
visitor *n* visiteur
visual *adj* visuel
visualize *v* visualiser
vital *adj* vital
vitality *n* vitalité
vitamin *n* vitamine
vivacious *adj* vigoureux
vivid *adj* vivide
vocabulary *n* vocabulaire
vocation *n* vocation
vogue *n* vogue
voice *n* voix
void *adj* annulé; vide
volatile *adj* volatile
volcano *n* volcan
volleyball *n* volleyball
voltage *n* voltage
volume *n* volume; quantité

volunteer *n* volontaire
vomit *v* vomir
vomit *n* vomi
vote *v* voter
vote *n* vote
voting *n* scrutin
vouch for *v* se porter garant
voucher *n* bon
vow *v* faire voeu
vowel *n* voyelle
voyage *n* voyage
voyager *n* voyageur
vulgar *adj* vulgaire
vulgarity *n* vulgarité
vulnerable *adj* vulnérable
vulture *n* vautour

wafer *n* gaufrette
wag *v* remuer
wage *n* salaire
wagon *n* wagon
wail *v* gémir
wail *n* plainte
waist *n* taille
wait *v* attendre
waiter *n* serveur

waiting *n* attente
waitress *n* serveuse
waive *v* renoncer
wake up *iv* se réveiller
walk *v* marcher
walk *n* marche
walkout *n* grève
wall *n* mur
wallet *n* portefeuille
walnut *n* noix
walrus *n* morse
waltz *n* valse
wander *v* se promener
wanderer *n* voyageur
wane *v* diminuer
want *v* vouloi
war *n* guerre
ward *n* service
warden *n* directeur
wardrobe *n* garde-robe
warehouse *n* entrepôt
warfare *n* guerre
warm *adj* chaud
warm up *v* réchauffer
warmth *n* chaleur
warn *v* avertir
warning *n* avertissement
warp *v* déformer
warped *adj* déformé
warrant *v* justifier
warrant *n* mandat
warranty *n* garantie

warrior *n* guerrier
warship *n* navire de guerre
wart *n* verrue
wary *adj* prudent
wash *v* laver
washable *adj* lavable
wasp *n* guêpe
waste *v* gaspiller
waste *n* gaspillage
waste basket *n* poubelle
wasteful *adj* gaspilleur
watch *n* montre
watch *v* regarder
watch out *v* faire attention
watchful *adj* vigilant
watchmaker *n* horloger
water *n* eau
water *v* arroser
water down *v* arroser
waterfall *n* chute d'eau
waterheater *n* chauffe-eau
watermelon *n* pastèque
waterproof *adj* imperméable
watertight *adj* étanche
watt *n* watt
wave *n* vague; signe
waver *v* trembler
wavy *adj* ondulé
wax *n* cire
way *n* chemin; façon
way in *n* entrée
way out *n* sortie

W

we *pro* nous
weak *adj* faible
weaken *v* affaiblir
weakness *n* faiblesse
wealth *n* richesse
wealthy *adj* riche
weapon *n* arme
wear *n* vêtements; usure
wear *iv* s'user; porter
wear down *v* user; saper
wear out *v* épuiser; user
weary *adj* fatigué
weather *n* temps
weave *iv* tisser
web *n* toile; réseau
web site *n* site web
wed *iv* marier
wedding *n* mariage
wedge *n* cale
Wednesday *n* mercredi
weed *n* mauvaise herbe
weed *v* désherber
week *n* semaine
weekday *adj* jour de semaine
weekend *n* fin de semaine
weekly *adv* hebdomadaire
weep *iv* pleurer
weigh *v* peser
weight *n* poids
weird *adj* bizarre
welcome *v* accueillir
welcome *n* bienvenue

weld *v* souder
welder *n* soudeur
welfare *n* bien-être
well *n* puit
well-known *adj* connu
well-to-do *adj* aisé
west *n* ouest
westerner *adj* occidental
wet *adj* mouillé
whale *n* baleine
wharf *n* embarcadère
what *adj* quel
whatever *adj* n'importe quel
wheat *n* blé
wheel *n* roue
wheelbarrow *n* brouette
wheelchair *n* chaise roulante
when *adv* quand
whenever *adv* n'importe quand
where *adv* où
whereas *c* tandis que
whereupon *c* où
wherever *c* n'importe où
whether *c* si
which *adj* quel
while *c* pedant
whim *n* caprice
whine *v* pleurnicher
whip *v* fouetter; cravacher
whip *n* fouet
whirl *v* tournoyer
whirlpool *n* tourbillon

whiskers *n* moustache
whisper *v* chuchoter
whisper *n* chuchotement
whistle *v* siffler
whistle *n* sifflet
white *adj* blanc
whiten *v* blanchir
whittle *v* tailler
who *pro* qui
whoever *pro* n'importe qui
whole *adj* entier
wholehearted *adj* dévoué
wholesale *n* vente en gros
wholesome *adj* sain
whom *pro* qui
why *adv* pourquoi
wicked *adj* malfaisant
wickedness *n* méchanceté
wide *adj* large
widely *adv* largement
widen *v* élargir
widespread *adj* étendu
widow *n* veuve
widower *n* veuf
width *n* largeur
wield *v* brandir; manier
wife *n* femme
wig *n* perruque
wiggle *v* tortiller
wild *adj* sauvage
wild boar *n* sanglier
wilderness *n* désert

wildlife *n* faune
will *n* volonté; testament
willfully *adv* délibérément
willing *adj* volontaire
willingly *adv* volontairement
willingness *n* volonté
willow *n* saule
wily *adj* futé
wimp *adj* lavette
win *iv* gagner
win back *v* récupérer
wind *n* vent
wind *iv* sepenter
wind up *v* finir
winding *adj* tortueux
windmill *n* moulin
window *n* fenêtre
windpipe *n* trachée-artère
windshield *n* pare-brise
windy *adj* venteux
wine *n* vin
winery *n* vignoble
wing *n* aile
wink *n* clin d'oeil
winner *n* gagnant
winter *n* hiver
wipe *v* essuyer
wipe out *v* anéantir
wire *n* fil; câble
wireless *adj* sans fil
wisdom *n* sagesse
wise *adj* sage

wish v souhaiter
wish n souhait
wit n esprit
witch n sorcière
witchcraft n sorcèlerie
with pre avec
withdraw v retirer; soustraire
withdrawal n retrait
withdrawn adj renfermé
wither v flétrir
withhold iv retenir
within pre dans
without pre sans
withstand v résister
witness n témoin
witty adj spirituel
wives n femmes
wizard n magicien
wobble v trembler
woes n voeux
wolf n loup
woman n femme
womb n utérus
women n femmes
wonder v se demander
wonder n merveille
wonderful adj merveilleux
wood n bois
wooden adj en bois
wool n laine
woolen adj en laine
word n mot

wording n formulation
work n travail
work v travailler
work out v faire du sport
workable adj maniable
workbook n cahier d'exercices
worker n travailleur
workshop n atelier
world n monde
worldly adj avisé
worldwide adj mondialement
worm n ver
worn-out adj épuisé
worrisome adj angoissant
worry v soucier
worry n souci
worse adj pire
worsen v s'empirer
worship n culte
worst adj le pire
worth adj valoir
worthless adj sans valeur
worthwhile adj bon
worthy adj valable
would-be adj future
wound n blessure
wound v blesser
woven adj tissé
wrap v envelopper
wrap up v finir
wrapping n emballage
wrath n fureur

wreath *n* couronne
wreck *v* détruire
wreckage *n* épave
wrench *n* clé
wrestle *v* lutter
wrestler *n* lutteur
wrestling *n* lutte
wretched *adj* malheureux
wring *iv* essorer
wrinkle *v* froisser
wrinkle *n* ride
wrist *n* poignet
write *iv* écrire
write down *v* noter
writer *n* écrivain
writhe *v* se dégager
writing *n* écriture
written *adj* écrit
wrong *adj* faux

X-mas *n* Noël
X-ray *n* radiographie

yacht *n* yacht
yam *n* patate douce
yard *n* jardin
yarn *n* laine
yawn *n* baillement
yawn *v* bailler
year *n* an
yearly *adv* annuel
yearn *v* languir
yeast *n* levure
yell *v* crier
yellow *adj* jaune
yes *adv* oui
yesterday *adv* hier
yet *c* pourtant
yield *v* céder, rapporter
yield *n* rendement
yoke *n* joug
yolk *n* jaune d'oeuf
you *pro* tu; vous
young *adj* jeune
youngster *n* jeune
your *adj* ton; ta; tes
yours *pro* le tien; le vôtre
yourself *pro* toi-même
youth *n* jeunesse
youthful *adj* jeune

W
X
Y

zap *v* écraser; détruire
zeal *n* zèle
zealous *adj* zélé
zebra *n* zèbre
zero *n* zéro

zest *n* zeste
zinc *n* zinc
zip code *n* code postal
zipper *n* fermeture éclair
zone *n* zone
zoo *n* zoo
zoology *n* zoologie

Z

French-English

Bilingual Dictionaries, Inc.

Abbreviations

a - article - un/une
adj - adjective - adjectif
adv - adverb - adverbe
c - conjunction - conjonction
e - exclamation - exclamation
m - masculine (noun) - masculin (nom)
f - feminine (moun) - féminin (nom)
pre - preposition - préposition
pro - pronoun - pronom
v - verb - verbe

abandon *m* abandonment
abandonner *v* abandon
abasourdi *adj* dazed
abasourdir *v* daze
abat-jour *m* lampshade
abattage *m* slaughter
abattre *v* gun down
abattu *adj* despondent
abbaye *f* abbey
abbé *m* abbot
abdication *f* abdication
abdiquer *v* abdicate
abdomen *m* abdomen
abeille *f* bee
aberration *f* aberration
abhorer *v* abhor
abîme *m* abyss
abîmer *v* deface
abolir *v* abolish
abominable *adj* heinous
abondance *f* abundance
abondant *adj* plentiful
abonder *v* abound
abonnement *m* subscription
abordable *adj* affordable
aboyer *v* bark
abréger *v* abridge
abréviation *f* abbreviation
abri *m* shelter

abricot *m* apricot
abriter *v* shelter
abrogation *f* repeal
abroger *v* abrogate
abrupt *adj* blunt
abruptement *adv* abruptly
abrutissant *adj* mindless
absence *f* absence
absent *adj* absent
absolu *adj* outright
absolut *adj* absolute
absolution *f* absolution
absolver *v* acquit
absorbant *adj* absorbent
absorber *v* absorb
absoudre *v* absolve
abstenir *v* abstain
abstinence *f* abstinence
abstrait *adj* abstract
absurde *adj* absurd
abus *m* abuse
abuser *v* abuse
abusif *adj* abusive
abyssal *adj* abysmal
académie *f* academy
accalmie *f* lull
accélérateur *m* accelerator
accélérer *v* accelerate
accendentel *adj* accidental
accent *m* accent, stress
acceptable *adj* acceptable
acceptation *f* acceptance

accès *m* access
accessible *adj* accessible
accessoire *m* attachment
accident *m* accident
acclamation *f* cheers
acclamer *v* acclaim
accomlir *v* fulfill
accommodant *adj* amenable
accomplir *v* accomplish
accomplissement *m* achievement
accord *m* accord
accordéon *m* accordion
accorder *v* bestow, tune
accouchement *m* delivery
accpter *v* accept
accrocher *v* clip, catch
accrocher à *v* hold on to
accroître *v* heighten
accroupir *v* crouch
accueillir *v* welcome
accumulation *f* buildup
accumuler *v* accumulate, pile up
accusation *f* accusation
accusé *m* defendant
accuser *v* accuse
acharné *adj* relentless
achat *m* purchase
acheter *v* buy
acheteur *m* buyer
achèvement *m* completion
acide *m* acid
acidité *f* acidity

acier *m* steel
aclimatiser *v* acclimatize
acolyte *m* henchman
acompte *m* down payment
acoustique *adj* acoustic
acoutumer *v* accustom
acquisition *f* acquisition
acquitement *m* acquittal
acre *m* acre
acrobate *m* acrobat
acte *m* deed
acteur *m* actor
actif *adj* active
action *f* action, share
actionnaire *m* shareholder
activation *f* activation
activement *adv* busily
activer *v* activate
activité *f* activity
actrice *f* actress
actualiser *v* update
actuel *adj* actual, current
actuellement *adv* currently
adaptable *adj* adaptable
adaptateur *m* adapter
adaptation *f* adaptation
adapter *v* adapt
addiction *f* addiction
addition *f* addition
additionel *adj* additional
adéquat *adj* adequate
adhérer *v* adhere

adhésif *adj* sticky
adhésion *f* membership
adieu *m* farewell
adjacent *adj* adjoining
adjectif *f* adjective
admettre *v* admit
administrer *v* administer
admirable *adj* admirable
admiral *m* admiral
admirateur *m* admirer
admiration *f* admiration
admirer *v* admire
admissible *adj* admissible
admonestation *f* admonition
admonester *v* admonish
adolescence *f* adolescence
adolescent *m* adolescent
adopter *v* adopt
adoptif *adj* adoptive
adoption *f* adoption
adorable *adj* adorable
adoration *f* adoration
adorer *v* adore, like
adoucir *v* mellow, soften
adresse *f* address
adresser *v* address
adroit *adj* deft
adulation *f* adulation
adulte *m* adult
adultère *m* adultery
adverbe *m* adverb
adversaire *m* adversary

adverse *adj* adverse
adversité *f* adversity
aérer *v* air
aérodrome *m* airfield
aéroplane *m* aeroplane
aéroport *m* airport
afecter *v* allocate
affable *adj* affable
affaiblir *v* weaken
affaire *f* deal
affaires *f* stuff
affamer *v* starve
affecter *v* affect
affection *f* affection
affectioné *adj* affectionate
affectueux *adj* caring, fond
affiche *f* bill, sign
affiliation *f* affiliation
affilier *v* affiliate
affinité *f* affinity
affirmative *adj* affirmative
affirmer *v* affirm, claim
affliction *f* affliction
affligé *adj* sorrowful
affligeant *adj* distressing
affliger *v* afflict, distress
affluence *f* affluence
affluent *adj* affluent
afflux *m* influx
affréter *v* charter
affreux *adj* awful, dire
affront *m* affront, snub

affronter *v* affront
âge *m* age
âge d'or *m* heyday
agence *f* agency
agenda *m* agenda
agent *m* agent
agglomeré *v* agglomerate
aggravation *f* aggravation
aggravé *v* aggravate
aggresseur *m* aggressor
aggressif *adj* aggressive
aggression *f* aggression
agile *adj* agile
agir *v* act
agitateur *m* agitator
agitation *f* hustle
agité *adj* restless
agneau *m* lamb
agnostique *mf* agnostic
agonie *f* agony
agonisant *adj* agonizing
agoniser *v* agonize
agrafe *f* staple
agrafer *v* staple
agrafeuse *f* stapler
agrandir *v* magnify
agréable *adj* agreeable
agresser *v* mug
agression *f* mugging
agriculture *f* agriculture
agriculturel *adj* agricultural
agripper *v* grip

aide *f* aid, help
aider *v* aid, help
aigle *m* eagle
aigre *adj* sour
aigrir *v* embitter
aiguille *f* needle
aiguillonner *v* goad
aiguiser *v* sharpen
ail *m* garlic
aile *f* fender, wing
ailleurs *adv* elsewhere
aimable *adj* kind, likable
aimant *m* magnet
aimer *v* love
aine *f* groin
aîné *adj* senior
ainsi *adv* thus
ainsi nommé *adj* so-called
air *m* air
aisé *adj* well-to-do
aisselle *f* armpit
ajournement *m* postponement
ajourner *v* adjourn
ajouter *v* add
ajustable *adj* adjustable
ajustement *m* adjustment
ajuster *v* adjust
alarme *f* alarm
alcolique *adj* alcoholic
alcolisme *m* alcoholism
alcool *m* booze
alerte *f* alert

alerter *v* alert
algèbre *m* algebra
alignement *m* alignment
aligner *v* align, line up
alimenter *v* fuel
allée *f* alley
allée de garage *f* driveway
allégation *f* allegation
allégeance *f* allegiance
allégorie *f* allegory
alléguer *v* allege
Allemagne *f* Germany
allemand *adj* German
aller *iv* go
allergie *f* allergy
allergique *adj* allergic
alliage *m* alloy
alliance *f* alliance
allié *adj* allied
allié *m* ally
allier *v* ally
alligator *m* alligator
allocation *f* allotment
allonger *v* lengthen
allumé *adv* alight
allumer *v* fire, switch on
allumette *f* match
allure *f* allure
allusion *f* allusion
almanac *m* almanac
alors *adv* then
alphabet *m* alphabet

altercation *f* altercation
alternative *f* alternative
alterner *v* alternate
Altesse *f* Highness
altitude *f* altitude
aluminum *m* aluminum
amande *f* almond
amant *m* lover
amarrer *v* dock
amasser *v* amass
amateur *adj* amateur
ambassadeur *m* ambassador
ambigu *adj* ambiguous
ambitieux *adj* ambitious
ambition *f* ambition
ambivalent *adj* ambivalent
ambulance *f* ambulance
âme *f* soul
amélioration *f* improvement
améliorer *adj* better, improve
amende *f* fine
amendement *m* amendment
amer *adj* bitter
amèrement *adv* bitterly
Américain *adj* American
amertume *f* bitterness
ami *m* friend
amiable *adj* amiable
amical *adj* amicable
amitié *f* friendship
amitiés *f* regards
ammoniaque *m* ammonia

amnésie _f_ amnesia
amnéstie _f_ amnesty
amoindrir _v_ lessen
amorphe _adj_ amorphous
amortir _v_ amortize
amour _f_ love
amour-propre _m_ self-esteem
amphibien _adj_ amphibious
amphithéâtre _m_ amphitheater
ample _adj_ ample, loose
amplificateur _m_ amplifier
amplifier _v_ amplify
ampoule _f_ blister, bulb
amputation _f_ amputation
amputer _v_ amputate
amusant _adj_ amusing
amusement _m_ fun
amuser _v_ amuse
amygdale _f_ tonsil
an _m_ year
analgésique _m_ painkiller
analogie _f_ analogy
analphabète _adj_ illiterate
analyse _f_ analysis
analyser _v_ analyze
ananas _m_ pineapple
anarchie _f_ anarchy
anarchiste _m_ anarchist
anatomie _f_ anatomy
ancêtre _m_ ancestor
anchois _m_ anchovy
ancien _m_ elder

ancienneté _f_ seniority
ancient _adj_ ancient
ancre _f_ anchor
âne _m_ donkey
anéantir _v_ annihilate
anecdote _f_ anecdote
anémie _f_ anemia
anémique _adj_ anemic
anésthésie _f_ anesthesia
ange _m_ angel
angélique _adj_ angelic
angine _m_ angina
Anglais _adj_ English
angle _f_ angle
Angleterre _f_ England
Anglican _adj_ Anglican
angoissant _adj_ worrisome
angoisse _f_ anguish
animal _m_ animal
animateur _m_ broadcaster
animation _f_ animation
animé _adj_ lively
animer _v_ animate
animosité _f_ animosity
anneau _m_ ring
année _f_ year
annexe _f_ annex
annexion _f_ annexation
anniversaire _m_ anniversary
annonce _f_ announce
annoncement _m_ announcement
annoncer _v_ herald

annonceur *m* announcer
annotation *f* annotation
annoter *v* annotate
annuaire *m* directory
annuel *adj* annual, yearly
annulation *f* annulment
annulé *adj* void
annuler *v* annul, cancel
anonimat *m* anonymity
anonyme *adj* anonymous
anorma *adj* abnormal
anormalité *f* abnormality
antagoniser *v* antagonize
antécédent *m* antecedent
antécédents *m* antecedents
antenne *f* antenna
antérieur *adj* prior
antibiotique *m* antibiotic
anticipation *f* anticipation
anticiper *v* anticipate
antidote *m* antidote
antilope *f* antelope
antipathie *f* antipathy
antiquité *f* antiquity
antirouille *adj* rust-proof
antre *f* den
anxiété *f* anxiety
anxieux *adj* anxious, uneasy
août *m* August
apathie *f* apathy
apéritif *m* aperitif
aplatir *v* flatten

apocalypse *f* apocalypse
apostolique *adj* apostolic
apostrophe *f* apostrophe
apôtre *m* apostle
appaisement *m* appeasement
appaiser *v* appease
apparaître *v* appear
appareil *m* device
appareil photo *m* camera
apparemment *adv* apparently
apparence *f* appearance
apparent *adj* apparent
apparenté *adj* related
apparition *f* apparition
appartement *m* apartment
appartenir *v* belong
appât *m* bait
appâter *v* lure
appauvri *adj* impoverished
appel *m* appeal, call
appelle *v* call
appeller *v* call out
appendice *f* appendix
appendicite *f* appendicitis
appétit *m* appetite
applaudir *v* applaud
applicable *adj* applicable
applicant *m* applicant
appliquer *v* smear, apply
appontement *m* dock
apport *m* input
apporter *iv* bring

apposer *v* affix
appréciable *adj* enjoyable
apprécier *v* appreciate
appréhender *v* apprehend
appréhensif *adj* apprehensive
appréhension *f* uneasiness
apprendre *v* learn
apprenti *m* apprentice
appris *adj* learned
apprivoiser *v* tame
approbation *f* approval
approche *f* approach
approcher *v* approach
approfondir *v* deepen
approprié *adj* suitable
approuver *v* approve
approximatif *adj* approximate
appuyer *v* lean on
après *pre* after
après-midi *m* afternoon
aproblème *m* matter
aptitude *f* aptitude
aquarium *m* aquarium
aquatique *adj* aquatic
aqueduc *m* aqueduct
aquérir *v* acquire
Arabique *adj* Arabic
arable *adj* arable
araignée *f* spider
arbitrage *m* arbitration
arbitraire *adj* arbitrary
arbitre *m* referee

arbitrer *v* arbitrate
arbre *m* tree
arbuste *m* shrub
arc *m* arc, bow
arc-en-ciel *m* rainbow
archaéologie *f* archaeology
archaïque *adj* archaic
arche *f* arch
archevêque *m* archbishop
architecte *m* architect
architecture *f* architecture
archive *f* archive
arctique *adj* arctic
ardent *adj* ardent
ardeur *f* ardor
ardoise *f* slate
ardu *adj* arduous
arène *f* arena
arête *f* ridge
argent *m* money
argent de poche *m* allowance
argenterie *f* silverware
argile *f* clay
argument *m* argument, point
argumenter *v* dispute
aride *adj* arid
aristocracie *f* aristocracy
aristocrate *m* aristocrat
arithmétique *f* arithmetic
arme *f* arm, weapon
armé *adj* armed
arme à feu *f* firearm

arme de poing *f* handgun
armée *f* army
armements *m* armaments
armer *v* arm
armistice *f* armistice
armure *f* armor
arnaquer *v* defraud
aromatique *adj* aromatic
arracher *v* tear, rip off
arrangement *m* arrangement
arranger *v* arrange
arrestation *f* arrest
arrêt *m* stop
arrêter *v* halt, stop
arriéré *m* rear
arriéré *adj* rear
arrivant *m* newcomer
arrivée *f* arrival
arriver *v* arrive, happen
arriviste *adj* pushy
arrogance *f* arrogance
arrogant *adj* arrogant
arrondissement *m* borough
arroser *v* sprinkle, water
arsenal *m* arsenal
arsenique *m* arsenic
art *m* art, craft
artère *f* artery
arthrite *f* arthritis
artichaut *m* artichoke
article *m* article
articulation *f* articulation

articuler *v* articulate
artificiel *adj* artificial
artillerie *f* artillery
artisan *m* craftsman
artisanat *m* craft
artisant *m* artisan
artiste *m* artist
artistique *adj* artistic
as *m* ace
asaillir *v* mob
ascenceur *m* elevator
ascendance *f* ancestry
ascétique *adj* ascetic
aspect *m* aspect, facet
asperge *f* asparagus
asphyxie *f* asphyxiation
asphyxier *v* asphyxiate
aspiration *f* aspiration
aspirer *v* aspire
aspirine *f* aspirin
assaillant *m* assailant
assaillir *v* assail, beset
assassin *m* assassin
assassinat *m* assassination
assassiner *v* assassinate
assaut *m* assault
assemblée *f* assembly
assembler *v* assemble
asseoir *v* sit
assez *adv* enough
assiéger *v* besiege
assiette *f* plate

assigner *v* assign
assimilation *f* assimilation
assimiler *v* assimilate
assis *adj* seated
assistance *f* assistance
assistant *m* helper
assister *v* assist, attend
association *f* association
associer *v* associate
assoiffé *adj* thirsty
assommer *v* stun
assorti *adj* assorted
assortiment *m* assortment
assortir *v* match
assoupir *v* doze
assourdir *v* deafen
assourdissant *adj* deafening
assumer *v* assume
assurance *f* assurance
assurer *v* assure, insure
astérisque *m* asterisk
astéroïde *f* asteroid
asthmatique *adj* asthmatic
asthme *m* asthma
astiquer *v* spruce up
astreinte *f* constraint
astrologie *f* astrology
astrologiste *m* astrologer
astronaute *m* astronaut
astronome *m* astronomer
astronomie *f* astronomy
astronomique *adj* astronomic

astucieux *adj* astute
asyle *m* asylum
atelier *m* workshop
aterrir *v* land
aterrissage *m* landing
athée *m* atheist
athéisme *m* atheism
athlète *m* athlete
athlètique *adj* athletic
atmosphère *f* atmosphere
atome *m* atom
atomique *adj* atomic
atout *m* asset
atroce *adj* atrocious
atrocité *f* atrocity
atrophier *v* atrophy
attaché *adj* attached
attacher *v* attach, fasten
attachment *m* attachment
attaquant *m* attacker
attaque *f* attack, seizure
attaquer *v* attack
attarder *v* linger
atteindre *v* attain, reach
attelle *f* splint
attendre *v* await, wait
attente *f* expectation
attentif *adj* attentive
attention *f* attention
attention! *v* beware
attentionné *adj* thoughtful
attenuant *adj* attenuating

atténuante *adj* extenuating
attenué *v* attenuate
attester *v* attest
attibutions *v* remit
attirant *adj* appealing
attirer *v* attract, entice
attraction *f* attraction
attraper *v* snatch
attrayant *adj* eye-catching
attribuer *v* attribute
attrister *v* sadden
au dessous *adv* below
au hasard *adv* randomly
au lieu de *adv* instead
au nom de *adv* behalf (on)
au revoir *e* bye
aube *f* dawn
auberge *f* inn
aucun *adj* neither
aucun *pre* none
audace *f* audacity
audacieux *adj* audacious
au-delà de *adv* beyond
au-dessus de *pre* above
audible *adj* audible
audience *f* audience
auditer *v* audit
auditeur *m* listener
audition *f* hearing
auditorium *m* auditorium
augmentation *f* increase
augmenter *v* increase, raise

aujourd'hui *adv* today
aumône *f* alms
auparavant *adv* previously
aussi *adv* also, too
austère *adj* austere
austèrité *f* austerity
autant *adv* as
autel *m* altar
auteur *m* author
authenticité *f* authenticity
authentifier *v* authenticate
authentique *adj* authentic
auto *f* auto
autocollant *m* sticker
autographe *m* autograph
automatique *adj* automatic
automne *m* autumn, fall
automobile *f* automobile
autonome *adj* autonomous
autonomie *f* autonomy
autopsie *f* autopsy
autorisation *f* authorization
autoriser *v* authorize
autoritaire *adj* bossy
autorité *f* authority
autoroute *f* freeway
autour *pre* around
autre *adj* other
autrefois *adv* formerly
autrement *adv* otherwise
autruche *f* ostrich
auvent *m* awning

auxiliaire *adj* auxiliary
avalanche *f* avalanche
avaler *v* engulf, swallow
avaler d'un coup *v* gulp down
avance *f* advance
avancer *v* advance
avant *adv* before
avant *pre* before
avantage *m* advantage
avant-garde *m* vanguard
avant-goût *m* foretaste
avant-propos *m* foreword
avare *adj* greedy
avare *m* miser
avarice *f* avarice
avarié *adj* tainted
avec *pre* with
avent *m* Advent
aventure *f* adventure
aventurer *v* venture
avenue *f* avenue
averse *f* downpour
aversion *f* dislike
avertir *v* warn
avertissement *m* warning
aveu *m* admission
aveugle *adj* blind
aveuglément *adv* blindly
aveugler *v* blind
aviateur *m* aviator
aviation *f* aviation
avide *adj* avid

avidité *f* greed
avion *m* airplane
avise *f* cove
avise *adj* worldly
avocat *m* attorney
avoine *m* oatmeal
avoir *v* have
avoir faim *adj* hungry
avoir peur *adj* afraid
avoir soif *v* thirst
avortement *m* abortion
avorter *v* abort
avoué *adj* avowed
avouer *v* concede
avril *m* April
axe *m* axis
axiome *m* axiom
azote *m* nitrogen

B

babiller *v* babble
babysitter *f* babysitter
bâcler *v* botch
bacon *m* bacon
bactérie *f* bacteria
badge *m* badge
bafouillage *v* stammer

bagarre *f* brawl
baguette *f* baguette
baie *f* bay
baigner *v* bathe
baignoire *f* bathtub
baillement *m* yawn
bailler *v* yawn
bailleur *m* lessor
bâilloner *v* gag
bain *m* bath
baïonnette *f* bayonet
baisse *f* drop
baisser *v* dim, duck
balafre *f* slash
balais *m* broom
balance *f* balance, scale
balancer *v* balance, swing
balançoire *f* swing
balayer *v* sweep
balcon *m* balcony
baleine *f* whale
balise *f* beacon, flare
baliverne *f* nonsense
ball *f* ball
balle *f* bullet, pellet
balustrade *f* rail
bambou *m* bamboo
banal *adj* trivial
banaliser *v* trivialize
banalité *f* banality
banane *f* banana
banc *m* bench

banc d'église *m* pew
bandage *m* bandage
bande *f* gang
bandeau *m* band
bander *v* bandage
bander les yeux *v* blindfold
banderole *f* banner
bandit *m* bandit
banlieue *f* suburb
bannir *v* ban, banish
bannissement *m* banishment
banque *f* bank
banquet *m* banquet
baptême *m* baptism
baptiser *v* baptize
bar *m* bar
barbare *m* barbarian
barbarique *adj* barbaric
barbarisme *m* barbarism
barbe *f* beard
barbecue *m* barbecue
barbier *m* barber
barbu *adj* bearded
baromètre *m* barometer
barrage *m* barrage, dam
barre *f* bar
barrer *v* bar
barricade *f* barricade
barrière *f* barrier
bas *adj* low
basculer *v* flip, topple
base *f* base, basis

B

baseball *m* baseball
baser *v* base
basketball *m* basketball
bassin *m* basin
bastonnade *f* beating
bataille *f* battle, fight
batailler *v* battle
batalion *m* battalion
bâtard *m* bastard
bateau *m* boat, ship
bâton *m* baton, stick
batte *f* bat
battement *m* beat, throb
batterie *f* drum
battre *v* defeat, beat
battu *adj* beaten
baume *m* balm
bavard *adj* talkative
bazar *m* bazaar
beau *adj* good-looking
beaucoup *adv* lot, much
beaucoup *adj* lots, many
beau-fils *m* stepson
beau-frère *m* brother-in-law
beau-père *m* father-in-law
beauté *f* beauty
beaux-parents *m* in-laws
bébé *m* baby
bec *m* beak
beffroi *m* belfry
bel homme *adj* handsome
Belge *adj* Belgian

Belgique *f* Belgium
bélier *m* ram
belle-fille *f* daughter-in-law
belle-mère *f* mother-in-law
belle-soeur *f* sister-in-law
belligérant *adj* belligerent
bénédiction *f* benediction
bénéfice *m* benefit
bénéficiaire *m* beneficiary
bénéficier *v* benefit
bénéfique *adj* beneficial
béni *adj* blessed
bénidiction *f* blessing
bénin *adj* benign
bénir *v* bless
béquille *f* crutch
berceau *m* cradle, crib
béret *m* beret
berger *m* shepherd
besoin *m* need
bestial *adj* bestial
bestialité *f* bestiality
bétail *m* livestock
bête *f* beast
béton *m* concrete
betterave *f* beet
beurre *m* butter
bible *f* bible
bibliographie *f* bibliography
bibliothécaire *m* librarian
bibliothéque *f* library
biblique *adj* biblical

B

bicyclette *f* bicycle
bide *m* gut
bidonville *m* slum
bien *m* assets
bien *adv* fine
bien que *c* although
bien s'entendre *v* get along
bien-aimé *adj* beloved
bien-être *d* welfare
bienfaiteur *m* benefactor
bienheureux *adj* blissful
biens *m* goods
bienséance *f* etiquette
bientôt *adv* shortly, soon
bienveillance *f* benevolence
bienveillant *adj* gracious
bienvenue *m* welcome
bière *f* beer
bigamie *f* bigamy
bigot *adj* bigot
bigoterie *f* bigotry
bijou *m* jewel
bijouterie *f* jewelry store
bijoutier *m* jeweler
bile *f* bile
bilingue *adj* bilingual
billard *m* pool, billiards
bimestriel *adj* bimonthly
biographie *f* biography
biologie *f* biology
biologique *adj* biological
biscuit *m* biscuit

bison *m* bison
bisous *m* kiss
bitume *m* asphalt
bizarre *adj* bizarre, weird
blague *f* joke, gag
blaguer *v* joke
blâmer *v* blame
blanc *adj* white
blanc d'oeuf *m* egg white
blanchir *v* whiten
blasphème *m* blasphemy
blasphémerer *v* blaspheme
blé *m* wheat
blessant *adj* hurtful
blessé *adj* hurt
blesser *v* wound
blessure *f* injury, wound
bleu *m* bruise
bleu *adj* blue
bleu marrine *adj* navy blue
blizzard *m* blizzard
bloc *m* block
blocus *m* blockade
blond *adj* blond
bloquer *v* block, obstruct
blottir *v* huddle
blouse *f* blouse
bluffer *v* bluff
blush *m* blush
bobine *f* spool
bocal *m* jar
bœuf *m* ox, beef

B

boire *v* drink
bois *m* lumber, wood
bois de chauffage *m* firewood
boisson *f* drink
boite *f* box, can
boîte aux lettres *f* mailbox
boiter *v* limp
boiteux *adj* lame
bol *m* bowl
bombardement *m* bombing
bombarder *v* bomb
bombe *f* bomb
bon *adj* good
bon marché *adj* cheap
bonbon *m* candy
bond *m* skip
bondé *adj* crowded
bondir *v* leap
bonheur *m* happiness
bonjour *e* hello
bonne affaire *f* bargain
bonne volonté *f* goodwill
bonté *f* goodness
bonus *m* bonus
bord *m* brim
bord (a) *adv* aboard
bord de mer *adj* seaside
bordel *m* brothel, mess
bosse *f* bump, bulge
bossu *m* hunchback
bossu *adj* hunched
botanie *f* botany

botte *f* boot
bouc émissaire *m* scapegoat
bouche *f* mouth
bouche d'aération *f* vent
boucher *m* butcher
boucher *v* plug, block
boucherie *f* butchery
boucle *f* buckle, curl
bouclé *adj* curly
boucle d'oreille. *f* earring
boucler *v* buckle up
bouclier *m* shield
boue *f* mud
boueux *adj* muddy
bouffée *f* puff
bouffi *adj* puffy
bouger *v* budge, shift
bougie *f* candle
bouillir *v* boil
bouilloire *f* kettle
bouillon *m* broth
boulanger *m* baker
boulangerie *f* bakery
boule *f* ball
boulette *f* meatball
boulevard *m* boulevard
bouleversant *adj* shattering
bouleverser *v* upset
bourbier *m* bog
bourde *f* blunder
bourdonnement *m* buzz
bourdonner *v* buzz

bourgeois *adj* bourgeois
bourgeon *m* bud
bourse *f* grant
boussole *f* compass
bout du doigt *m* fingertip
bouteille *f* bottle
bouton *m* button, pimple
boutonnière *f* buttonhole
boutton *m* bud
boxe *f* boxing
boxeur *m* boxer
boycotter *m* boycott
bracelet *m* bracelet
braises *f* embers
brancard *m* stretcher
branche *f* branch
branché *adj* trendy
brancher *v* plug
brandir *v* wield
branlant *adj* shaky
brasser *v* brew
brasserie *f* brewery
brave *adj* brave
bravement *adv* bravely
bravoure *f* bravery
bref *adj* brief
bretelles *f* suspenders
brevet *m* patent
bride *f* bridle
briefing *m* briefing
brièvement *adv* briefly
brièveté *f* brevity

brigade *f* brigade
brillant *adj* glossy, shiny
briller *v* shine
brilliant *adj* brilliant
brique *f* brick
briquet *m* lighter
brise *f* breeze
briser *v* shatter, smash
Britanique *adj* British
brochure *f* brochure
broder *v* embroider
broderie *f* embroidery
bronchite *f* bronchitis
bronze *m* bronze
bronzé *adj* tanned
brosse *f* brush
brosser *v* brush
brouette *f* wheelbarrow
brouillard *m* fog, haze
brouillé *adj* scrambled
brouiller *v* blur
brouillon *m* draft
brouter *v* browse
bruiner *v* drizzle
bruit *m* noise, sound
brûler *v* burn, scorch
brûlure *f* burn
brume *f* mist
brumeux *adj* foggy, misty
brun *adj* brown
brunch *m* brunch
brune *adj* brunette

B
C

brusque *adj* brusque
brutal *adj* brutal
brutaliser *v* brutalize
brutalité *f* brutality
bruyamment *adv* loudly
bruyant *adj* loud, noisy
bûche *f* log
budget *m* budget
buffle *m* buffalo
buisson *m* bush
bulle *f* bubble
bulletin *m* newsletter
bureau *m* desk, office
bureaucrate *m* bureaucrat
bureaucratie *f* bureaucracy
bus *m* bus
buse *f* buzzard
buste *m* bust
but *m* goal
butin *m* booty, loot
buvable *adj* drinkable
buveur *m* drinker

C

cabine *f* booth, cabin
cabinet *m* chamber
cable *m* cable
câble *m* wire
cabosser *v* dent
cabrer *v* rear
cacahuète *f* peanut
cacao *m* cocoa
caché *adj* hidden
cacher *v* hide
cachet postal *m* postmark
cadavre *m* corpse
cadeau *m* gift
cadenas *m* padlock
cadran *m* dial
cadre *m* frame
cafard *m* cockroach
café *m* coffee
caféine *f* caffeine
cafétéria *f* cafeteria
cage *f* cage
cahier *m* notebook
caille *f* quail
cailler *v* curdle
caillot *m* clot
caissier *m* cashier
cajoler *v* coax
calamité *f* calamity
calcaire *m* limestone

calcul *m* calculation
calculatrice *f* calculator
calculer *v* calculate
cale *f* wedge
calendrier *m* calendar
caler *v* stall
calibre *m* caliber
calibrer *v* calibrate
calice *m* chalice
câliner *v* cuddle
calmar *m* squid
calme *adj* calm, still
calmer *v* soothe, settle
calomnie *f* calumny
calomnier *v* malign
calorie *f* calorie
camarade *m* comrade
cambriolage *m* burglary
cambrioler *v* burglarize
cambrioleur *m* burglar
camelote *f* junk
camion *m* truck
camionnette *f* pickup
camouflage *m* camouflage
camoufler *v* camouflage
camp *m* camp
campagnard *adj* folksy
campagne *f* countryside
camper *v* camp
canabis *m* pot
canal *m* canal
canapé *m* couch

canard *m* duck
canarie *m* canary
cancer *m* cancer
cancereux *adj* cancerous
candeur *f* candor
candidat *m* candidate
candidature *f* candidacy
candide *adj* candid
canevas *m* canvas
canevaser *v* canvas
caniveau *m* gutter
canne *f* cane
cannelle *f* cinnamon
cannibale *m* cannibal
canoë *m* canoe
canon *m* cannon
canoniser *v* canonize
canular *m* hoax
canyon *m* canyon
caoutchouc *m* rubber
cap *m* cape
capabicité *f* capability
capable *adj* capable
capacité *f* capacity
cape *f* cloak, cape
capitaine *m* captain
capitale *f* capital
capitaliser *v* capitalize
capitalisme *m* capitalism
capitulation *f* surrender
capituler *v* surrender
caporal *m* corporal

C

caprice *m* whim
capsule *f* capsule
captif *m* captive
captiver *v* captivate
captivité *f* captivity
capture *f* capture
capturer *v* capture
capuchon *m* hood
caractère *m* character
caractères *m* type
caractéristique *m* feature
carat *m* carat
caravane *f* caravan
carburant *m* fuel
carburateur *m* carburetor
carcasse *f* carcass
cardiaque *adj* cardiac
cardiologie *f* cardiology
carême *m* Lent
caresse *f* caress
caresser *v* caress, fondle
cargaison *f* shipment
cargo *m* cargo
caricature *f* caricature
carie *f* decay
carnage *m* carnage
carnet de vol *m* log
carotte *f* carrot
carré *adj* square
carré *m* square
carreau *m* tile
carrefour *m* crossroads

carrière *f* career, quarry
carte *f* card
carte postale *f* postcard
carton *m* cardboard
cartouche *f* cartridge
cas *m* instance, case
cascade *f* cascade
caserne *f* barracks
casino *m* casino
casque *m* helmet
casquette *f* cap
cassable *adj* breakable
cassé *adj* broken
casser *v* break
casserole *f* pan
cassette *f* tape
caste *f* caste
castor *m* beaver
cataclisme *m* cataclysm
catacombe *f* catacomb
catalogue *m* catalog
cataloguer *v* catalog
cataracte *f* cataract
catastrophe *f* catastrophe
catéchisme *m* catechism
catégorie *f* category
catégorique *adj* adamant
cathédrale *f* cathedral
Catholicisme *m* Catholicism
catholique *adj* catholic
cauchemar *m* nightmare
cause *f* cause

cause (a) *pre* because of
cause (a) *adv* owing to
causer *v* cause
caution *f* bail
cavalerie *f* cavalry
cave *f* cave, cellar
caverne *f* cavern
cavité *f* cavity
ce soir *adj* this
ce soir *adv* tonight
cécité *f* blindness
céder *v* give in, relent
ceintre *m* hanger
ceinture *f* belt
célébration *f* celebration
célèbre *adj* famous
célébrer *v* celebrate
célébrité *f* celebrity
céleri *m* celery
céleste *adj* celestial
célibat *m* celibacy
célibataire *m* bachelor
cendre *f* cinder, ash
cendrier *m* ashtray
censure *f* censorship
censurer *v* censure
cent *adj* hundred
centenaire *m* centenary
centième *adj* hundredth
centime *m* cent
centimètre *m* centimeter
centrale *adj* central

centraliser *v* centralize
centre *m* center, focus
centre commercial *m* mall
centrer *v* center
centre-ville *m* downtown
cependant *c* however
céramique *f* ceramic
cerceuil *m* casket, coffin
cercle *m* circle
céréale *f* cereal
cérébrale *adj* cerebral
cérémonie *f* ceremony
cerf-volant *m* kite
cerise *f* cherry
certain *adj* certain
certificat *m* certificate
certifier *v* certify
certitude *f* certainty
cérumen *m* earwax
cerveau *m* brain
ces *adj* these
cesser *v* cease
cessez-le-feu *m* cease-fire
c'est-à-dire *adv* namely
ceux-là *adj* those
chacal *m* jackal
chacun *adv* apiece
chagrin *m* sorrow, grief
chahuter *v* heckle
chahuteur *adj* boisterous
chaine *f* chain, channel
chaine de magasin *f* franchise

chair *f* flesh
chaise *f* chair
chaise roulante *f* wheelchair
chalet *m* chalet
chaleur *f* heat, warmth
challenge *m* challenge
chambre *f* bedroom, room
chameau *m* camel
champ *m* scope
champ de mines *m* minefield
champignon *m* mushroom
champion *m* champion
chance *f* luck, chance
chanceler *v* sway
chancelier *m* chancellor
chances *f* odds
chanceux *adj* lucky
chandelier *m* candlestick
changement *m* change, shift
changer *v* alter, change
chanson *f* song
chant de Noël *m* carol
chant scandé *m* chant
chantage *m* blackmail
chanter *v* sing
chanteur *m* singer
chantier naval *m* shipyard
chaos *m* chaos
chaotique *adj* chaotic
chapeau *m* hat
chapel *f* chapel
chapelain *m* chaplain

chapitre *m* chapter
chaque *adj* each, every
charade *f* charade
charbon *m* coal
charge *f* charge, load
chargé *adj* loaded
charge (a) *adj* dependent
charger *v* load
chario *m* carriage
charisme *m* charisma
charitable *adj* charitable
charité *f* charity
charmant *adj* charming
charme *m* appeal
charmer *v* charm
charnel *adj* carnal
charnière *f* hinge
charrette *f* cart
charte *f* charter
charter *m* charter
chasse *f* hunting
chasse à l'homme *f* manhunt
chasser *v* dispel, hunt
chasseur *m* hunter
chaste *adj* chaste
chasteté *f* chastity
chat *m* cat
chateau *m* castle
châtier *v* chastise
châtiment *m* chastisement
chaton *m* kitten
chatouillement *m* tickle

chatouiller *v* tickle
chatouilleux *adj* ticklish
chaud *adj* hot, warm
chaudière *f* boiler
chauffage *m* heating
chauffe-eau *m* waterheater
chauffer *v* heat
chauffeur *m* chauffeur
chaussée *f* pavement
chaussette *f* sock
chaussure *f* shoe
chaussures *f* footwear
chauve *adj* bald
chauve-souris *f* bat
chavirer *v* capsize
check-up *m* check up
chef *m* chef, chief
chef-d'œuvre *m* masterpiece
chemin *m* path, way
chemin de fer *m* railroad
cheminée *f* chimney
chemise *f* shirt
chêne *m* oak
chenille *f* caterpillar
chèque *m* check
chèquier *m* checkbook
cher *adj* dear, pricey
chercher *v* seek
chercheur *m* research
chéri *adj* darling
chérir *v* cherish
cheval *m* horse

chevalier *m* knight
chevaucher *v* overlap
cheveux *m* hair
cheville *f* ankle
chèvre *f* goat
chevreau *m* kid
chevreuil *m* venison
chewing gum *m* bubble gum
chez *pre* to
chic *adj* posh
chien *m* dog
chien de chasse *m* hound
chiffon *m* rag
chiffre *m* digit
chimie *f* chemistry
chimique *adj* chemical
chimiste *m* chemist
chimpanzé *m* chimpanzee
chiot *m* puppy
chirurgical *adv* surgical
chirurgien *m* surgeon
choc *m* shock
chocolat *m* chocolate
chœur *m* chorus
choisir *v* choose, pick
choix *m* choice
choléra *m* cholera
choléstérole *m* cholesterol
chômage *m* unemployment
chômeur *adj* unemployed
choquant *adj* shocking
choqué *adj* shaken

C

choquer v madden, shock
chorale f choir
chose f thing
choses f stuff
chou m cabbage
chou fleur m cauliflower
choyer v pamper
christianisme m Christianity
chrétien adj christian
chronique adj chronic
chronique f chronicle
chronologie f chronology
chronométrer v time
chuchotement m whisper
chuchoter v whisper
chute f fall
chute de neige f snowfall
chute d'eau f waterfall
chuter v plunge
ci-après adv hereafter
cible f target
cicatrice f scar
cidre m cider
ciel m sky
cigare m cigar
cigarette f cigarette
cigogne f stork
cil m eyelash
ciment m cement
cimetière m cemetery
cinéma m cinema
cinq adj five

cinquante adj fifty
cinquième adj fifth
cirage m shoepolish
circonciser v circumcise
circoncision f circumcision
circonstance f circumstance
circuit m circuit
circulaire adj circular
circulation f circulation
circuler v circulate
cire f polish, wax
cirque m circus
ciseau m chisel
ciseaux m scissors
citation f subpoena
citer v quote
citerne f cistern
citoyen m citizen
citoyenneté f citizenship
citron m lemon
citron vert m lime
citrouille f pumpkin
civil adj civil
civilisation f civilization
civiliser v civilize
civique adj civic
clair adj light
claire adj clear
clairement adv clearly
clairsemé adj sparse
clan m clan
clandestin adj clandestine

claque *f* slap, smack
claquer *v* slam
clarification *f* clarification
clarifier *v* clarify
clarinette *f* clarinet
clarté *f* clearness
classe *f* class
classer *v* classify, file
classique *adj* classic
clause *f* clause
clavicule *f* collarbone
clavier *m* keyboard
clé *f* wrench, key
clémence *f* clemency
clérgé *m* clergy
clérical *adj* clerical
client *m* client
clientèle *f* clientele
cliff *m* cliff
cligner *v* blink
clignoter *v* flicker
climat *m* climate
climatique *adj* climatic
clin *m* decline
clin d'oeil *m* wink
clinique *f* clinic
cliquer *v* click
cloche *f* bell
cloître *m* cloister
clonage *m* cloning
cloner *v* clone
clôture *f* enclosure

clou *m* tack
clown *m* clown
club *m* club
coagulation *f* coagulation
coaguler *v* coagulate
coalition *f* coalition
cocaïne *f* cocaine
cochon *m* pig
cockpit *m* cockpit
cocktail *m* cocktail
cocotte *f* casserole
code *m* code
code postal *m* zip code
codifier *v* codify
coéfficient *m* coefficient
coercition *f* coercion
coeur *m* heart
coexister *v* coexist
coffre *m* trunk
cogner *v* knock, punch
cohabiter *v* cohabit
cohérent *adj* coherent
cohésion *f* cohesion
coi *adj* speechless
coiffeur *m* hairdresser
coin *m* corner
coincé *adj* uptight
coincidence *f* coincidence
coincider *v* coincide
col *m* collar
colère *f* anger
colier *m* necklace

C

C

colique _f_ colic
colis postaux _m_ parcel post
collaborateur _m_ collaborator
collaboration _f_ collaboration
collaborer _v_ collaborate
collant _m_ pantyhose
collapser _v_ collapse
collatéral _adj_ collateral
colle _f_ glue
collecteur _m_ collector
collection _f_ collection
collectioner _v_ collect
collègue _m_ colleague
coller _v_ glue, paste
colline _f_ hill
collision _f_ collision
colombe _f_ dove
colon _m_ settler
côlon _m_ colon
colonel _m_ colonel
colonial _adj_ colonial
colonie _f_ colony
colonisation _f_ colonization
coloniser _v_ colonize
colonne _f_ column, spine
coloré _adj_ colorful
colorier _v_ color
colossal _adj_ colossal
coma _m_ coma
combat _m_ combat
combatant _m_ combatant
combattant _m_ fighter

combattre _v_ combat
combinaison _f_ combination
combine _f_ plan, trick
combiner _v_ combine
combustible _m_ combustible
combustion _f_ combustion
come-back _m_ comeback
comédie _f_ comedy
comédien _m_ comedian
comestible _adj_ edible
comète _f_ comet
comique _adj_ comical
comité _m_ council
commandant _m_ commander
commande _f_ order
commandement _m_ commandment
commander _v_ command
comme _c_ as
comme _pre_ like
commémorer _v_ commemorate
commencer _v_ begin, start
comment _adv_ how
commentaire _m_ comment
commenter _v_ comment
commerçant _m_ trader
commerce _m_ business
commercial _adj_ commercial
commettre _v_ commit
commissaire _m_ auctioneer
commission _f_ errand
commode _adj_ convenient
commode _f_ dresser

commodité *f* convenience
commodités *f* amenities
commun *adj* common
communication *f* communication
communion *f* communion
communiquer *v* communicate
communisme *m* communism
communiste *m* communist
communauté *f* community
compact *adj* compact
compagnie *f* company
companion *m* companion
comparable *adj* comparable
comparaison *f* comparison
comparatif *adj* comparative
comparer *v* compare
compartiment *m* compartment
compassion *f* compassion
compassioné *adj* compassionate
compatibilité *f* compatibility
compatible *adj* compatible
compatir *v* sympathize
compatriote *m* compatriot,
countryman
compensation *f* compensation
compenser *v* compensate
compétence *f* competence
compétent *adj* competent
compétiteur *m* competitor
compétitif *adj* competitive
compétition *f* competition
complainte *f* lament

complaisance *f* leniency
complaisant *adj* lenient
complément *m* complement
complet *adj* complete
complètement *adv* quite
compléter *v* complete
complexe *m* complex
complexion *f* complexion
complexité *f* complexity
complication *f* complication
complice *m* accomplice
complicité *f* complicity
compliment *m* compliment
compliqué *adj* intricate
compliquer *v* complicate
complot *m* plot
comploter *v* plot
comportement *m* behavior
comporter *v* behave
composant *m* component
composer *v* compose
compositeur *m* composer
composition *f* composition
compost *m* compost
compréhensible *adj* understandable
compréhensif *adj* comprehensive
compréhension *f* understanding
comprendre *v* understand
compression *f* compression
comprimé *m* tablet
comprimer *v* compress
compromettre *v* compromise

C

compromis _m_ compromise
compromis _v_ consist
comptabilité _m_ account
comptable _m_ accountant
compte _mf_ account
compter _v_ count, reckon
compter sur _v_ reckon on
comptoir _m_ counter
compulsif _adj_ compulsive
compulsion _f_ compulsion
comté _m_ county
comtesse _f_ countess
concentration _f_ concentration
concentrer _v_ concentrate
concentrique _adj_ concentric
concept _m_ concept
conception _f_ conception
concernant _pre_ concerning
concerner _v_ pertain
concert _m_ concert
concession _f_ concession
concevoir _v_ conceive
concierge _m_ janitor
conciliant _adj_ compliant
concilier _v_ conciliate
concis _adj_ concise
concluant _adj_ conclusive
conclure _v_ conclude
conclusion _f_ conclusion
concocter _v_ concoct
concoction _f_ concoction
concombre _m_ cucumber

concomitant _adj_ concurrent
concours _m_ contest
concret _adj_ concrete
concurrent _m_ contender
condamnation _f_ conviction
condamné _adj_ doomed
condamner _v_ condemn
condensation _f_ condensation
condenser _v_ condense
condiment _m_ condiment
condition _f_ condition
condition que (a) _c_ providing that
conditionel _adj_ conditional
condoléances _f_ condolences
condomner _v_ sentence
conducteur _m_ driver
conduire _v_ conduct, drive
conduit _m_ duct
conduite _f_ conduct
cone _m_ cone
conférence _f_ lecture
conférer _v_ confer
confesser _v_ confess
confesseur _m_ confessor
confession _f_ confession
confessionnal _m_ confessional
confiance _f_ confidence
confident _m_ confidant
confidentiel _adj_ confidential
confier _v_ confide, entrust
confirmation _f_ confirmation
confirmer _v_ confirm

confiscate _v_ confiscate
confisquer _v_ impound
confiture _f_ conserve, jam
conflictuel _adj_ contentious
conflit _m_ conflict
confondre _v_ confound, baffle
conforme _adj_ consistent
conformer _v_ conform
conformer à _v_ abide by
conformiste _adj_ conformist
conformité _f_ conformity
confort _m_ comfort
confortable _adj_ comfortable
confromer _v_ comply
confrontation _f_ confrontation
confronter _v_ confront
confusion _f_ confusion
congédiement _m_ discharge
congédier _v_ discharge
congélateur _m_ freezer
congeler _v_ freeze
congenial _adj_ congenial
congestion _f_ congestion
congestionné _adj_ congested
congrégation _f_ congregation
congrès _m_ congress
conjointement _adv_ jointly
conjonction _f_ conjunction
conjugal _adj_ conjugal
conjuger _v_ conjugate
conjurer _v_ beseech
connaissance _f_ knowledge

connecter _v_ connect
connection _f_ connection
connoter _v_ connote
connu _adj_ well-known
conquérant _m_ conqueror
conquérir _v_ conquer
conquête _f_ conquest
consacrer _v_ consecrate
conscience _f_ awareness, consciousness
consciencieux _adj_ conscious
conscient _adj_ aware
conscrit _m_ conscript
consécration _f_ consecration
consécutif _adj_ consecutive
conseil _m_ advice, counsel
conseiller _v_ counsel
conseiller _m_ counselor
conseils _m_ guidance
consensus _m_ consensus
consentement _m_ consent
consentir _v_ assent, consent
conséquence _f_ consequence
conséquent _adj_ consequent
conservateur _adj_ conservative
conservateur _m_ curator
conservation _f_ conservation
conserver _v_ conserve
considér _adj_ considerate
considérable _adj_ significant
considérer _v_ consider
consistance _f_ consistency

consolation *f* consolation
consoler *v* console
consolider *v* consolidate
consommateur *m* consumer
consommation *f* consumption
consommer *v* consume
consomne *f* consonant
conspirateur *m* conspirator
conspiration *f* conspiracy
conspirer *v* conspire
constance *f* constancy
constancy *adj* constant
constant *adj* steady
constellation *f* constellation
consternation *f* dismay
consterner *v* dismay
constipation *f* constipation
constipé *adj* constipated
constiper *v* constipate
constituer *v* constitute
constitution *f* constitution
constructeur *m* builder
constructif *adj* constructive
construction *f* construction
construire *v* build
consul *m* consul
consulat *m* consulate
consultation *f* consultation
consulter *v* consult
contact *m* contact, touch
contacter *v* contact
contagieux *adj* contagious

contamination *f* contamination
contaminer *v* contaminate
conte *m* tale
contempler *v* contemplate
contemporain *adj* contemporary
contenance *f* countenance
contenir *v* contain
content *adj* glad
contenter *v* content
contenu *m* contents
conteur *m* teller
contexte *m* context
contigent *adj* contingent
continent *m* continent
continental *adj* continental
contingence *f* contingency
continu *adj* continuous
continuation *f* continuation
continuel *adj* ongoing
continuer *v* continue
continuité *f* continuity
contour *m* contour, outline
contourner *v* bypass
contracter *v* contract
contraction *f* contraction
contradiction *f* contradiction
contradictoire *adj* conflicting
contraindre *v* constrain
contrainte *f* constraint
contraire *adj* contrary
contraire *m* opposite
contrarier *v* thwart

contraste *m* contrast
contraster *v* contrast
contrat *m* contract
contre *pre* against, versus
contrebande *f* contraband
contrebandier *m* smuggler
contrecarrer *v* counteract
contrecœur (a) *adv* grudgingly
contredfait *adj* counterfeit
contredire *v* contradict
contrefaire *v* counterfeit
contremaître *m* foreman
contretemps *m* setback
contribuable *m* contributor
contribuer *v* contribute
contribution *f* contribution
contrition *f* contrition
contrôle *m* assessment
contrôler *v* check, control
controverse *f* controversy
controversé *adj* controversial
convaincant *adj* compelling
convaincre *v* convince
convainquant *adj* convincing
convalescent *adj* convalescent
convenable *adj* decent
convenir *v* convene
convenir de *v* agree
convention *f* convention
conventionnel *adj* conventional
converger *v* converge
conversation *f* conversation

converser *v* converse
conversion *f* conversion
converti *m* convert
convertir *v* convert
conviction *f* conviction, faith
convoi *m* convoy
convulser *v* convulse
convulsion *f* convulsion
cool *adj* cool
coopérative *adj* cooperative
coopérer *v* cooperate
coordinateur *m* coordinator
coordination *f* coordination
coordiner *v* coordinate
copain *m* buddy, pal
copie *f* copy
copier *v* copy
copieux *adj* hearty
copropriété *f* condo
coq *m* cock, rooster
coque *f* hull
coquillages *f* shellfish
coquille *f* shell
coquille de noix *f* nut-shell
coquin *m* rascal
corbeau *m* raven
corbillard *m* hearse
corde *f* rope, string
cordial *adj* cordial
cordon *m* cordon
coriace *adj* tough
corneille *f* crow

cornet *m* cornet
corollaire *m* corollary
coronaire *adj* coronary
corporel *adj* bodily
corps *m* frame, body
corpulent *adj* corpulent
corpuscle *m* corpuscle
correct *adj* correct, proper
correctement *adv* properly
correction *f* correction
corréler *v* correlate
correspondant *m* correspondent
correspondre *v* correspond
corrida *f* bull fight
corridor *m* corridor
corriger *v* correct
corroborer *v* corroborate
corroder *v* corrode
corrompre *v* corrupt
corrompu *adj* corrupt
corruption *f* bribery
cosmétique *m* cosmetic
cosmique *adj* cosmic
cosmonaute *m* cosmonaut
costume *m* costume, suit
côte *f* coast, rib
côté *m* side
côté (a) *adj* next door
côte à côte *adv* abreast
côté de (a) *pre* beside
côtelette *f* chop
côtier *adj* coastal

cotisation *f* dues
coton *m* cotton
cou *m* neck
couche *f* coat, layer
coucher du soleil *m* sunset
couchette *f* berth
coude *m* elbow
coudre *v* sew, stitch
couler *v* sink, go under
couleur *f* color
couloir *m* hallway
coup *m* blow, coup
coup de bec *mf* peck
coup de chaleur *m* heatstroke
coup de couteau *m* stab
coup de feu *m* gunshot
coup de poing *m* punch
coup de soleil *m* sunburn
coup d'oeil *m* glance, look
coup monté *m* setup
coupable *m* culprit
coupable *adj* guilty
coupe *f* haircut
couper *v* carve, chop, slash
couple *m* couple
coupon *m* coupon
coupure *f* cut, clipping
cour *f* court, yard
courage *m* courage
courageux *adj* courageous
couramment *adv* fluently
courbe *f* curve

courber *v* curb, curve
coureur *m* runner
courge *v* squash
courir *v* run
couronne *f* wreath
couronnement *m* coronation
courrant d'air *m* draft
courrier *m* mail, post
courronne *f* crown
courronnement *m* crowning
courronner *v* crown
cours *m* class
course *f* race, course
courses *f* groceries
coursier *m* courier
court *adj* short
courtois *adj* courteous
cousin *m* cousin
coussin *m* cushion
cout *m* cost
couteau *m* knife
couter *v* cost
couteux *adj* costly
coutiser *v* court
coutoisie *f* courtesy
coutume *m* custom
couture *f* seam, sewing
couturière *f* seamstress
couvent *m* convent
couvercle *m* cover, lid
couvert *adj* overcast
couverts *m* cutlery

couverture *f* blanket, cover
couvre-feu *m* curfew
couvrir *v* cover
co-voiturer *v* commute
cowboy *m* cowboy
crabe *m* crab
crachin *m* drizzle
craie *f* chalk
crainte *f* awe
craintif *adj* fearful
crampe *f* cramp, pang
cramponner *v* cling
crane *m* crane
crâne *m* skull
crapaud *m* toad
craquant *adj* crusty
craquer *v* crack
crasse *f* filth, grime
crasseux *adj* filthy
cratère *m* crater
cravacher *v* whip
cravate *f* necktie
crayon *m* crayon, pencil
créateur *m* creator
créatif *adj* creative
création *f* creation
créativité *f* creativity
créature *f* creature
crèche *f* nursery
crédibilité *f* credibility
crédible *adj* credible
crédit *m* credit

créditeur *m* creditor
crédule *adj* gullible
créer *v* create
crématorium *m* crematorium
crème *f* cream
crèmeux *adj* creamy
crépu *adj* fuzzy
crépuscule *m* sundown
crête *f* crest
crétin *adj* moron
creu *adj* hollow
creuser *iv* dig
crevaison *f* blowout
crevette *f* prawn, shrimp
cri *m* cry, shout
criard *adj* lurid
cricket *m* cricket
crier *v* scream, yell
crime *m* crime
criminel *adj* criminal
crique *f* creek
criquet *m* locust
cris *m* shouting
crise *f* crisis
cristal *m* crystal
critère *m* criterion
critique *adj* critical
critique *f* criticism, critique
critiquer *v* criticize
crochet *m* bracket, hook
crocodile *m* crocodile
croire *v* believe

croisade *f* crusade
croisé *m* crusader
croiser *v* intersect
croiseur *m* destroyer
croissance *f* growth
croissant *adj* increasing
croix *f* cross
croquant *adj* crunchy
crosse *f* hilt
croustillant *adj* crispy
croûte *fm* crust
croyable *adj* believable
croyance *f* belief, faith
croyant *m* believer
cru *adj* raw
cruauté *f* cruelty
cruche *f* jug
crucial *adj* crucial, critical
crucifier *v* crucify
crucifix *m* crucifix
crucifixion *f* crucifixion
cruel *adj* cruel
cube *m* block, cube
cubique *adj* cubic
cueillir *v* pick, pluck
cuillère *f* spoon
cuillère à café *f* teaspoon
cuillère à soupe *f* tablespoon
cuillerée *f* spoonful
cuir *m* leather
cuir chevelu *m* scalp
cuirassé *m* battleship

cuire *m* sting
cuire au four *v* bake
cuisine *f* kitchen, cuisine
cuisiner *v* cook
cuisinier *m* cook
cuisinière *f* stove
cuisse *f* thigh
cuivre *m* copper
culbuter *v* overturn
culminer *v* culminate
culot *fm* crust
culpabilité *f* guilt
culte *m* worship
cultivé *adj* genteel
cultiver *v* cultivate
culture *f* cultivation
culturel *adj* cultural
curable *adj* curable
cure *f* cure
cure-dents *m* toothpick
curieux *adj* curious
curiosité *f* curiosity
cutter *m* cutter
cyanure *m* cyanide
cycle *m* cycle
cycliste *m* cyclist
cyclone *m* cyclone
cygne *m* swan
cylindre *m* cylinder
cynicisme *m* cynicism
cynique *adj* cynic
cyprès *m* cypress

D

daigner *v* deign
daim *m* deer
dalle *f* slab
dame *f* lady
damnation *f* damnation
Danemark *m* Denmark
danger *m* danger
dangereux *adj* dangerous
dans *pre* in, within
danse *f* dance
danser *v* dance
date *f* date
dater *v* date
dauphin *m* dolphin
d'autre *adv* else
de *pre* from, of
dé *m* dice
de bon goût *adj* tasteful
de côté *adv* sideways
de courte durée *adj* shortlived
de l'est *adj* eastern
de loin *adv* afar
de mauvais goût *adj* tasteless
de nos jours *adv* nowadays
de plus *pre* besides
de plus *adv* moreover
de près *adv* closely
de retour *adv* back
de secours *adj* spare**

C
D

de travers *adj* crooked
de valeur *adj* valuable
déballer *v* unpack, unwrap
débandade *f* stampede
débarquer *v* disembark
débarrasser *v* scrap
débarrasser de *v* rid of
débat *m* debate
débattre *v* debate
débit *m* debit
débiteur *m* debtor
déboîter *v* pull out
déborder *v* boil over
déboulonner *v* debunk
débourser *v* disburse
debout *adj* upright
déboutonner *v* unbutton
débraillé *adj* sloppy
débrancher *v* unplug
débriefer *v* debrief
début *m* start, outset
débutant *m* beginner
décadence *f* decadence
décapiter *v* behead
décédé *adj* deceased
décéder *v* pass away
décembre *m* December
décendre *v* pull down
décennie *f* decade
déception *f* deception
décevant *adj* disappointing
décevoir *v* disappoint

déchaîner *v* unleash
décharge *f* dump, landfill
décharger *v* unload
déchéance *f* degradation
déchets *m* rubbish
déchiffrer *v* decipher
déchiqueté *adj* ragged
déchiqueter *v* shred
déchirer *v* rip, tear
décider *v* decide
décimal *adj* decimal
déciminer *v* decimate
décisif *adj* decisive
décision *f* decision
déclaration *f* declaration
déclarer *v* declare
déclarer forfait *v* forfeit
déclencher *v* set off, trigger
déclin *m* slump
déclinaison *f* declension
décline *v* ebb
décliner *v* decline
décollage *m* lift-off
décoller *v* lift off, take off
décolorer *v* bleach
décombres *m* rubble
décompresser *v* chill out
décompte *m* countdown
déconcerter *v* bewilder
décongeler *v* defrost, thaw
déconnecter *v* disconnect
décontracté *adj* relaxed

décor *m* décor
décoratif *adj* decorative
décorer *v* decorate
décorum *m* decorum
découler *v* stem
découper *v* cut out
découragé *adj* dejected
décourageant *adj* discouraging
découragement *m* discouragement
décourager *v* discourage
découverte *f* discovery
découvrir *v* discover
décrépit *adj* decrepit
décret *m* decree
décréter *v* decree
décrire *v* describe
dédaigner *v* shun
dédain *m* disdain
dédicacer *v* dedicate
déductible *adj* deductible
déduction *f* deduction
déduire *v* deduce, deduct
déesse *f* goddess
défaillance *f* malfunction
défaillir *v* falter
défaire *v* undo
défaite *f* defeat
défaut *m* defect, flaw
défavorable *adj* unfavorable
défectueux *adj* defective
défendre *v* defend
défense *f* defense

défenseur *m* defender
défi *m* dare
déficient *adj* deficient
déficit *m* deficit
défier *v* challenge
défigurer *v* disfigure
défini *adj* definite
définir *v* define
définitif *adj* definitive
définition *f* definition
déformation *f* distortion
déformé *adj* warped
déformer *v* deform, distort
déformité *f* deformity
défraîchi *adj* faded, shabby
défrayer *v* defray
dégager *v* writhe
dégâts *m* damage
dégel *m* thaw
dégénéré *adj* degenerate
dégénérer *v* degenerate
dégonfler *v* deflate
dégouliner *v* drip, trickle
dégoût *m* disgust
dégoûtant *adj* disgusting
dégradant *adj* degrading
dégradation *f* disrepair
dégrader *v* degrade
degré *mm* degree
déguisement *m* disguise
déguiser *v* disguise
dehors *adv* out

déjà _adv_ already
déjeuner _m_ lunch
délabré _adj_ derelict
délai _m_ delay
délecter _v_ revel
déléguation _f_ delegation
délégué _m_ delegate
déléguer _v_ delegate
délibérément _adv_ willfully
délibérer _v_ deliberate
délicat _adj_ delicate
délicieux _adj_ delicious
délinquance _f_ delinquency
délinquant _adj_ delinquent
délit _m_ misdemeanor
délivrer _v_ serve
délocalisation _f_ relocation
délocaliser _v_ relocate
déloyal _adj_ disloyal
déloyauté _f_ disloyalty
déluge _m_ deluge
demain _adv_ tomorrow
demande _f_ inquiry, request
demander _v_ ask, demand
démangeaison _f_ itchiness
démanger _v_ itch
démarrage _m_ kickoff
démasquer _v_ unmask
démêlant _m_ conditioner
démêler _v_ disentangle
déménager _v_ move out
démener _v_ exert

dément _adj_ insane
démentir _v_ deny
demi-frère _m_ stepbrother
demi-soeur _f_ stepsister
démission _f_ resignation
démissionner _v_ resign
démocratie _f_ democracy
démocratique _adj_ democratic
démolir _v_ demolish
démolition _f_ demolition
démon _m_ demon
démonstratif _adj_ demonstrative
démonter _v_ dismantle
démontrer _v_ demonstrate
démoraliser _v_ demoralize
démuni _adj_ destitute
dénaturer _v_ adulterate
dénégation _f_ denial
dénicher _v_ unearth
dénigrer _v_ denigrate
dénominateur _m_ denominator
dénoncer _v_ denounce
dénouer _v_ let down, untie
denrée _f_ foodstuff
dense _adj_ dense
densité _f_ density
dent _f_ tooth
dentaire _adj_ dental
dentelle _f_ lace
dentier _m_ dentures
dentiste _m_ dentist
dents _f_ teeth

déodorant *m* deodorant
dépanner *v* bail out
dépanneuse *f* tow truck
départ *m* departure
département *m* department
dépassé *adj* outdated
dépasser *v* protrude
dépêcher *v* rush
dépendance *f* dependence
dépendant *adj* addicted
dépendre *v* depend
dépense *f* spending
dépenser *iv* spend
déplacer *v* move, transfer
déplaire *v* displease
déplaisant *adj* displeasing
dépliant *m* leaflet
déplier *v* unfold
déploiement *m* deployment
déplorable *adj* deplorable
déplorer *v* deplore
déployer *v* deploy
déportation *f* deportation
déporter *v* deport
déposer *v* depose
dépôt *m* deposit, depot
dépravation *f* depravity
dépraver *adj* deprave
dépréciation *f* depreciation
déprécier *v* depreciate
dépression *f* depression
déprimant *adj* depressing

déprimer *v* depress
depuis *pre* since
depuis que *c* since
déraciner *v* uproot
déraillement *m* derailment
dérailler *v* derail
dérangé *adj* deranged
déranger *v* disturb
dérivatif *adj* derivative
dérivé *m* by-product
dériver *v* derive
dernier *adj* last, latter
dernier-cri *adj* up-to-date
dernièrement *adv* lately
dérogation *f* dispensation
déroutant *adj* confusing
derrière *pre* behind
dès que *c* once
désaccord *m* disagreement
désagréable *adj* nasty
désamorcer *v* defuse
désapprobation *f* disapproval
désapprouver *v* disapprove
désarçonner *v* dismount
désarmement *m* disarmament
désarmer *v* disarm
désastre *m* disaster
désastreux *adj* disastrous
désavantage *m* disadvantage
descendance *f* descent
descendant *m* descendant
descendre *v* descend, get off

descente *adv* downhill
descriptif *adj* descriptive
description *f* description
désenchanté *adj* disenchanted
déséquilibre *m* imbalance
désert *m* desert
désert *adj* deserted
déserter *v* desert
déserteur *m* deserter
désertique *adj* barren
désespéré *adj* hopeless
désespoir *m* despair
déshabiller *v* undress
désherber *v* weed
déshériter *v* disown
déshonorer *v* disgrace
déshydrater *v* dehydrate
désigner *v* designate
désillusion *f* disillusion
désinfectant *m* disinfectant
désinfecter *v* disinfect
désintégration *f* disintegration
désintégrer *v* disintegrate
désintéressé *adj* disinterested
désir *m* desire
désirable *adj* desirable
désirer *v* desire, lust
désister *v* desist
désobéir *v* disobey
désobéissan *adj* disobedient
désobéissance *f* disobedience
désobéissant *adj* naughty

désobligeant *adj* derogatory
désolation *f* desolation
désolé *adj* bleak, stark
désoler *adj* desolate
désordonné *adj* messy
désordre *m* disorder, mess
désorganisé *adj* disorganized
désorienté *adj* disoriented
despote *m* despot
despotique *adj* despotic
desserrer *v* loosen
dessert *m* dessert
dessin *m* drawing
dessin animé *m* cartoon
dessinateur *m* draftsman
dessiner *iv* draw
dessous *m* bottom
dessus *m* top
dessus de lit *m* bedspread
destin *m* destiny
destinataire *m* addressee
destination *f* destination
destructif *adj* destructive
destruction *f* destruction
désuétude *f* disuse
désunion *f* disunity
détachable *adj* detachable
détaché *adj* unattached
détacher *v* detach
détail *m* detail
détecter *v* detect
détecteur *m* detector

détective *m* detective
détendu *adj* slack
détention *f* confinement
détenu *m* inmate
détergent *m* detergent
détérioration *f* deterioration
détériorer *v* deteriorate
détérmination *f* determination
détérminer *v* determine
détestable *adj* detestable
détester *v* detest, loathe
détonateur *m* detonator
détonation *f* detonation
détour *m* detour
détournement *m* hijack
detourner *v* bypass, divert
détourner *v* hijack
détrempé *adj* soggy
détresse *f* distress
détriment *m* detriment
détroit *m* strait
détruire *v* destroy, wreck
dette *f* debt
deuil *m* mourning
deux *adj* two
deux-points *m* colon
dévaloriser *v* mark down
dévaluation *f* devaluation
dévaluer *v* devalue
devant *m* front
devanture *f* frontage
dévastation *f* devastation

dévaster *v* devastate
développement *m* development
développer *v* develop
devenir *iv* become, get
déviation *f* deviation
dévier *v* deviate
devise *f* motto, currency
dévoiler *v* unveil
devoir *m* duty
devoir *v* must, have to, owe
devoirs *m* homework
dévorer *v* devour
dévoué *adj* wholehearted
dévouement *m* dedication
diabète *m* diabetes
diabètique *adj* diabetic
diable *m* devil
diabolique *adj* evil
diacre *m* deacon
diagnostic *m* diagnosis
diagnostiquer *v* diagnose
diagonal *adj* diagonal
diagramme *m* diagram
dialecte *m* dialect
dialogue *m* dialogue
diamant *m* diamond
diamètre *m* diameter
diarrhée *f* diarrhea
dictateur *m* dictator
dictatorial *adj* dictatorial
dictature *f* dictatorship
dicter *v* dictate

dictionnaire *m* dictionary
dicton *m* saying
Dieu *m* God
diffamation *f* libel
diffamer *v* defame
différence *f* difference
différencier *v* distinguish
différent *adj* different
différer *v* differ
difficile *adj* difficult
difficulté *f* difficulty
diffuser *v* broadcast
digérer *v* digest
digestif *adj* digestive
digestion *f* digestion
dignifier *v* dignify
dignitaire *m* dignitary
dignité *f* dignity
dilapidé *adj* dilapidated
dilemme *m* dilemma
diligence *f* diligence
diligent *adj* diligent
diluer *v* dilute
dimanche *m* Sunday
dimension *f* dimension
dimininuer *v* diminish
diminuer *v* decrease, wane
diminution *f* decrease
diner *m* diner
dîner *v* dine
dingue *adj* nutty
dinosaure *m* dinosaur

diocèse *m* diocese
diplomate *m* diplomat
diplomatie *f* diplomacy
diplomatique *adj* diplomatic
diplôme *m* diploma
dire *v* say
direct *adj* direct
directeur *m* director
direction *f* direction, lead
direction est *adj* eastbound
directive *f* guidelines
dirigeant *f* leader, ruler
diriger *v* direct, rule
diriger vers *v* head for
discerner *v* discern
disciple *m* follower
discipline *f* discipline
discontinuer *v* discontinue
discordant *adj* discordant
discorde *f* discord, strife
discothèque *f* club
discréditer *v* discredit
discret *adj* discreet
discrétion *f* discretion
discrimination *f* discrimination
discriminer *v* discriminate
discussion *f* discussion
discutable *adj* debatable
discuter *v* argue, discuss
disgrâce *f* disgrace
disloquer *v* dislocate
disparaître *v* vanish

disparité *f* disparity
disparition *f* disappearance
disparu *adj* extinct
dispenser *v* dispense
disperser *v* scatter, disperse
dispersion *f* dispersal
disponibilité *f* availability
disponible *adj* available
disposer *v* dispose
disposition *f* lay
disprove *v* disprove
disputer *v* contend
disqualifier *v* disqualify
disque *m* record
disquette *f* disk
dissemblable *adj* dissimilar
disséminer *v* disseminate
dissidence *v* dissident
dissident *adj* dissident
dissimuler *v* conceal
dissiper *v* dispel, squander
dissolu *adj* dissolute
dissolution *f* dissolution
dissonant *adj* dissonant
dissoudre *v* dissolve
dissuader *v* dissuade
dissuasion *f* deterrence
distance *f* distance
distancier *v* outrun
distant *adj* aloof, distant
distiller *v* distill
distinct *adj* distinct

distinctif *adj* distinctive
distinction *f* distinction
distingué *adj* ladylike
distraction *f* amusement
distraire *v* distract
distribuer *v* distribute
distribution *f* distribution
district *m* district
divaguer *v* digress
divergence *f* discrepancy
diverger *v* disagree
divers *adj* diverse, varied
diversifier *v* diversify
diversion *f* diversion
diversité *f* diversity
divertir *v* entertain
divertissant *adj* entertaining
divertissement *m* entertainment
dividence *f* dividend
divin *adj* divine
divinité *f* divinity
diviser *v* divide, split
divisible *adj* divisible
division *f* division
divorce *m* divorce
divorcée *f* divorcee
divorcer *v* divorce
divulger *v* divulge
dix *adj* ten
dix-huit *adj* eighteen
dixième *f* tenth
dix-neuf *adj* nineteen

dix-sept *adj* seventeen
docile *adj* docile, meek
docilité *f* docility
docteur *m* doctor
doctrine *f* doctrine
document *m* document
documentaire *m* documentary
documentation *f* documentation
dogmatique *adj* dogmatic
doigt *m* finger
doigt de pied *m* toe
doléance *f* grievance
dollar *m* dollar, buck
domaine *m* arena
dome *m* dome
domestique *adj* domestic
domestiquer *v* domesticate
dominant *adj* domineering
dominateur *adj* overbearing
domination *f* domination
dominer *v* dominate
dominion *f* dominion
donation *f* donation
donc *adv* hence
donjon *m* dungeon
données *f* data
donner *iv* give
donneur *m* donor
doper *v* dope
doré *adj* golden
dorer *v* bask
dormir *iv* sleep

dortoire *m* dormitory
dos *m* back
dos-d'âne *m* bump
dose *f* dosage
dossier *m* dossier, file
dot *f* dowry
douane *f* customs
double *adj* double, dual
doubler *v* double
doublure *f* lining
doucement *adv* softly
douceur *f* smoothness
douche *f* shower
doué *adj* gifted
douillet *adj* cozy
douleur *f* ache
douloureux *adj* harrowing
doute *m* doubt
douter *v* doubt
douteux *adl* doubtful
doux *adj* gentle, sweet
douzaine *f* dozen
douze *adj* twelve
douzième *adj* twelfth
doyen *m* dean
dragon *m* dragon
dramatique *adj* dramatic
dramatiser *v* dramatize
drapeau *m* flag
draps *m* sheets
drastique *adj* drastic
dresser *v* break in

dressing *m* dressing
drogue *f* dope
droguer *v* drug
droit *adj* straight, right
droit d'auteur *m* copyright
droite *f* right
droite (a) *adv* right
drôle *adj* funny
dscendre *v* come down
dû *adj* due
du dessous *pre* below
du sud *adj* southern
duc *m* duke
duchesse *f* duchess
duel *m* duel
dûment *adv* duly
duper *v* dupe, fool
dur *adj* harsh, hard
durable *adj* durable,
durcir *v* toughen
durée *f* duration, span
durement *adv* harshly
durer *v* last, outlast
dureté *f* hardness
duveteux *adj* furry
dynamique *adj* dynamic
dynamite *f* dynamite
dynastie *f* dynamite

eau *f* water
eau-de-cologne *f* cologne
eau-de-vie *f* brandy
ébauche *f* design
ébaucher *v* draft
éblouir *v* dazzle
éblouissant *adj* dazzling
ébouillanter *v* scald
écaille *f* scale
eccentrique *adj* eccentric
ecclésiastique *m* clergyman
échafaudage *m* scaffolding
échange *m* swap
échanger *v* exchange, trade
échangeur *m* interchange
échantillon *m* sample
échapper *v* escape
écharde *f* splinter
écharpe *f* scarf
échauffourée *f* skirmish
échec *m* failure
échelle *f* ladder
écho *m* echo
échouer *v* fail
éclabousser *v* splash
éclair *m* lightning
éclairage *f* lighting
éclairer *v* light
éclat *m* glare

D
E

E

éclatant *adj* vibrant
éclater *v* break out
éclats d'obus *m* shrapnel
éclipse *f* eclipse
éclipser *v* outshine
écœurant *adj* sickening
écœurer *v* sicken
école *f* school
écologie *f* ecology
économe *adj* thrifty
économie *f* economy
économies *f* savings
économique *adj* economical
économiser *v* economize
écorce *f* bark
écorcher *v* skin, scrape
écorchure *f* graze
écoulement *m* flow
écouler *v* elapse
écouter *v* heed, listen
écouteurs *m* earphones
écran solaire *m* screen
écrasant *adj* crushing
écraser *v* crush, mash
écrémer *v* skim
écrier *v* cry out
écriere *v* write
écrit *adj* written
écriture *f* handwriting
écrivain *m* writer
écureuil *m* squirrel
édifice *m* edifice

éditer *v* edit
éditeur *m* publisher
édition *f* edition
édredon *m* comforter
éducatif *adj* educational
éducation *f* upbringing
éduquer *v* educate
effacer *v* erase, clear
effaceur *m* eraser
effaré *adj* aghast
effective *adj* effective
effectuer *v* carry out
efféminé *adj* sissy
effet *m* effect
effets personnels *m* belongings
efficace *adj* efficient
efficacité *f* effectiveness
effigie *f* effigy
effondrement *m* collapse
effondrer *v* plummet
effort *m* effort
effrayant *adj* frightening
effrayer *v* frighten, scare
effronté *adj* cheeky
effroyable *adj* gruesome
égal *adj* equal
égaliser *v* tie
égalité *f* equality
égarer *v* misplace, stray
égayer *v* cheer up
église *f* church
égoïsme *m* egoism

égoïste *m* egoist
égout *m* drainage
égoutter *v* drain, strain
égratignure *f* graze
éjecter *v* eject
élargir *v* broaden, widen
élargissement *m* enlargement
élastique *adj* elastic
élection *f* election
électricien *m* electrician
électricité *f* electricity
électrifier *v* electrify
électrique *adj* electric
électrocuter *v* electrocute
électroménager *m* appliance
électronique *adj* electronic
élégance *f* elegance
élégant *adj* elegant
élément *m* element
élémentaire *adj* basic
éléphant *m* elephant
élévation *f* elevation
élève *m* pupil
élever *v* elevate, raise
éligible *adj* eligible
éliminer *v* eliminate
élir *v* elect
elle *pro* she, her
elle-même *pro* herself
éloquence *f* eloquence
éluder *v* elude
élusive *adj* elusive

émacié *adj* emaciated
émanciper *v* emancipate
émaner *v* emanate
emballage *m* wrapping
emballer *v* pack
embarcadère *m* pier
embarquer *v* embark
embassade *f* embassy
embaumer *v* embalm
embellir *v* beautify
embêtant *adj* annoying
embêter *v* annoy, bother
emblème *m* emblem
embourber *v* bog down
embout *m* nozzle
embouteillage *m* bottleneck
embouteiller *v* bottle
embrasser *v* kiss
embrayage *m* clutch
embryon *m* embryo
embûche *f* pitfall
émeraude *f* emerald
emerger *v* emerge
émettre *v* emit
émietter *v* crumble
émigrant *m* emigrant
émigrer *v* emigrate
éminent *adj* leading
émission *f* broadcast
émotion *f* emotion
émotionel *adj* emotional
émoussé *adj* blunt

E

empaqueter _v_ bundle
emparer _v_ take over
empêcher _v_ prevent
empereur _m_ emperor
emphase _f_ pomposity
empiéter _v_ encroach
empiler _v_ heap, pile
empire _m_ empire
empirer _v_ worsen
emploi _m_ employment
employé _m_ clerk
employer _v_ employ
employeur _m_ employer
empoigner _v_ seize
empoisonant _m_ poisoning
empoisoner _v_ poison
empreinte _f_ impression, print
emprisonner _v_ imprison
emprunt _m_ mortgage
emprunter _v_ borrow
en alternance _adj_ alternate
en arrière _adv_ backwards
en avant _pre_ ahead
en avoir marre _adj_ fed up
en bas _adv_ down
en bois _adj_ wooden
en boîte _adj_ canned
en bonne santé _adj_ healthy
en colère _adj_ mad
en direct _adj_ live
en effet _adv_ indeed
en face _adv_ opposite

en fait _adv_ actually
en feu _adj_ ablaze
en gras _adj_ bold
en haut _adv_ upstairs
en laine _adj_ woolen
en partie _adv_ partly
en pièces _adv_ asunder
en plaisantant _adv_ jokingly
en plein ciel _m_ midair
en profondeur _adv_ in depth
en quelque sorte _adv_ somehow
en route _adj_ bound for
en vain _adv_ vainly
encadrer _v_ frame
encastré _adj_ built-in
enceinte _f_ compound
enceinte _v_ expect
encens _m_ incense
encercler _v_ encircle
enchainer _v_ chain
enchanter _v_ enchant
enchanteur _adj_ enchanting
enchère _f_ bid
enchères _f_ auction
enchèrir _v_ bid
enchevêtrement _m_ tangle
enchevêtrer _v_ entangle
enclave _f_ enclave
enclume _f_ anvil
encombrant _adj_ cumbersome
encombrer _v_ burden
encore _adv_ again, still

encore plus *c* even more
encourager *v* encourage
encre *f* ink
encyclopédie *f* encyclopedia
endeuillé *adj* bereaved
endommagé *adj* corrupt
endommager *v* damage
endormi *adj* asleep
endossement *m* endorsement
endosser *v* endorse
endroit *m* place, spot
endurcir *v* harden
endurer *v* endure
énergie *f* energy
énergique *adj* energetic
énervé *adj* edgy
énerver *v* anger
enfance *m* childhood
enfant *m* child
enfantin *adj* childish
enfants *m* children
enfer *m* hell
enfermer *v* enforce
enfiler *v* thread
enfin *adv* lastly
enflé *adj* bloated
enfler *v* bloat, swell
enflure *f* swelling
enforcer *v* enforce
enfuir *v* run away
engagé *adj* committed
engagement *m* commitment

engager *v* enlist, hire
engelures *f* frostbite
englober *v* encompass
engloutir *v* gobble, guzzle
engorger *v* clog
engouement *m* gusto
engouffrer *v* bolt
engourdi *adj* numb
engraisser *v* fatten
enjamber *v* span
enjeu *m* stake
enlacer *v* intertwine
enlèvement *m* abduction
enlever *v* abduct
ennemi *m* enemy
ennui *m* boredom
ennuis *m* trouble
ennuyant *adj* boring
ennuyé *adj* bored
ennuyer *v* bore
ennuyeux *adj* dull, tedious
énorme *adj* enormous
enquérir *v* inquire
enquête *f* inquest
enquêter *v* investigate
enraciné *adj* ingrained
enrager *v* enrage
enregistrement *m* recording
enregistrer *v* check in, record
enrichir *v* enrich
enseignant *m* teacher
enseigner *v* teach**

E

E

ensemble *adv* together
ensoleillé *adj* sunny
ensorceler *v* bewitch
entaille *f* gash
entasser *v* cram, crowd
entendre *v* hear
enterprise *f* enterprise
enterrement *m* burial
enterrer *v* bury
en-tête *f* heading
enthousiasme *m* enthusiasm
enthousiasmer *v* enthuse
enthousiaste *adj* eager
entier *adj* entire, whole
entièrement *adv* fully
entorse *v* sprain
entourer *v* surround
entrailles *f* bowels, guts
entraînement *m* practice
entraîner *v* practise
entrainer *v* coach
entraineur *m* coach, trainer
entrave *f* hindrance
entraver *v* hinder
entre *pre* between
entrée *f* entry, admission
entreposage *m* storage
entreposer *v* store
entrepôt *m* warehouse
entrepreneur *m* entrepreneur
entreprise *f* firm
entrer *v* come in, enter

entre-temps *adv* meantime
entretenir *v* service
entretien *m* maintenance
entrevoir *v* glimpse
entrouvert *adj* ajar
énumérer *v* list, detail
envahir *v* invade
envahisseur *m* invader
enveloppe *f* envelope
enveloppé *adj* shrouded
envelopper *v* envelop
envergure *f* span
envie *f* envy, urge
envier *v* envy
envieux *adj* envious
environ *adv* about
environnement *m* environment
environs *m* surroundings
envisager *v* envisage
envoyé *m* envoy
envoyer *v* send
épais *adj* thick, dense
épaisseur *f* thickness
épaissir *v* thicken
épanchement *m* outpouring
épanouir *v* blossom
épargner *v* spare
épaule *f* shoulder
épave *f* wreckage
épée *f* sword
épeler *v* spell
éperdu *adj* distraught

éperdument *adv* madly
éperon *m* spur
éperonner *v* spur
épice *f* spice
épicé *adj* spicy
épices *f* seasoning
épidémie *f* epidemic
épine *f* thorn
épineux *adj* thorny
épingle *f* pin
épis *f* ear
épisode *m* episode
épitaphe *m* epitaph
épître *m* epistle
éponge *f* sponge
époque *f* epoch
époustoufflant *adj* breathtaking
épouvantable *adj* horrendous
époux *m* spouse
épreuve *f* hardship
épuisant *adj* exhausting
épuisé *adj* worn-out
épuisement *m* exhaustion
épuiser *v* exhaust
équateur *m* equator
équation *f* equation
équilibre *m* equilibrium
équipage *m* crew
équipe *f* team
équipement *m* equipment
équité *f* fairness
équivalent *adj* equivalent

équivaloir à *v* amount to
éradiquer *v* eradicate
ère *f* era
ériger *v* erect
ermitage *m* retreat
ermite *m* hermit
erreur *f* error, mistake, slip
erroné *adj* erroneous
éruption *f* eruption
escabeau *m* stepladder
escalade *f* climbing
escalader *v* climb
escalier *m* staircase
escalier roulant *f* escalator
escaliers *m* stairs
escapade *f* escapade
escargot *m* snail
esclavage *m* slavery
esclave *m* slave
escrime *f* fencing
escroc *m* swindler
escroquer *v* swindle
escroquerie *f* scam
espace *m* space
espace aérien *m* airspace
espacer *v* space out
espadon *m* swordfish
Espagne *f* Spain
Espagnol *m* Spaniard
espérance *f* expectancy
espiègle *adj* mischievous
espièglerie *f* mischief

E

espion *m* spy
espionage *m* espionage
espionner *v* spy
espoir *m* hope, prospect
esprit *m* mind, spirit, wit
esquisse *f* sketch
esquisser *v* sketch
essai *m* essay, trial
essaim *m* swarm
essayer *v* try
esse *f* linchpin
essence *f* essence, gas
essentiel *adj* essential
essentiel *m* bulk
essieu *m* axle
essorer *v* wring
essoufler *v* wind
essuyer *v* wipe
est *m* east
ésthetique *adj* aesthetic
estimation *f* appraisal
estime *v* esteem
estimer *v* estimate, assess
estomac *m* stomach
estomper *v* fade, recede
estropier *v* cripple, maim
estuaire *m* estuary
et *c* and
étable *f* stable
établi *adj* entrenched
établir *v* establish
étage *m* story

étagère *f* shelf
étain *m* tin
étalage *m* array, display
étalement *v* sprawl
étaler *v* spread, smear
étanche *adj* airtight
étancher *v* quench
étape *f* step
état *m* status, state
étau *m* clamp
été *m* summer
éteindre *v* put out, turn off
étendre *v* expand, stretch
étendu *adj* widespread
étendue *f* extent, stretch
éternel *adj* everlasting
éternité *f* eternity
éternuement *m* sneeze
éternuer *v* sneeze
ethique *adj* ethical
étincelle *f* spark
étiquette *f* label, tag
étoffe *m* material
étoile *f* star
étonnant *adj* astonishing
étonner *v* astonish
étouffant *adj* stifling
étouffer *v* stifle, smother
étourdi *adj* dizzy
étrange *adj* strange
étranger *m* foreigner
étranger *adj* foreign

étrangler *v* choke, strangle
être *m* being
être *v* be
être capable de *adj* able
être en retard *v* fall behind
être habitué à *adj* used to
être humain *m* human being
être né *v* be born
étreindre *v* embrace
étreinte *v* embarraas
étreinte *f* embrace, hug
étroit *adj* narrow
étroitement *adv* narrowly
étudiant *m* student
étudier *v* study
euphorie *f* euphoria
Europe *f* Europe
Européen *adj* European
eux-mêmes *pro* themselves
évacuer *v* evacuate
évader *v* evade
évaluations *f* feedback
évaluer *v* evaluate
évanouir *v* faint
évaporer *v* evaporate
évasif *adj* evasive
évasion *f* avoidance
eveillé *adj* awake
éveiller *v* arouse
événement *m* event
éventualité *f* eventuality
évêque *m* bishop

évidemment *adv* obviously
évidence *f* evidence
évident *adj* obvious
évitable *adj* avoidable
éviter *v* avert, avoid
évoluer *v* evolve
évolution *f* evolution
évoquer *v* evoke, refer to
ex *adj* former
exact *adj* accurate
exactitude *f* accuracy
exagéré *adj* overdone
exagérer *v* exaggerate
exaltant *adj* exhilarating
exalté *adj* ecstatic
exalter *v* exalt
examen *m* scrutiny
examination *f* examination
examiner *v* examine
exasperer *v* exasperate
excellence *f* excellence
excellent *adj* excellent
exceller *v* excel
exception *f* exception
exceptionae *adj* exceptional
excès *m* excess, glut
excessif *adj* excessive
excitant *adj* exciting
excitation *f* excitement
exciter *v* arouse
exclamer *v* exclaim
exclu *adj* outcast

exclure *v* exclude
exclusion *f* dismissal
excuse *f* apology, excuse
excuser *v* apologize
exécuter *v* execute
exemplaire *adj* exemplary
exemple *m* example
exemplifier *v* exemplify
exempt *adj* exempt
exemption *f* exemption
exercer *v* exercise, exert
exercice *m* exercise, drill
exhorter *v* exhort
exigeant *adj* demanding
exiger *v* require
exigu *adj* cramped
exile *m* exile
exiler *v* exile
existence *f* existence
exister *v* exist
exode *f* exodus
exonérer *v* exonerate
exorbitant *adj* exorbitant
exorciste *m* exorcist
exotique *adj* exotic
expansion *f* expansion
expédient *adj* expedient
expédier *v* dispatch
expéditeur *m* sender
expédition *f* expedition
expérience *f* experience
expert *adj* expert

expiation *f* atonement
expier *v* atone, expiate
expiration *f* expiration
expirer *v* expire
explicite *adj* explicit
expliquer *v* explain
exploit *m* feat, exploit
exploitation *f* farming
exploiter *v* exploit
explorateur *m* explorer
explorer *v* explore
exploser *v* burst, explode
explosif *adj* explosive
explosion *f* explosion
exporter *v* export
exposé *adj* exposed
exposer *v* display, expose
exposition *f* exhibition
exprès *adj* express
exprès *adv* purposely
expressément *adv* expressly
expression *f* expression
exprimer *v* express
exproprier *v* expropriate
expulser *v* evict, expel
expulsion *f* expulsion
exquis *adj* exquisite
exsuder *v* exude
extase *f* ecstasy
extension *f* extension
extérieur *adj* exterior, outer
exterminer *v* exterminate

externe adj external
extorquer v extort
extortion f extortion
extra adv extra
extrader v extradite
extradition f extradition
extraire v extract, mine
extrait m excerpt
extravagance f extravagance
extravagant adj extravagant
extrême adj extreme
extrêmement adv exceedingly
extrémiste adj extremist
extrémités f extremities
extroverti adj extroverted
exultant adj jubilant
exulter v exult

fable f fable
fabricant m maker
fabriquer v fabricate
fabuleux adj fabulous
façade m front, pretense
facette f facet
facile adj easy
facilement adv easily

facilité f ease
faciliter v facilitate
façon f way
facteur m factor
factuel adj factual
facture f invoice, bill
facturer v charge
faculté f faculty
fade adj bland
faible adj faint, feeble, weak
faiblesse f weakness
faille f rift
faillite f bankruptcy
faim f hunger
faire v do, make
faire allusion v hint
faire appel v appeal
faire attention v watch out
faire circuler v pass around
faire confiance v trust
faire du chantage v blackmail
faire du sport v work out
faire escale v stop over
faire face v face up to
faire faillite v bankrupt
faire fuir v scare away
faire irruption v burst into
faire un bleu v bruise
faire voeu v vow
faisable adj feasible
faisan m pheasant
fait m fact

E
F

fait main *adj* handmade
fait maison *adj* homemade
falsification *f* forgery
falsifier *v* fake, falsify
familier *adj* familiar
famille *f* family
famine *f* starvation
fan *m* fan
fanatique *adj* fanatic
fantasie *f* fantasy
fantastique *adj* fantastic
fantôme *m* ghost
farce *f* stuffing, filling
fardeau *m* burden
farine *f* flour
fascinant *adj* riveting
fasciner *v* fascinate
fatal *adj* fatal
fatidique *adj* fateful
fatigue *f* fatigue
fatigué *adj* tired
fauché *adj* broke
faucille *f* sickle
faucon *m* hawk
faune *f* wildlife
fausse-couche *f* miscarriage
faute *f* blame, fault
faux *adj* fake, untrue
favorable *adj* conducive
favori *adj* favorite
féculents *m* starch
fédéral *adj* federal

fée *f* fairy
feindre *v* feign
félicitations *f* congratulations
féliciter *v* congratulate
fêlure *f* cleft
femelle *f* female
féminin *adj* feminine
femme *f* female, woman
femme au foyer *f* wife
femmes *f* women
fendre *v* crack, splinter
fenêtre *f* window
fente *f* slot
fer *m* iron
ferme *f* farm
ferme *adj* forceful
fermé *adj* closed
fermement *adv* forcibly
ferment *m* ferment
fermenter *v* ferment
fermer *v* close, shut
fermerutre *f* closure
fermeté *f* firmness
fermeture éclair *f* zipper
fermier *m* farmer
féroce *adj* ferocious
férocité *f* ferocity
ferry *m* ferry
fertile *adj* fertile
fertiliser *v* fertilize
fertilité *f* fertility
fervent *adj* fervent

fessée *f* spanking
fesser *v* spank
fesses *f* butt
festif *adj* festive
festivité *f* festivity
fête *f* feast
fétide *adj* fetid, foul
feu *m* fire
feu croisé *m* crossfire
feu d'artifice *m* fireworks
feu de camp *m* campfire
feu de joie *m* bonfire
feuille *f* leaf
feuille de vigne *f* grapevine
feutre *m* marker
février *m* February
fiable *adj* reliable
fiançailles *f* engagement
fiancé *m* fiancé
fiasco *m* flop
fibre *f* fiber
ficelle *f* string
fiche *f* card
fictif *adj* fictitious
fiction *f* fiction
fidèle *adj* faithful
fidélité *f* fidelity
fier *adj* proud
fier *v* trust
fièrement *adv* proudly
fierté *f* pride
fièvre *f* fever

fièvrieux *adj* feverish
figue *f* fig
fil *m* cord, thread
fil dentaire *m* floss
file *f* lane
filer *v* spin
filet *m* sirloin
fileuse *f* spinster
fille *f* daughter, girl
film *m* film, movie
fils *m* son
filtre *m* filter
filtrer *v* filter
fin *f* end, ending
fin *adj* fine, thin, slim
fin de semaine *f* weekend
final *adj* final
finalement *adv* eventually
finaliser *v* finalize
finance *v* finance
financier *adj* financial
finir *v* end, finish
Finlande *f* Finland
Finnois *adj* Finnish
fiord *m* fjord
fissure *f* crack, split
fixe *adj* stationary
fixer *v* gaze, stare
flageller *v* flog
flagrant *adj* conspicuous
flamboyant *adj* flamboyant
flame *f* flame

F

flanc *m* flank
flash *m* flash
flatter *v* flatter, pander
flatterie *f* flattery
flatteur *adj* complimentary
flèche *f* arrow
fléchette *f* dart
fléchir *v* flex
flemmard *adj* slob
flétrir *v* wither
fleur *f* flower
fleurir *v* bloom
fleuve *m* river
flexible *adj* flexible
flirter *v* flirt
flocon de neige *m* snowflake
flot (a) *adv* afloat
floter *v* float
flotte *f* fleet
flou *adj* blurred
fluctuer *v* fluctuate
fluide *m* fluid
flûte *f* flute
foetus *m* fetus
foi *f* creed
foie *m* liver
foin *m* hay
foire *f* fair
folie *f* craziness
foncé *adj* dark
fonction *f* function
fonctionner *v* work

fond *m* bed
fond de teint *m* foundation
fondamental *adj* fundamental
fondateur *m* founder
fonder *v* fund
fonderie *f* foundry
fondre *v* melt
fonds *m* funds
fontaine *f* fountain
football *m* football
force *f* force, strength
forcer *v* coerce, force
foret *m* drill
forêt *f* forest
forgé *adj* trumped-up
forger *v* forge, mint
forgeron *m* blacksmith
formaliser *v* formalize
formalité *f* formality
format *m* format
formation *f* formation
forme *f* shape, form
formel *adj* formal
formellement *adv* formally
former *v* shape, train
formidable *adj* formidable
formulation *f* wording
formule *f* formula
formuler *v* frame
fort *m* fort, strong
forteresse *f* fortress
fortifier *v* fortify

fortuit *adj* coincidental
fortune *f* fortune
fortuné *adj* fortunate
fosse *f* bunker
fossé *m* ditch
fossile *m* fossil
fou *adj* crazy
fouchette *f* fork
foudre *f* thunderbolt
fouet *m* lash, scourge
fouetter *v* lash
fougueux *adj* fiery
fouiller *v* excavate
foule *f* crowd, mob
foulure *f* twist
four *m* oven
fourberie *f* guile
fourche *f* pitchfork
fourmis *f* ant
fourneau *m* furnace
fournir *v* furnish, provide
fournisseur *m* supplier
fourrure *f* fur
fourvoyer *v* mislead
foutaises *f* crap
foyer *m* hearth
fracas *m* crash
fraction *f* fraction
fracture *f* fracture
fracturer *v* rupture
fragement *m* chip
fragile *adj* brittle, fragile

fragilité *f* frailty
fragment *m* fragment
fraîcheur *f* freshness
frais *adj* cool, fresh
frais *m* fee, expense
frais de scolarité *m* tuition
fraise *f* strawberry
fraiser *v* drill
framboise *f* raspberry
franc *adj* outspoken
français *adj* French
France *f* France
franchement *adv* frankly
franchise *f* frankness
frange *f* fringe
frappant *adj* striking
frapper *v* batter, hit, smack
fraternel *adj* brotherly
fraternité *f* brotherhood
fraude *f* fraud
fraudulent *adj* fraudulent
fredonner *v* hum
freezer *m* icebox
frégate *f* frigate
frein *m* brake
freiner *v* brake
freins *m* break
frêne *m* ash
frénésie *f* frenzy
frénétique *adj* frenzied
fréquence *f* frequency
fréquent *adj* frequent

F

fréquenter *v* frequent
frère *m* brother
frères *m* brethren
fri *adj* fried
fri *v* fry
friction *f* friction
frigide *adj* frigid
frigorifier *v* refrigerate
frisson *m* shudder
frissonner *v* shiver
frites *f* fries
frivole *adj* frivolous
froid *m* chill
froid *adj* chilly, cold
froideur *f* coldness
froisser *v* crease, wrinkle
fromage *m* cheese
froncer *v* frown
front *m* forehead
frontal *adv* head-on
frontière *f* frontier, border
frottement *m* friction
frotter *v* rub
fructueux *adj* fruitful
frugal *adj* frugal
frugalité *f* frugality
fruit *m* fruit
fruité *adj* fruity
fruits de mer *m* seafood
frustration *f* frustration
frustrer *v* frustrate
fugitif *m* fugitive

fuir *iv* flee, leak
fuite *f* flight, leakage
fumé *adj* smoked
fumer *v* fumigate
fumeur *m* smoker
fumier *m* dung, manure
funérailles *f* funeral
fureur *f* furor, fury
furieusement *adv* furiously
furieux *adj* furious, irate
furtif *adj* stealthy
fusible *m* fuse
fusil *m* rifle
fusillade *f* gunfire
fusion *f* fusion, merger
fusionner *v* merge
fût *m* keg
futé *adj* wily
futile *adj* futile
futilité *f* futility
futur *m* future
future *adj* forthcoming

G

gâcher v spoil
gâchette f trigger
gadget m gadget
gaffe f goof
gaffer v goof
gagnant m winner
gagne-pain m livelihood
gagner v earn, gain
gai adj cheerful
gain m gain
galaxie f galaxy
galet m pebble
gallant adj gallant
galon m gallon
galop v gallop
galvaniser v galvanize
gamme f range
gangrène f gangrene
gangster m gangster
gant m glove
garage m garage
garagiste m mechanic
garant m guarantor
garantie f warranty
garçon m boy
garde m guard
garde-manger m pantry
garder v hang on
garde-robe f wardrobe

gardien m guardian
gare f station
garer v park
gargariser v gargle
garnir v garnish
garnison f garrison
garniture f garnish
gars m lad
gaspillage m waste
gaspiller v squander, waste
gaspilleur adj wasteful
gastrique adj gastric
gâteau m cake
gateau sec m cookie
gâterie f treat
gaufrette f wafer
gaze m gauze
gazon m sod, turf
géant m giant
geindre v groan
gel m frost
gelé adj freezing, frozen
gémir v moan
gémissement m groan
gênant adj troublesome
gencive f gum
gendre m son-in-law
gène m gene
général m general
généraliser v generalize
générateur m generator
génération f generation

G

générer *v* generate

générique *adj* generic

générosité *f* generosity

génétique *adj* genetic

génial *adj* genial

génie *m* genius

génocide *m* genocide

genou *m* knee

genoux *m* lap

genre *m* gender

gens *m* people

gentiment *adv* kindly

gentleman *m* gentleman

géographie *f* geography

geôlier *m* jailer

géologie *f* geology

géométrie *f* geometry

gérer *v* manage

germe *m* germ

germer *v* sprout

gérondif *m* gerund

gestation *f* gestation

geste *m* gesture

gesticuler *v* gesticulate

geyser *m* geyser

gibet *m* gallows

gifler *v* slap

gigantesque *adj* gigantic

gingembre *m* ginger

girafe *m* giraffe

gitan *m* gypsy

glace *f* ice

glacé *adj* icy

glacial *adj* frosty

glacier *m* glacier

glaçon *m* ice cube

gladiateur *m* gladiator

glan *m* acorn

glande *f* gland

glas *m* toll

glissant *adj* slippery

glisser *iv* slide, slip

glisser *v* creep

globalement *adv* overall

globe *m* globe

globule *f* globule

gloire *f* glory

glorieux *adj* glorious

glorifier *v* glorify

glossaire *m* glossary

glousser *v* chuckle

glouton *m* glutton

glucose *m* glucose

golf *m* gulf

gomme *m* gum

gonfler *v* inflate

gorge *f* gorge, throat

gorille *m* gorilla

gospel *m* gospel

goudron *m* tar

gouffre *m* chasm

goulée *f* gulp

gourde *f* canteen

gourmandise *f* delicacy

goût *m* flavor, taste
goûter *v* taste
goutte *f* drip, drop
gouttière *f* gutter
gouvernail *m* rudder
gouvernement *m* government
gouverner *v* govern
gouverneur *m* governor
grabuge *m* havoc
grâce *f* grace
gracieux *adj* graceful
grade *m* rank
graduel *adj* gradual
grain *m* grain
grain de beauté *m* mole
graine *f* seed
graisse *f* fat, grease
graisser *v* grease
graisseux *adj* fatty
grammaire *f* grammar
gramme *m* gram
grand *adj* big, tall
Grande Betagne *f* Britain
grandeur *f* greatness
grandiose *adj* awesome
grand-mère *f* grandmother
grand-papa *m* granddad
grand-parents *m* grandparents
grand-père *m* grandfather
granite *m* granite
graphique *m* chart, graphic
grappe *f* cluster

gratifiant *adj* gratifying
gratifier *v* gratify
gratitude *f* gratitude
gratte-ciel *m* skyscraper
gratter *v* scrape, scratch
gratuit *adj* free
graufrer *v* emboss
grave *adj* serious, grave
gravement *adv* badly
graver *v* engrave
gravier *m* gravel
gravir *v* climb
gravité *f* gravity
graviter *v* gravitate
gravure *f* engraving
Grèce *f* Greece
grecque *adj* Greek
greffe *f* graft
greffer *v* graft
grégaire *adj* gregarious
grêle *f* hail
grêler *v* hail
grenade *f* grenade
grenier *m* attic
grenouille *f* frog
grève *f* strike
gribouiller *v* scribble
griffe *f* claw
grignoter *v* nibble
gril *m* grill
grillage *m* mesh
grille-pain *m* toaster

G

griller *v* broil, grill
grillon *m* cricket
grimace *f* grimace
grinçant *adj* squeaky
grincement *m* creak
grincer *v* creak, grind
grincheux *adj* cranky
grippe *f* flu
gris *adj* gray
grisâtre *adj* grayish
grondement *m* rumble
gronder *v* rumble
gros *adj* fat
grossesse *f* pregnancy
grosseur *f* lump
grossier *adj* crass, coarse
grossièrement *adv* grossly
grotesque *adj* grotesque
grotte *f* grotto
groupe *m* band, group
grumeau *m* lump
guarantie *f* guarantee
guarantir *v* guarantee
guêpe *f* wasp
guérillero *f* guerrilla
guérir *v* heal, cure
guérisseur *m* healer
guerre *f* war
guerrier *m* warrior
guetter *v* look out
gueule *f* muzzle
guichet *m* box office

guide *m* guide
guider *v* guide
guilde *f* guild
guillemet *m* quotation
guillotine *f* guillotine
guirlande *f* garland
guitare *f* guitar
gymnase *m* gymnasium
gynécologie *f* gynecology

habile *adj* shrewd
habillement *m* apparel
habiller *v* dress
habitable *adj* habitable
habitant *m* inhabitant
habitation *f* dwelling
habiter *v* dwell, live
habitude *m* habit
habituel *adj* customary
hache *f* ax
hacher *v* mince
hachette *f* hatchet
haie *f* hurdle
haine *f* hatred
haineux *adj* hateful
haïr *v* hate

G
H

haleter *v* gasp
hall *m* hall, lobby
halluciner *v* hallucinate
hamac *m* hammock
hamburger *m* hamburger
hameau *m* hamlet
hameçon *m* hook
hanche *f* hip
handicap *m* handicap
hanter *v* haunt, stalk
harcèlement *m* harassment
harceler *v* harass, hassle
haricot *m* bean
haricot rouge *m* kidney bean
haricot vert *m* green bean
harmonie *f* harmony
harmoniser *v* harmonize
harpe *f* harp
harpon *m* harpoon
hasard *m* hazard
hashish *m* hashish
hâte *f* haste
hâter *v* hasten
hâtif *adj* hasty
hausse *f* appreciation
haut *adj* high
hautain *adj* haughty
haute voix (a) *adv* aloud
hautement *adv* highly
haut-parleur *f* loudspeaker
hélicoptère *m* helicopter
hémisphère *m* hemisphere

hémorragie *f* bleeding
héraut *m* herald
herbe *f* grass, herb
héréditaire *adj* hereditary
hérésie *f* heresy
hérétique *adj* heretic
héritage *m* heritage
hériter *v* inherit
héritier *m* heir
héritière *f* heiress
hermétique *adj* hermetic
hernie *f* hernia
héroïne *f* heroin
héroïque *adj* heroic
héroïsme *m* heroism
héros *m* hero
hésitant *adj* hesitant
hésitation *f* hesitation
hésiter *v* hesitate
heure *f* hour
heureux *adj* happy
heurter *v* run into
hibou *m* owl
hideux *adj* hideous
hier *adv* yesterday
hier soir *adv* last night
hiérarchie *f* hierarchy
hilarant *adj* hilarious
hispanique *adj* Hispanic
hisser *v* hoist
histoire *f* history
historien *m* historian

hiver *m* winter
hocher *v* nod
holdup *m* holdup
Hollande *f* Holland
holocauste *m* holocaust
homard *m* lobster
homélie *f* homily
homicide *m* homicide
hommage *m* homage
homme *m* man, fellow
homme d'affaires *m* businessman
hommes *m* men
homologue *m* counterpart
honnête *adj* honest
honnêteté *f* honesty
honneur *f* honor
honte *f* shame
honteux *adj* shameful
hooligan *m* hooligan
hôpital *m* hospital
hoquet *m* hiccup
horaire *m* schedule
horizon *f* horizon
horizontal *adj* horizontal
horloge *f* clock
horloger *m* watchmaker
hormone *f* hormone
horreur *f* horror
horrible *adj* horrible
horrifier *v* horrify
hôspitaliser *v* hospitalize
hôspitalité *f* hospitality

hostile *adj* hostile
hostilité *f* hostility
hôte *m* host
hôtel *m* hotel
hôtesse *f* hostess
huées *f* outcry
huissier *m* bailiff
huit *adj* eight
huitième *adj* eighth
huître *f* oyster
humain *adj* human
humanité *f* mankind
humanités *f* humanities
humble *adj* humble
humblement *adv* humbly
humecter *v* moisten
humeur *f* mood
humide *adj* damp, humid
humidité *f* moisture
humiliant *adj* demeaning
humilier *v* humiliate
humilité *f* humility
humoristique *adj* humorous
humour *m* humor
hurlement *m* howl
hurler *v* screech, shriek
hutte *f* hut
hydraulique *adj* hydraulic
hydrogène *f* hydrogen
hyène *f* hyena
hygiène *f* hygiene
hymne *m* anthem, hymn

hypnose *f* hypnosis
hypnotiser *v* hypnotize
hypocrisie *f* hypocrisy
hypocrite *adj* hypocrite
hypothèse *f* hypothesis
hystérie *f* hysteria
hystérique *adj* hysterical

iceberg *m* iceberg
ici *adv* here
icône *m* icon
idéal *adj* ideal
idée *f* idea, thought
idemne *adj* unhurt
identifier *v* identify
identique *adj* identical
identité *f* identity
idéologie *f* ideology
idiome *m* idiom
idiot *adj* dumb, fool
idolatrie *f* idolatry
idole *m* idol
ignorance *f* ignorance
ignorant *adj* ignorant
ignorer *v* ignore
il *pro* he

il y a *adv* there
île *f* island
illégal *adj* illegal
illégitime *adj* illegitimate
illicite *adj* illicit
illimité *adj* unlimited
illisible *adj* illegible
illogique *adj* illogical
illuminer *v* illuminate
illusion *f* illusion
illustration *f* illustration
illustre *adj* illustrious
illustrer *v* illustrate
ils *pro* they
image *f* image
imagination *f* imagination
imaginer *v* imagine
imbattable *adj* unbeatable
imitation *f* imitation
imiter *v* imitate
immaculer *adj* immaculate
immatriculer *v* matriculate
immature *adj* immature
immaturité *f* immaturity
immédiate *adj* immediate
immense *adj* huge
immensité *f* immensity
immergé *adj* sunken
immerger *v* immerse
immérité *adj* undeserved
immersion *f* immersion
immeuble *m* building

H
I

immigrant *m* immigrant
immigration *f* immigration
immigrer *v* immigrate
imminent *adj* imminent
immobile *adj* motionless
immobiliser *v* immobilize
immoral *adj* immoral
immoralité *f* immorality
immortalité *f* immortality
immortel *adj* immortal
immuable *adj* immutable
immunisé *adj* immune
immuniser *v* immunize
immunité *f* immunity
impact *m* impact
impacter *v* impact
impair *adj* odd
impartial *adj* unbiased
impasse *f* stalemate
impatience *f* impatience
impatient *adj* impatient
impeccable *adj* spotless
impératrice *f* empress
imperfection *f* blemish
impérial *adj* imperial
impérialisme *m* imperialism
imperméable *m* raincoat
impersonnel *adj* impersonal
impertinence *f* impertinence
impertinent *adj* impertinent
impertubabilité *f* coolness
impétueux *adj* impetuous

impie *adj* godless
impitoyable *adj* ruthless
implacable *adj* implacable
implanter *v* implant
implémenter *v* implement
implication *f* implication
implicite *adj* implicit
impliqué *v* involved
impliquer *v* entail, imply
implorer *v* implore
impopulaire *adj* unpopular
importance *f* importance
important *adj* major
importation *f* importation
importer *v* import
imposant *adj* imposing
imposer *v* impose
imposition *f* imposition
impossibilité *f* impossibility
impossible *adj* impossible
imposteur *m* sham
impotent *adj* impotent
imprécis *adj* imprecise
imprégner *v* permeate
impression *f* printing
impressionner *v* impress
imprévisible *adj* unpredictable
imprévu *adj* unexpected
imprimante *f* printer
imprimer *v* print
improbable *adj* unlikely
impromptu *adv* impromptu

impropre *adj* improper
improviser *v* improvise
imprudent *adj* reckless
impudent *adj* shameless
impulse *f* impulse
impulsif *adj* impulsive
impunité *f* impunity
impure *adj* impure
inabilité *f* inability
inaccessible *adj* inaccessible
inadapté *adj* inappropriate
inadéquat *adj* unfit
inadvertance *f* oversight
inaperçu *adj* unnoticed
inauguration *f* inauguration
inaugurer *v* inaugurate
incalculable *adj* countless
incapable *adj* unable
incapaciter *v* incapacitate
incarcérer *v* jail
incarner *v* embody
incertain *adj* uncertain
incessant *adj* incessant
incidemment *adv* incidentally
incident *m* incident
incinérer *v* cremate
incision *f* incision
inciter *v* incite, prod
inclination *f* inclination
incliner *v* incline, tilt
inclure *v* include
inclus *adv* inclusive

incohérent *adj* incoherent
incompatible *adj* incompatible
incompétence *f* incompetence
incompétent *adj* inept
incomplet *adj* incomplete
inconfortable *adj* uncomfortable
inconnu *adj* unknown
inconscient *adj* unconscious
inconsistent *adj* inconsistent
inconstant *adj* fickle
incontestable *adj* unmistakable
incontesté *adj* undisputed
incontinence *f* incontinence
inconvénient *m* drawback
inconvénient *adj* inconvenient
incorporer *v* incorporate
incorrect *adj* incorrect
incorrigible *adj* incorrigible
incrédulité *f* disbelief
incrément *m* increment
incriminer *v* incriminate
incroyable *adj* incredible
incrusté *adj* inlaid
inculper *v* charge, indict
inculte *adj* uneducated
incurable *adj* incurable
indécence *f* indecency
indécis *adj* undecided
indécision *f* indecision
indéfectible *adj* unfailing
indéfini *adj* indefinite
indélicat *adj* insensitive

I

indemniser *v* indemnify
indémnité *f* indemnity
indéniable *adj* undeniable
indépendent *adj* independent
indéssif *adj* indecisive
index *m* index
indicateur *m* informer
indicatif *m* code
indication *f* indication
indice *m* clue, hint
indifférence *f* indifference
indifférent *adj* indifferent
indigent *adj* indigent
indigestion *f* indigestion
indiquer *v* indicate
indirect *adj* indirect
indiscret *adj* indiscreet
indiscretion *f* indiscretion
indispensable *adj* indispensable
indisposé *adj* indisposed
indisputable *adj* indisputable
indivisible *adj* indivisible
indoctriner *v* indoctrinate
indolore *adj* painless
induire *v* induce
indulgent *adj* indulgent
industrie *f* industry
inefficace *adj* ineffective
inégal *adj* unequal
inégalité *f* inequality
inévitable *adj* inevitable
inexact *adj* inaccurate

inexcusable *adj* inexcusable
inexperienced *adj* inexperienced
inexplicable *adj* inexplicable
inexprimable *adj* unspeakable
infallible *adj* infallible
infâme *adj* infamous
infanterie *f* infantry
infatigable *adj* tireless
infatigant *adj* tiresome
infecter *v* infect
infectieux *adj* infectious
infection *f* infection
inférer *v* infer
inférieur *adj* inferior
infesté *adj* infested
infidèle *adj* unfaithful
infidélité *f* infidelity
infiltration *f* infiltration
infiltrer *v* infiltrate
infini *adj* infinite
infirme *m* invalid
infirmer *v* sap
infirmerie *f* infirmary
infirmier *f* nurse
infirmité *f* disability
inflammable *adj* flammable
inflammation *f* inflammation
inflation *f* inflation
inflexible *adj* inflexible
infliger *v* inflict
influence *f* influence
influent *adj* influential

infondé *adj* groundless
informateur *m* informant
information *f* information
informations *f* news
informel *adj* informal
informer *v* inform, brief
infraction *f* breach
infructueux *adj* unsuccessful
infusion *f* infusion
ingénieur *m* engineer
ingéniosité *f* ingenuity
ingester *v* ingest
ingrat *adj* ungrateful
ingratitude *f* ingratitude
ingrédient *m* ingredient
inhabitable *adj* inhabitable
inhaler *v* inhale
inhospitalier *adj* unfriendly
inhumain *adj* inhuman
inique *adj* sinful
initiale *adj* initial
initialement *adv* initially
initiales *f* initials
initiative *f* initiative
initier *v* initiate
injecter *v* inject
injection *f* injection
injurier *v* injure
injuste *adj* unfair, unjust
injustement *adv* unfairly
injustice *f* injustice
injustifié *adj* unjustified

inné *adj* innate
innocence *f* innocence
innocent *adj* innocent
innovation *f* innovation
innumérable *adj* innumerable
inoccupé *adj* unoccupied
inoffensif *adj* harmless
inondation *f* flooding
inonder *v* flood
inopportun *adj* untimely
inoubliable *adj* unforgettable
inquiétant *adj* alarming
inquiéter *v* concern
inquiétude *f* concern
inquisition *f* inquisition
insanité *f* insanity
insatiable *adj* insatiable
inscription *f* enrollment
inscrire *v* enroll
insecte *m* bug, insect
insécurité *f* insecurity
insélparable *adj* inseparable
insensé *adj* meaningless
insérer *v* insert
insertion *f* insertion
insetimable *adj* invaluable
insignifiant *adj* insignificant
insinuation *f* insinuation
insinuations *f* innuendo
insinuer *v* insinuate
insipide *adj* insipid
insistance *f* insistence

I

insister *v* insist
insolence *f* rudeness
insolent *adj* insolent
insoluble *adj* insoluble
insomnie *f* insomnia
insouciant *adj* carefree
inspecter *v* inspect
inspecteur *m* inspector
inspection *f* inspection
inspiration *f* inspiration
inspirer *v* inspire
instabilité *f* instability
instable *adj* unstable
installation *f* installation
installer *v* install, settle
instant *m* instant
instiller *v* instil
instinct *m* instinct
institut *v* institute
institution *f* institution
instructeur *m* instructor
instruire *v* instruct
insuffisance *f* deficiency
insuffisant *adj* inadequate
insulte *f* insult
insulter *v* insult
insupportable *adj* unbearable
insurrection *f* insurgency
intact *adj* intact
intégration *f* integration
intégrer *v* integrate
intégrité *f* integrity

intelligence *f* sense
intelligent *adj* clever
intemporel *adj* timeless
intense *adj* intense, hectic
intensif *adj* intensive
intensifier *v* intensify
intensité *f* intensity
intention *f* intention
intercéder *v* intercede
intercepter *v* intercept
intercession *f* intercession
interdiction *f* ban
interdire *v* forbid
intéressant *adj* interesting
intéressé *adj* interested
intérêt *m* interest
interférence *f* interference
intérieur *adv* inland
intérieur *adj* interior, inner
intermédiaire *m* intermediary
interner *v* intern
interposer *v* interfere
interprétateur *m* interpreter
interprétation *f* interpretation
interpréter *v* interpret
interroger *v* interrogate
interrompre *v* interrupt
interrupteur *m* switch
interruption *f* interruption
intervalle *f* interval
intervenir *v* intervene
intervention *f* intervention

intervertir *v* switch
interview *f* interview
intestin *m* intestine
intime *adj* intimate
intimider *v* intimidate
intimité *f* intimacy
intolérable *adj* intolerable
intolérance *f* intolerance
intouchable *adj* untouchable
intoxiqué *adj* intoxicated
intraveineux *adj* intravenous
intrépide *adj* intrepid
intriguant *adj* intriguing
intrigue *f* intrigue
intrinsèque *adj* intrinsic
introduction *f* introduction
introduire *v* introduce
introverti *adj* introvert
intrus *m* intruder
intrusion *f* intrusion
intuition *f* intuition
inutile *adj* useless
invalider *v* invalidate
invasion *f* invasion
inventaire *m* inventory
inventer *v* invent
invention *f* invention
inverse *adj* averse
inverse *m* reverse
inversé *adv* upside-down
inversement *adv* conversely
investigation *f* investigation

investir *v* invest
investisseur *m* investor
invincible *adj* invincible
invisible *adj* invisible
invitation *f* invitation
invité *m* guest
inviter *v* invite
invoquer *v* invoke
iode *f* iodine
irelandais *adj* Irish
Irelande *f* Ireland
ironie *f* irony
ironique *adj* ironic
irrationnal *adj* irrational
irréaliste *adj* unrealistic
irréel *adj* unreal
irrefutable *adj* irrefutable
irrégulie *adj* bumpy
irrégulier *adj* irregular
irréparable *adj* irreparable
irréprochable *adj* blameless
irrésistible *adj* irresistible
irrespect *m* disrespect
irrespectueux *adj* disrespectful
irréversible *adj* irreversible
irrévocable *adj* irrevocable
irrigation *f* irrigation
irriguer *v* irrigate
irritant *adj* irritating
irrité *adj* sore
irriter *v* irritate
irruption *f* outbreak

Islamique *adj* Islamic
isolation *f* isolation
isolé *adj* remote
isolement *m* seclusion
isoler *v* isolate
Italie *f* Italy
Italien *adj* Italian
italique *adj* italics
itinéraire *m* itinerary
ivoire *m* ivory
ivresse *f* drunkenness

J

jackpot *m* jackpot
jaguar *m* jaguar
jalousie *f* jealousy
jaloux *adj* jealous
jamais *adv* ever, never
jambe *f* leg
jambon *m* ham
jante *f* rim
janvier *m* January
Japon *m* Japan
Japonais *adj* Japanese
jardin *m* garden, yard
jardinier *m* gardener
jarretière *f* garter

jasmin *m* jasmine
jaune *adj* yellow
jaune d'œuf *m* yolk
javel *f* bleach
je *pro* I
jeans *m* jeans
jetable *adj* disposable
jeter *v* discard, toss
jeton *m* token
jeu *m* game, play, set
jeudi *m* Thursday
jeune *adj* young
jeune *m* youngster
jeune fille *f* maiden
jeunes mariés *adj* newlywed
jeunesse *f* youth
jeux olympiques *m* olympics
joie *f* joy
joindre *v* join
joint *m* joint
joli *adj* pretty
jonction *f* junction
jongleur *m* juggler
joue *f* cheek
jouer *v* perform, play
jouet *m* toy
joueur *m* player, gambler
joug *m* yoke
jour *m* day
journal *m* newspaper
journal intime *m* diary
journaliste *m* journalist

jouyeuse *adv* joyful
jovial *adj* jovial
joyeux *adj* joyful
jubilant *adj* elated
judaïsme *m* Judaism
judicieux *adj* judicious
juge *m* judge
jugement *m* judgment
Juif *m* Jew
Juif *adj* Jewish
juillet *m* July
juin *m* June
jumeau *m* twin
jumelles *f* binoculars
jument *f* mare
jungle *f* jungle
jupe *f* skirt
jupon *m* slip
jurer *v* swear
jury *m* jury
jus *m* juice
jusqu'à *pre* until
jusqu'ici *adv* hitherto
juste *adj* right, just
justement *adv* justly
justice *f* justice
justifier *v* justify
juteux *adj* juicy
juvénile *adj* juvenile

kangarou *m* kangaroo
karaté *m* karate
kidnapper *v* kidnap
kidnappeur *m* kidnapper
kidnapping *m* kidnapping
kilogramme *m* kilogram
kilomètre *m* kilometer
kilowatt *m* kilowatt
kiosque *m* newsstand
klaxon *m* horn
klaxonner *v* honk
kyste *m* cyst

J
K
L

la *pro* her
là *adv* there, here
labo *m* lab
labourer *v* plow
labyrinthe *m* labyrinth
lac *m* lake
lacet *m* shoelace
lâche *m* coward
lâcher *v* release
lâcheté *f* cowardice

lacune *f* loophole
lagune *f* lagoon
laid *adj* ugly
laideur *f* ugliness
laine *f* wool, yarn
laisse *f* leash
laisser *v* let
lait *m* milk
laiteux *adj* milky
laitue *f* lettuce
lambeau *m* shred
lame *f* blade
lampadaire *m* streetlight
lampe *f* lamp
lampe de poche *f* flashlight
lance *f* spear
lancement *m* launch
lancer *v* cast, hurl, throw
langage *m* language
langue *f* tongue
languir *v* languish
lanterne *f* lantern
lapin *m* rabbit
lard *m* lard
large *adj* wide, large
large d'esprit *adj* broadminded
largement *adv* widely
largeur *f* breadth, width
larme *f* tear
larmoyant *adj* tearful
larynx *m* larynx
lascif *adj* lustful

laser *m* laser
latéral *adj* lateral
latitude *f* latitude
lavable *adj* washable
lavabo *m* basin
laver *v* wash
laverie *f* laundry
lavette *adj* wimp
lave-vaisselle *m* dishwasher
laxative *adj* laxative
le long de *pre* alongside
le pire *adj* worst
le tien *pro* yours
lécher *v* lick
leçon *f* lesson
lecteur *m* reader
lecture *f* reading
légal *adj* lawful, legal
légaliserl *v* legalize
légalité *f* legality
légende *f* legend
léger *adj* mild, light
légèrement *adv* lightly
légiférer *v* legislate
légion *f* legion
législateur *m* lawmaker
législation *f* legislation
législature *f* legislature
légitime *adj* legitimate
léguer *v* bequeath
légume *m* vegetable
lent *adj* slow

lentement *adv* slowly
lentille *f* lense, lentil
l'envers (a) *adv* inside out
léopard *m* leopard
lépre *f* leprosy
lépreux *m* leper
les deux *adj* both
l'étranger (a) *adv* abroad
lettre *f* letter
lettré *adj* literate
lettre capitale *f* capital letter
leucémie *f* leukemia
lever *v* get up, stand
lever du soleil *m* sunrise
levier *m* lever
lèvre *m* lip
lévrier *m* greyhound
levure *f* yeast
lézard *m* lizard
liaison *f* liaison, affair
libération *f* liberation
libérer *v* free
liberté *f* freedom
libraire *m* bookseller
librairie *f* bookstore
libre *adj* free
licence *f* licence
licencier *v* fire, lay off
lié *adj* bound
liège *m* cork
lien *m* bond, tie
lier d'amitié *v* befriend

lieutenant *m* lieutenant
lieux *m* scene
lièvre *m* hare
ligament *m* ligament
ligne *f* line
ligue *f* league
lime *f* file
limer *v* file
limitation *f* limitation
limite *f* boundary, limit
limiter *v* limit
limonade *f* lemonade
linceul *m* shroud
linge *m* linen
lingerie *f* lingerie
lingot *m* ingot
lion *m* lion
lionne *f* lioness
liqueur *f* liqueur, liquor
liquidation *f* liquidation
liquide *m* liquid, cash
liquider *v* liquidate
lire *v* read
lisible *adj* legible
lisse *adj* smooth
lisser *v* smooth
liste *f* list
lit *m* bed
lit de mort *m* deathbed
lit superposé *m* bunk bed
litanie *f* litany
literie *f* bedding

L

litière _f_ litter
litiges _m_ litigation
litre _m_ liter, litre
littéral _adj_ literal
littéralement _adv_ literally
littérature _f_ literature
littoral _m_ seashore
liturgie _f_ liturgy
livide _adj_ livid
livraison _f_ delivery
livre _m_ book
livre _f_ pound
livrer _v_ deliver
lobby _m_ lobby
local _adj_ local
localiser _v_ localize
locataire _m_ tenant
location _f_ location
logement _m_ lodging
logique _f_ logic
logique _adj_ logical
loi _f_ law, statute
loin _adv_ away, far
lointain _adj_ faraway
loisir _m_ leisure
loiter _v_ loiter
long _adj_ lengthy
longterme _adj_ long-term
longitude _f_ longitude
longueur _f_ length
loquet _m_ latch
lorgner _v_ covet

l'original (a) _adv_ originally
lotion _f_ lotion
lotterie _f_ lottery
louable _adj_ praiseworthy
louange _f_ praise
louche _adj_ seedy
louer _v_ lease, praise
loufoque _adj_ silly
loup _m_ wolf
lourd _adj_ heavy
lourdeur _f_ heaviness
loutre _f_ otter
loyal _adj_ loyal
loyauté _f_ loyalty
loyer _m_ rent
lubrication _f_ lubrication
lubrifier _v_ lubricate
lubrique _adj_ prurient
lucarne _f_ skylight
lucide _adj_ lucid
lucratif _adj_ lucrative
lueur _f_ gleam
luge _f_ sleigh
lugubre _adj_ dismal
lui (a) _pro_ his
luire _v_ gleam, glow
lumière _f_ light
lumineux _adj_ luminous
l'un l'autre _adj_ each other
lunatique _adj_ lunatic
Lundi _m_ Monday
lune _f_ moon

lune de miel *f* honeymoon
lunettes *f* eyeglasses
lunettes de soleil *f* sunglasses
lustre *m* chandelier
lustrer *m* polish
lutte *f* contest, struggle
lutter *v* struggle
lutteur *m* wrestler
luxe *m* luxury
luxuriant *adj* lush
luxurieux *adj* luxurious
lyncher *v* lynch
lynx *m* lynx

mâcher *v* munch
machine *f* machine
mâchoire *f* jaw
maçon *m* mason
madame *f* madam
magasin *m* shop, store
magazine *f* magazine
magicien *m* magician
magie *f* magic
magique *adj* magical
magistrat *m* magistrate
magnat *m* tycoon

magnétique *adj* magnetic
magnétisme *m* magnetism
magnifique *adj* magnificent
mai *m* May
maigre *adj* meager, skinny
maille *f* stitch
maillé *adj* sleazy
maillon *m* link
maillot *m* jersey
main *f* hand
maintenant *adv* now
maintenir *v* maintain
maire *m* mayor
mairie *f* city hall
mais *c* but
maïs *m* corn
maison *f* home, house
maître *m* master
maître nageur *m* lifeguard
maîtresse *f* mistress
maîtrise *f* mastery
maîtriser *v* master
majesté *f* majesty
majestueux *adj* majestic
majeur *m* major
majordome *m* butler
majorité *f* majority
mal *m* evil, harm
mal *adv* badly
mal comprendre *v* misunderstand
mal de tête *m* headache
mal poli *adj* impolite

L
M

malade *adj* ill, sick
maladie *f* ailment, disease
maladif *adj* unhealthy
maladresse *f* clumsiness
maladroit *adj* clumsy
malaise *m* unrest
malchance *f* misfortune
malchanceux *adj* unlucky
mâle *m* male
malfaisant *adj* wicked
malgré *c* despite
malheureux *adj* wretched
malhonnête *adj* crooked
malhonnêteté *f* deceit
malice *f* malice
malignité *f* malignancy
malléable *adj* pliable
malmener *v* mistreat
malnutrition *f* malnutrition
malodorant *adj* smelly
malsain *adj* unsafe
maltraitance *f* mistreatment
malveillant *adj* malevolent
maman *f* mom
mamelon *m* nipple
mammifère *m* mammal
mammouth *m* mammoth
manche *f* sleeve
mandarine *f* tangerine
mandat *m* mandate, warrant
mandataire *m* proxy
mander *v* summon

mangeoire *f* manger
manger *iv* eat
maniable *adj* workable
maniaque *adj* maniac
manie *f* mannerism
manier *v* wield
manière *f* manner
manières *f* manners
manifeste *adj* patent
manifester *v* manifest
manipuler *v* handle
manivelle *f* crank
mannequin *m* dummy
manœuvre *f* maneuver
manoir *m* mansion
manquante *adj* missing
manque *m* lack, miss
manquer *v* lack, miss
manteau *m* coat
manuel *m* handbook
manuel *adj* manual
manuscrit *m* manuscript
maquillage *m* makeup
marais *m* swamp
marauder *v* pilfer
marbre *m* marble
marchander *v* haggle
marchandise *f* merchandise
marchant *m* dealer
marche *f* march, walk
marché *m* market
marcher *iv* tread

M

mardi *m* Tuesday
mare *f* pond
maréchal *m* marshal
marée *f* tide
marge *f* margin
marginal *adj* marginal
marguerite *f* daisy
mari *m* husband
mariage *m* marriage
marié *m* bridegroom
marié *adj* married
mariée *f* bride
marier *v* marry
marin *m* sailor
marine *adj* marine
mariner *v* marinate
marionnette *f* puppet
marital *adj* marital
marmelade *f* marmalade
marmonner *v* mumble
marnot *m* brat
marque *f* mark, brand
marquer *v* mark
marrine *f* navy
marron *m* chestnut
mars *m* March
marteau *m* hammer
marteler *v* pound
martyre *m* martyr
marxiste *adj* marxist
masculin *adj* masculine
masochisme *m* masochism

masque *m* mask
massacre *m* massacre
massage *m* massage
masse *f* mass
masser *v* massage
masseur *m* masseur
masseuse *f* masseuse
massif *adj* massive
mastiquer *v* chew
mât *m* flagpole
match *m* match
match nul *m* tie
matelas *m* mattress
matérialisme *m* materialism
matériel *m* gear
maternel *adj* maternal
maternité *f* maternity
maths *m* math
matière *f* subject
matin *m* morning
matraquer *v* club
matrimonie *f* matrimony
maturité *f* maturity
maudire *v* curse
mauvais *adj* bad
mauvaise herbe *f* weed
maxime *f* maxim
maximum *adj* maximum
mec *m* guy
mécaniser *v* mechanize
mécanisme *m* mechanism
mécène *m* patron

M

méchanceté *f* meanness
méchant *adj* mean
mèche *f* highlight
mécontent *adj* discontent
médaille *f* medal
médaillon *m* medallion
médecine *f* medicine
médiateur *m* mediator
médicament *m* medication
médicinal *adj* medicinal
médiéval *adj* medieval
médiocre *adj* mediocre
médiocrité *f* mediocrity
méditation *f* meditation
méditer *v* meditate
méfiance *f* distrust
méfiant *adj* distrustful
méfier *v* distrust
meilleur *adj* best
mélancolie *f* melancholy
mélange *m* blend
mélanger *v* blend
mêler *v* embroil
mélodie *f* melody
mélodieux *adj* melodic
melon *m* cantaloupe
membrane *f* membrane
membre *m* limb
mémé *f* granny
même si *c* even if
mémoire *f* memory
mémoires *m* memoirs

mémorable *adj* memorable
mémoriser *v* memorize
menace *f* menace
menacer *v* jeopardize
ménage *m* household
mendiant *m* beggar
mendier *v* beg
mener *v* lead
meneur *m* leader
méningite *f* meningitis
ménopause *f* menopause
menotte *f* handcuffs
mensonge *m* falsehood
menstruation *f* menstruation
mensuel *adv* monthly
mental *adj* mental
mentalement *adv* mentally
mentalité *f* mentality
menteur *adj* liar
menthe *f* mint
mention *f* mention
mentionner *v* mention
mentir *v* lie
menton *m* chin
menu *m* menu
menuiserie *f* carpentry
menuisier *m* carpenter
mépris *m* contempt
méprisant *adj* scornful
mépriser *v* despise
mer *f* sea
mercredi *m* Wednesday

M

mercure *m* mercury
mère *f* mother
méritant *adj* deserving
mérite *m* merit
mériter *v* deserve
merveille *f* marvel
merveilleux *adj* marvelous
mesquin *adj* petty
mesquinerie *f* pettiness
message *m* message
messager *m* messenger
Messie *m* Messiah
mesurer *v* gage, mesure
métal *m* metal
métallique *adj* metallic
métaphore *f* metaphor
météo *v* forecast
météore *f* meteor
méthode *f* method
méthodique *adj* methodical
méticuleux *adj* meticulous
métier à tisser *m* loom
mètre *m* meter
mètrique *adj* metric
métro *m* subway
métropole *f* metropolis
mettre *v* put, set
meuble *m* furniture
meubles *m* furnishings
meule de foin *f* haystack
meurtre *m* killing
meurtrier *m* murderer

mexicain *adj* Mexican
microbe *m* microbe
micro-onde *m* microwave
microphone *m* microphone
microscope *m* microscope
midi *m* noon
miel *m* honey
miette *f* crumb
mignon *adj* cute
migraine *f* migraine
migrant *m* migrant
mijoter *v* simmer
mi-journée *f* midday
mile *m* mile
milieu *m* middle
militant *adj* militant
millard *m* billion
millardaire *m* billionaire
mille *adj* thousand
millénaire *m* millennium
milligramme *m* milligram
millimètre *m* millimeter
million *m* million
millionaire *m* millionaire
mimer *v* mime
minable *adj* crappy
mince *adj* thin, lean
mine *m* mine
minerai *m* ore, mineral
mineur *m* miner
mineur *adj* petty
miniature *f* miniature

M

mini-jupe *f* miniskirt
minimiser *v* minimize
minimum *adj* least
ministère *m* ministry
ministre *m* minister
minorité *f* minority
minuit *m* midnight
minuscule *adj* tiny
minute *f* minute
minutieux *adj* thorough
miotiver *v* motivate
miracle *m* miracle
miraculeux *adj* miraculous
mirage *m* mirage
miraillette *f* machine gun
miroir *m* looking glass
miser *v* stake
misérable *adj* miserable
miséricordieux *adj* merciful
missile *m* missile
mission *f* mission
missionaire *m* missionary
mite *f* moth
mitiger *v* mitigate
mixeur *m* blender
mixture *f* mixture
mobile *adj* mobile
mobiliser *v* mobilize
mode *f* fad, mode
mode de vie *m* lifestyle
modèle *m* model
modération *f* moderation

modérer *adj* moderate
moderne *adj* modern
moderniser *v* modernize
modeste *adj* modest
modestie *f* modesty
modification *f* alteration
modifier *v* amend
module *m* module
moelle *f* bone marrow
moi-même *pro* myself
moindre *adj* lesser
moine *m* friar
moineau *m* sparrow
moins *adj* less
moins de *adj* fewer
moins de (a) *pre* barring
moins que (a) *c* unless
mois *m* month
moisi *adj* moldy
moisissure *f* mildew
moissonner *v* reap
moitié *f* half
molaire *f* molar
molécule *f* molecule
molester *v* maul
moment *m* moment
momie *f* mummy
mon *adj* my
monarchie *f* monarchy
monarque *m* monarch
monastère *m* monastery
monastique *adj* monastic

M

monde *m* world
monnaie *f* coin
monogamie *f* monogamy
monologue *m* monologue
monopolie *f* monopoly
monopoliser *v* monopolize
monotone *adj* monotonous
monotonie *f* monotony
monsieur *m* mister, sir
monstre *m* monster
monstrueux *adj* monstrous
mont *m* mount
montagne *f* mountain
montagneux *adj* mountainous
monter *v* go up, ride
monter à bord *v* board
montgolfière *f* balloon
montre *f* watch
montrer *v* show
monture *f* setting
monument *m* monument
monumental *adj* monumental
moquer *v* mock
moquerie *f* mockery
moquette *f* carpet
moral *adj* moral
moralité *f* ethics
morceau *m* piece, morsel
mordre *v* bite
morose *adj* gloomy
morosité *f* gloom
morphine *f* morphine

morse *m* walrus
morsure *f* bite
mort *adj* dead
mort *f* death
mortalité *f* mortality
mortel *adj* deadly
mortier *m* mortar
mortification *f* mortification
mortifier *v* mortify
mortuaire *m* mortuary
morue *f* cod
mosaïque *f* mosaic
mosquée *f* mosque
mot *m* word
mot de passe *m* password
motel *m* motel
moteur *m* engine
motif *m* motive
moto *f* motorcycle
mots croisés *m* crossword
mouchoir *m* handkerchief
mouette *f* gull
mouillé *adj* wet
mouiller *v* moor
moule *m* mold
mouler *v* mold
moulin *m* mill
moulinet *m* reel
mourant *adj* dying
mourir *v* die
mousse *f* foam, moss
moustache *f* mustache

M

moustique *m* mosquito
moutarde *f* mustard
mouton *m* sheep
mouvement *m* move
moyen *m* means
moyenne *f* average
mucus *f* mucus
muet *adj* dumb
mulet *m* mule
multiple *adj* multiple
multiplication *f* multiplication
multiplier *v* multiply
multitude *f* multitude
munition *f* ammunition
munitions *f* munitions
mur *m* wall
mûr *adj* mature
mûre *f* blackberry
mûrir *v* ripen
murmure *m* murmur
murmurer *v* murmur
muscle *m* muscle
musée *m* museum
museler *v* muzzle
muselière *f* muzzle
musicien *m* musician
musique *f* music
musulman *adj* Muslim
muter *v* mutate
mutiler *v* mangle
mutiner *v* riot
mutinerie *f* mutiny

mutuellement *adv* mutually
myope *adj* myopic, shortsighted
mystère *m* mystery
mystérieux *adj* mysterious
mystifier *v* mystify
mystique *adj* mystic
mythe *m* myth

N

nageoire *f* fin
nager *v* swim
nageur *m* swimmer
naïf *adj* fond
nain *m* dwarf
naissance *f* birth
nana *m* chick
nappe *f* tablecloth
narcotique *m* narcotic
narine *f* nostril
narrer *v* narrate
natation *f* swimming
natif *adj* native
nation *f* nation
national *adj* national
nationaliser *v* nationalize
nationalité *f* nationality
natte *f* braid

M
N

nature _f_ nature
naturel _adj_ natural
naufrage _m_ shipwreck
naufragé _m_ castaway
nausée _f_ nausea
navigateur _m_ browser
navigation _f_ navigation
naviguer _v_ navigate
navire de guerre _m_ warship
né _adj_ born
ne...pas _adv_ not
néanmoins _adv_ nevertheless
nécessaire _adj_ necessary
nécessité _f_ necessity
nécessiter _v_ necessitate
nécessiteux _adj_ needy
Néerlandais _adj_ Dutch
nef _f_ nave
négatif _adj_ negative
négligence _f_ negligence
négligent _adj_ careless
négliger _v_ disregard, overlook
négociation _f_ bargaining
négocier _v_ negotiate
négotiation _f_ negotiation
neige _f_ snow
neiger _v_ snow
nerf _m_ nerve
nerveux _adj_ jumpy
net _adj_ clear-cut
nettoyant _m_ cleanser
nettoyer _v_ clean, mop

nettoyer à sec _m_ dryclean
neuf _adj_ nine
neutraliser _v_ neutralize
neutre _adj_ neutral
neuvième _adj_ ninth
neveu _m_ nephew
névrosé _adj_ neurotic
nez _m_ nose
niche _f_ kennel
nickel _m_ nickel
nicotine _f_ nicotine
nid _m_ nest
nid-de-poule _m_ pothole
nièce _f_ niece
nier _v_ disclaim
niminer _v_ nominate
n'importe où _c_ wherever
n'importe quand _adv_ whenever
n'importe quel _adj_ whatever
n'importe qui _pro_ anyone
n'importe quoi _pro_ anything
niveau _m_ level
niveler _v_ level
noble _adj_ lofty
noble _m_ nobleman
noblesse _f_ nobility
nocif _adj_ noxious
nocturne _adj_ nocturnal
Noël _f_ Christmas
noeud _m_ bow
noeud coulant _m_ noose
noir _adj_ black

N

noirceur *f* blackness
noisette *f* hazelnut
noix *f* walnut
noix de coco *f* coconut
nom *m* name
nom de famille *m* last name
nombre *m* number
nombre de mort *m* death toll
nombreux *adj* numerous
nombril *m* belly button
nomination *f* appointment
nommer *v* appoint
non plus *adv* either
non plus *c* nor
non-assisté *adj* singlehanded
non-fumeur *m* nonsmoker
nord *m* north
nord-est *m* northeast
nordique *adj* northern
normal *adj* normal
normalement *adv* normally
normaliser *v* normalize
norme *f* norm
Norvège *f* Norway
Norvègien *adj* Norwegian
nostalgie *f* longing
notable *adj* notable
notablement *adv* notably
notaire *m* notary
notation *f* notation
note *f* receipt
noter *v* write down

notification *f* notification
notifier *v* notify
notion *f* notion
notorieux *adj* notorious
nôtre *pro* ours
notre/nos *adj* our
nouer *v* tie
nourrice *f* nanny
nourrir *iv* feed
nourrissant *adj* nutritious
nourrisson *m* infant
nourriture *f* sustenance
nous *pro* us
nous-mêmes *pro* ourselves
nouveau *adj* brand-new
nouveau (a) *adv* afresh
nouveau-né *m* newborn
nouveauté *f* novelty
nouvelement *adv* newly
novembre *m* November
noyer *v* drown
nu *adj* bare, nude
nuage *m* cloud
nuageux *adj* cloudy
nuance *f* nuance
nucléaire *adj* nuclear
nudisme *m* nudism
nudiste *m* nudist
nudité *f* nudity
nuire *v* harm
nuisance *f* nuisance
nuisible *adj* damaging, harmful

N

nuit _f_ night
nul _adj_ null
nulpart _adv_ nowhere
nuptial _adj_ bridal
nutrition _f_ nutrition

oasis _m_ oasis
obéir _v_ obey
obéissance _f_ obedience
obéissant _adj_ obedient
obese _adj_ obese
objectif _m_ goal, target
objection _f_ objection
objet _m_ item, object
obligation _f_ obligation
obligatoire _adj_ compulsory
obligé _adj_ obliged
obliger _v_ compel, oblige
oblique _adj_ oblique, slanted
obliterer _v_ obliterate
oblongue _adj_ oblong
obscène _adj_ lewd
obscènité _f_ obscenity
obscurcir _v_ darken
obscure _adj_ obscure
obscurité _f_ darkness

obséder _v_ obsess
observation _f_ observation
observatoire _f_ observatory
observer _v_ observe
obsession _f_ obsession
obsolète _adj_ obsolete
obstacle _m_ obstacle
obstiné _adj_ stubborn
obstiner _adj_ obstinate
obstruction _f_ obstruction
obtenir _v_ obtain
occasion _f_ chance, occasion
occidental _adj_ westerner
occulte _adj_ occult
occupant _m_ occupant
occupation _f_ occupation
occupé _adj_ busy
occuper _v_ occupy, look after
océan _m_ ocean
octobre _m_ October
odeur _f_ odor, scent
odieux _adj_ obnoxious
odomètre _m_ odometer
odorant _adj_ fragrant
odyssée _m_ odyssey
œil _m_ eye
œillet _m_ carnation
œsophage _m_ esophagus
œuf _m_ egg
œuvre d'art _m_ artwork
offense _f_ offense
offenser _v_ offend

N
O

offensif *adj* offensive
officiel *adj* official
officier *m* officer
offrande *f* offering
offre *f* offer
offrir *v* offer
oie *f* goose
oignon *m* onion
oindre *v* anoint
oiseau *m* bird
oléoduc *m* pipeline
olive *f* olive
ombragé *adj* shady
ombre *f* shadow, shade
omelette *f* omelette
omettre *v* omit
omission *f* omission
once *f* ounce
oncle *m* uncle
on-dit *m* hearsay
ondulation *f* ripple
ondulé *adj* wavy
one cent *m* penny
ongle *m* fingernail
ongle de pied *m* toenail
onze *adj* eleven
onzième *adj* eleventh
opaque *adj* opaque
opéra *m* opera
opération *f* operation
opérer *v* operate
opiniâtreté *f* obstinacy

opinion *f* opinion
opium *m* opium
opportun *adj* timely
opportunité *f* expediency
opposé *adj* opposite
opposer *v* oppose
opposition *f* opposition
opprimé *m* underdog
opprimer *v* oppress
opter *v* opt for
opticien *m* optician
optimisme *m* optimism
optimiste *adj* optimistic
option *f* option
optionel *adj* optional
optique *adj* optical
opulence *f* opulence
or *m* gold
oracle *m* oracle
orage *m* thunderstorm
orageux *adj* stormy
oralement *adv* orally
orange *f* orange
orang-outang *m* orangutan
orateur *m* speaker
orbite *m* orbit
orchestre *m* orchestra
ordinaire *adj* ordinary
ordinairement *adv* ordinarily
ordinateur *m* computer
ordination *f* ordination
ordonné *adj* neat

O

ordonner *v* ordain
orée *f* threshold
oreille *f* ear
oreiller *m* pillow
oreillons *m* mumps
orfèvre *m* silversmith
organe *m* organ
organisation *f* organization
organiser *v* organize
organisme *m* organism
organiste *m* organist
orge *m* barley
orient *m* orient
oriental *adj* oriental
orientation *f* orientation
orienté *adj* oriented
original *adj* original
origine *f* origin
orme *f* elm
ornement *m* ornament
ornemental *adj* ornamental
orner *v* adorn
orphelin *m* orphan
orphelinat *m* orphanage
orthodoxe *adj* orthodox
orthographe *f* spelling
os *m* bone
oscillation *f* swing
osé *adj* daring
ostentatoire *adj* ostentatious
otage *m* hostage
other *adj* another

otite *f* earache
ou *c* or
où *adv* where
oubli *m* oblivion
oublier *v* forget
ouest *d* west
oui *adv* yes
ouragan *m* hurricane
ourlet *m* hem
ours *m* bear
ourson *m* cub
outil *m* tool
outrage *m* outrage
outrageant *adj* outrageous
outre-mer *adv* overseas
outrepasser *v* override
ouvert *adj* open
ouvert d'esprit *adj* open-minded
ouverture *f* opening
ouvre boîte *m* can opener
ouvreuse *f* usher
ouvrir *v* open, unlock
ovaire *m* ovary
oval *adj* oval
ovation *f* ovation
overdose *f* overdose
oxygène *m* oxygen

O

P

pacifier *v* pacify

pacte *m* pact

pagaille *f* shambles

pagayer *v* paddle

page *f* page

paiement *m* payment

païen *m* heathen, pagan

paille *f* straw

paillette *v* glitter

pain *m* bread, loaf

pair *f* pair

paisible *adj* peaceful

paix *m* peace

palace *m* palace

palais *m* palate

palan *m* hoist

pâle *adj* fair, pale

pâleur *f* paleness

palourde *f* clam

palpable *adj* palpable

paltry *adj* paltry

paludisme *m* malaria

panais *m* parsnip

pancréas *m* pancreas

panier *m* basket

panique *f* panic

panne *f* breakdown

panorama *m* panorama

pantalon *m* pants, trousers

panthère *f* panther

pantoufle *f* slipper

paon *m* peacock

papa *m* dad

papauté *f* papacy

Pape *m* Pope

paperasserie *f* paperwork

papeterie *f* stationery

papier *m* paper

papier de verre *m* sandpaper

papillon *m* butterfly

paque *m* bundle

Pâques *m* Easter

paquet *m* package

par *pre* by, per

par avion *n* airmail

par terre *m* floor

parabole *f* parable

parachute *m* parachute

parachutiste *m* paratrooper

parade *f* parade

paradis *m* heaven

paradisiaque *adj* heavenly

paradoxe *m* paradox

paragraphe *m* paragraph

parallèle *f* parallel

paralyser *v* paralyze

paralysie *f* paralysis

paramètre *m* parameters

paranoïde *adj* paranoid

parapluie *m* umbrella

parasite *m* parasite

parc *m* park
parce que *c* because
parchemin *m* parchment
parcourir *v* browse, roam
pardessus *m* overcoat
par-dessus *pre* over
pardon *m* forgiveness
pardonnable *adj* forgivable
pardonner *v* forgive
pare-brise *m* windshield
pare-chocs *m* bumper
pareil *adj* alike
pareillement *adv* likewise
parent *m* relative, folks
parenté *f* kinship
parenthèse *f* parenthesis
parents *m* parents
parer *v* counter
paresse *f* laziness
paresseux *adj* idle
parfait *adj* perfect
parfum *m* perfume
pari *m* bet
parier *v* bet, gamble
parité *f* parity
parjure *f* perjury
parking *m* parking
parlement *m* parliament
parler *v* speak, talk
parmis *pre* among
parois *f* parish
paroissien *m* parishioner

paroles *f* lyrics
part *f* share
part (a) *adv* apart, aside
partager *v* share
partager en deux *v* halve
partenaire *m* partner
partenariat *m* partnership
participant *m* contributor
participation *f* participation
participe *m* participle
participer *v* participate
particule *f* particle
particulier *adj* particular
partie *f* play, party
partiel *adj* partial
partielement *adv* partially
partir *v* leave, quit
partisan *m* supporter
partition *f* partition
pas *m* step
pas de porte *m* doorstep
passage *m* passage
passage couté *m* crosswalk
passager *m* passenger
passant *m* bystander
passe *f* pass
passé *adj* past
passeport *m* passport
passer *v* pass, get by
passe-temps *m* pastime
passif *adj* passive
passion *f* passion

P

passioné *adj* passionate
passionnant *adj* enthralling
passionner *v* enthrall
passoire *f* strainer
pastèque *f* watermelon
pasteur *m* preacher, priest
pasteuriser *v* pasteurize
pastoral *adj* pastoral
patate douce *f* yam
pate *f* pat
pâte *f* dough, paste
paternel *adj* fatherly
paternité *f* fatherhood
pathétique *adj* pathetic
patience *f* patience
patient *adj* patient
patin *m* skate
patiner *v* skate
patio *m* patio
pâtisserie *f* pastry
patriarche *m* patriarch
patricipation *f* contribution
patrie *f* homeland
patrimoine *m* patrimony
patriote *m* patriot
patriotique *adj* patriotic
patron *m* boss, pattern
patronage *m* patronage
patronner *v* patronize
patrouille *f* patrol
patte *f* paw
pattes *f* sideburns

pâturage *m* pasture
paume *f* palm
paupière *f* eyelid
pause *f* lapse, break
pauvre *m* poor
pauvrement *adv* poorly
pauvreté *f* poverty
pavé *m* cobblestone
pavillon *m* pavilion
pavot *m* poppy
payable *adj* payable
paye *f* paycheck
payer *v* pay
pays *m* country
paysage *m* scenery
paysan *m* peasant
Pays-Bas *m* Netherlands
péage *m* toll
peau *f* skin
péché *v* sin
pêche *f* peach
pécher *m* sin
pécheur *m* sinner
pédagogie *m* pedagogy
pédale *f* pedal
pedant *c* while
pédant *adj* pedantic
pédestrien *m* pedestrian
peigne *m* comb
peigner *v* comb
peindre *v* paint
peine *f* sentence

peiner v grieve
peintre m painter
peinture f paint, painting
pèlerin m pilgrim
pèlerinage m pilgrimage
pélican m pelican
pelle f shovel
pellicules f dandruff
peloton m platoon
pelouse f lawn
peluché adj plush
pelure f peel
pénaliser v penalize
pénalité f penalty
penchant m bias, leaning
pencher v lean
pendant pre during
pendantif m pendant
pendre v dangle, hang
pendule f pendulum
pénétrer v penetrate
péniche f barge
pénicilline f penicillin
péninsule f peninsula
pénitence f penance
pénitent m penitent
penser v think
pension f pension
pentagone m pentagon
pente f slope
pénurie f shortage
pépinière f nursery

percée f breakthrough
perception f perception
percer v pierce, drill
percevoir v perceive
percuter v crash
perdant m loser
perdrix f partridge
perdu adj stray
père m father
pérenne adj perennial
pereux adv cowardly
perfection f perfection
perforation f perforation
perforer v perforate
performance f performance
péril m peril
périlleux adj perilous
périmètre m perimeter
période f period
périphérie f fringe
périr v perish
périssable adj perishable
perle f pearl
perler v peel
permanent adj permanent
permettre v allow, permit
permission f permission
pernicieux adj pernicious
perpétrer v perpetrate
perroquet m parrot
perruque f wig
persécuter v persecute

P

persévérer *v* persevere
persil *m* parsley
persistance *f* persistence
persistant *adj* lingering
persister *v* persist
personnalité *f* personality
personne *pro* nobody
personne *f* person
personnel *m* staff
personnifier *v* personify
perspective *f* perspective
perspectives *f* outlook
persuader *v* persuade
persuasif *adj* persuasive
persuasion *f* persuasion
perte *f* loss
pertinent *adj* relevant
pertuber *v* disrupt
perturbant *adj* disturbing
perturbation *f* disruption
perturber *v* perturb
pervers *adj* perverse
pervertir *v* pervert
peser *v* weigh
pessimisme *m* pessimism
pessimiste *adj* pessimistic
peste *f* pest, plague
pesticide *m* pesticide
pétale *m* petal
pétard *m* firecracker
petit *adj* small, short
petit à petit *adv* little by little

petit ami *m* boyfriend
petit déjeuner *m* breakfast
petit pain *m* bun
petite *adj* petite
petite amie *f* girlfriend
petite enfance *f* infancy
petit-enfant *m* grandchild
petit-fils *m* grandson
pétition *f* petition
pétrifié *adj* petrified
pétrole *m* petroleum
peu fiable *adj* unreliable
peur *f* fear, scare
peut-être *adv* perhaps
phare *m* lighthouse
pharmacie *f* pharmacy
pharmacien *m* pharmacist
phase *f* phase
phénomène *m* phenomenon
philosophe *m* philosopher
philosophie *f* philosophy
phobie *f* phobia
phoque *m* seal
phosphore *m* phosphorus
photo *f* photo, picture
photocopie *f* photocopy
photocopieuse *f* copier
photographe *m* photographer
photographie *f* photography
photographier *v* photograph
phrase *f* phrase
physique *f* physics

P

physiquement *adv* physically
pianiste *m* pianist
piano *m* piano
pic *m* peak
pickpocket *m* pickpocket
picorer *v* peck, graze
piéce *f* part
pied *m* foot
pied nu *adj* barefoot
pied-de-biche *m* crowbar
piège *m* snare, trap
pièger *v* snare
piercing *m* piercing
pierre *f* rock, stone
pierre précieuse *f* gem
pierre tombale *f* tombstone
piétiner *v* trample
pieuvre *f* octopus
pieux *adj* devout, pious
pigeon *m* pigeon
pile *f* battery
pilier *m* pillar
pillage *v* pillage
piller *v* sack, plunder
pilleur *m* raider
pilote *m* pilot
pilule *f* pill
pin *m* pine
pinailleur *adj* nitpicking
pinceau *m* paintbrush
pincée *f* pinch
pincement *m* nip, pinch

pincer *v* nip, pinch
pinces *f* tongs
pincette *f* tweezers
pingouin *m* penguin
pinte *f* pint
pionnier *m* pioneer
pipe *f* pipe
piquant *adj* stinging
piquer *v* prick
piqûre *v* sting
pirate *m* pirate
pirate de l'air *m* hijacker
piraterie *f* piracy
pire *adj* worse
piscine *f* pool
piste *f* trail
pistolet *m* pistol
pitié *f* mercy, pity
pitoresque *adj* picturesque
pitoyable *adj* pitiful
pivoter *v* swivel
placard *m* closet, cabinet
place *f* lieu, square
plache *f* board
placide *adj* placid
plafond *m* ceiling
plage *f* beach
plaider *v* plead
plaie *f* sore
plaignant *m* plaintiff
plaindre *v* complain
plaine *f* plain

P

plainte *f* complaint, wail
plaisant *adj* pleasant
plaisir *m* pleasure
plan *m* blueprint, plan
planer *v* glide
planète *f* planet
planifier *v* plan
plante *f* plant
planter *v* plant
plaquer *v* tackle
plastique *m* plastic
plat *m* course, dish
plat *adj* flat
plateau *m* plateau
plate-forme *f* platform
platine *f* platinum
plâtre *m* plaster
plâtrer *v* plaster
plausible *adj* plausible
plein *adj* laden
plein air *adv* outdoors
pleurer *v* cry, weep
pleurnicher *v* whine
pleurs *m* crying
pleuvoir *v* rain
pli *m* pleat, crease
plié *adj* pleated
plier *v* bend, fold
plombé *adj* leaded
plomberie *f* plumbing
plombier *m* plumber
plongeon *m* plunge

plonger *v* dive, plunge
plongeur *m* diver
pluie *f* rain
plume *f* feather
pluriel *f* plural
plus *adj* more, plus
plus loin *adv* farther
plus tard *adv* later
plusieurs *adj* several
plutonium *m* plutonium
plutôt *adv* rather
pluvieux *adj* rainy
pneumonie *f* pneumonia
poche *f* pocket
poêle *f* frying pan
poème *m* poem
poèsie *f* poetry
poète *m* poet
poids *m* weight
poids plume *m* lightweight
poignant *adj* poignant
poignard *m* dagger
poignarder *v* stab
poignée *f* knob, handle
poignée de main *f* handshake
poignet *m* wrist
poilu *adj* hairy
poinçon *m* punch
poinçonner *v* punch
poing *m* fist
point *m* dot
point de vue *m* standpoint

pointe *f* point, tip
pointu *adj* pointed
poire *f* pear
pois *m* pea
poison *m* poison
poisson *m* fish
poitrine *f* bosom, chest
poivre *m* pepper
poivron *m* bell pepper
polaire *adj* polar
Polande *f* Poland
pole *m* pole
poli *adj* polite
police *f* police
policier *m* policeman
polir *v* polish
politesse *f* politeness
politicien *m* politician
politique *f* politics
pollen *m* pollen
polluer *v* pollute
pollution *f* pollution
Polonais *adj* Polish
polycopié *m* handout
polygamie *f* polygamy
polygamiste *adj* polygamist
pommade *f* ointment
pomme *f* apple
pomme de terre *f* potato
pommette *f* cheekbone
pompe *f* pump
pomper *v* pump

pompier *m* firefighter
ponctuel *adj* punctual
pondre *v* lay
pont *m* bridge
pontife *m* pontiff
popcorn *m* popcorn
populaire *adj* popular
populariser *v* popularize
population *f* population
porc *m* pork
porc verrat *m* hog
porcelaine *f* porcelain
porc-épic *m* porcupine
porchain *adj* coming
porche *m* porch
pore *m* pore
poreux *adj* porous
port *m* harbor, port
portable *adj* portable
porte *f* door, gate
porte de derrière *f* backdoor
porte-clés *m* key ring
portefeuille *m* wallet
porter *v* wear, carry
porter garant *v* vouch for
porter un otast *v* toast
porteur *m* porter
portion *f* portion
portrait *m* portrait
portugais *adj* Portuguese
Portugal *m* Portugal
pose *f* pose

P

posé *adj* composed
poser *v* pose
poseur *adj* phoney
position *f* position
positive *adj* positive
posséder *v* own
possession *f* possession
possibilité *n* possibility
possible *adj* possible
poste *f* post office, post
poster *v* mail
poster *m* poster
postérité *f* posterity
postiche *f* hairpiece
postier *m* mailman
postuler *v* apply for
pot *m* pot
pot de fleur *m* flowerpot
pot-de-vin *m* bribe
potelé *adj* chubby
potentiel *adj* potential
pou *m* lice
poubelle *f* bin, trash can
pouce *m* inch, thumb
poudre *f* powder
poulain *m* colt
poule *f* hen
poulet *m* chicken
poulie *f* pulley
poumon *m* lung
poupe *f* stern
poupée *f* doll

pour *pre* for
pour cent *adv* percent
pourboire *m* tip
pourcentage *m* percentage
pourchasser *v* pursue
pourquoi *adv* why
pourri *adj* rotten
pourrir *v* decay, rot
pourriture *f* rot
poursuite *f* chase, lawsuit
poursuivre *v* chase, sue
pourtant *c* nonetheless
pourvoir *v* cater to
pourvu que *adv* hopefully
pousse *f* shot
pousser *v* shove, push
poussière *f* dust
poussièreux *adj* dusty
poussin *m* chick
pouvoir *m* power
pouvoir *v* can, may
pragmatique *adj* pragmatist
prairie *f* prairie
pratiquant *adj* practising
pratique *adj* practical
pré *m* meadow
preamble *f* preamble
précaire *adj* precarious
précaution *f* precaution
précédent *m* precedent
précédent *adj* previous
précéder *v* precede

P

précepte m precept
prêcher v preach
précieux adj precious
précipice m precipice
précipitations f rainfall
précipiter v precipitate, dash
précis adj precise
précision f precision
précoce adj precocious
précurseur m precursor
prédécesseur m predecessor
prédicament m predicament
prédication f preaching
prédiction f prediction
prédilection f predilection
prédir v predict
prédire v foretell
prédisposé adj predisposed
prédominant adj paramount
prédominer v predominate
predre v lose
préempter v preempt
préface f preface
préférence f preference
préférer v prefer
préfixe m prefix
préfrabriquer v prefabricate
préhistorique adj prehistoric
préjudice m prejudice
prélever v levy
préliminaire adj preliminary
prélude m prelude

prématuré adj premature
préméditation f premeditation
prémédité v premeditate
premier adj first, premier
premier plan m foreground
prémisse f premise
prémonition f premonition
prendre v take, put
préoccupation f preoccupation
préoccuper v preoccupy
préparation f preparation
préparer v prepare
préposition f preposition
prérogative f prerogative
près pre near
présage m omen
prescription f prescription
prescrire v prescribe
présence f presence
présent adj present
présentation f presentation
présenter v present
présidence f presidency
président m chairman
présider v chair, preside
présomption f presumption
presque adv almost
pressant adj pressing
presse f press
presser v urge, press
presseux adj lazy
pression f pressure

P

prestige *m* prestige
présumer *v* presume
présupposer *v* presuppose
prêt *m* loan
prêt *adj* ready
prétendre *v* pretend
prétendument *adv* allegedly
prétention *f* pretension
prêter *v* lend, loan
prêtre *m* priest
prêtresse *f* priestess
prêtrise *f* priesthood
preuve *f* proof
prévaloir *v* prevail
préventif *adj* preventive
prévention *f* prevention
prévoyance *f* foresight
prier *v* pray
prière *f* prayer
primauté *f* primacy
primitif *adj* primitive
prince *m* prince
princesse *f* princess
principal *adj* leading, main
principe *m* principle
printemps *m* spring
prioritaire *m* priority
prise *f* plug, grip
prisme *m* prism
prison *m* jail, prison
prisonier *m* prisoner
privation *f* deprivation

privé *adj* deprived
priver *v* deprive
privilège *m* privilege
prix *m* fare, prize
probabilité *f* likelihood
probable *adv* likely
probatoire *f* probing
problèmatique *adj* problematic
problème *m* problem, matter
procéder *v* proceed
procédure *f* procedure
procès *m* trial
procession *f* procession
processus *m* process
prochain *adj* upcoming
proche *adj* nearby
proche de *pre* close to
proclamation *f* proclamation
proclamer *v* proclaim
procrastiner *v* procrastinate
procreate *v* procreate
procurer *v* procure
procureur *m* prosecutor
prodige *m* prodigy
prodigieux *adj* prodigious
prodiguer *v* lavish
productif *adj* productive
production *f* production
produire *v* produce
produits *m* product
profane *m* profane
profaner *v* desecrate

professer v profess
professeur m professor
profession f profession
professionel adj professional
profile m profile
profit m profit
profitable adj profitable
profiter v avail, profit
profond adj deep
profondeur f depth
progéniture f offspring
programme m program
programmer v schedule
programmeur m programmer
progrès m progress
progresser v progress
progressif adj progressive
prohibition f prohibition
proie f prey
projecteur m floodlight
projectile m projectile
projet m project
projeter v project
prologue m prologue
prolongé adj protracted
prolonger v prolong
promenade f promenade
promener v stroll
promesse f pledge
prometteur adj auspicious
promettre v pledge
prominent adj prominent

promotion f promotion
promouvoir v promote
pronom m pronoun
prononcer v pronounce
propagande f propaganda
propager v propagate
propension f propensity
prophète m prophet
prophétie f prophecy
proportion f proportion
propos de (a) pre about
proposer v propose
proposition f proposal
propre adj clean, own
propreté f cleanliness
propriétaire m owner
propriété f ownership
propulser v propel
prose f prose
prospectus m flier
prospère adj prosperous
prospérer v prosper
prospérité f prosperity
prostate f prostate
prostré adj prostrate
protection f protection
protéger v protect, protest
protéine f protein
proteste m protest
protester v object, protest
protocole m protocol
prototype m prototype

P

proue *f* prow
prouvé *adj* proven
prouver *v* prove
provenir *v* derive
proverbe *m* proverb
providence *f* providence
province *f* province
provision *f* provision
provisoire *adj* provisional
provocant *adj* defiant
provocation *f* provocation
provoquer *v* provoke
proximité *f* proximity
prudence *f* prudence
prudent *adj* careful, cautious
prune *f* plum
pruneau *m* prune
pseudonyme *m* pseudonym
psychiatre *m* psychiatrist
psychiatrie *f* psychiatry
psychique *adj* psychic
psychologie *f* psychology
psychopathe *m* psychopath
puant *adj* stinking
puanteur *f* stench, stink
puberté *f* puberty
publication *f* publication
publicité *f* advertising
publier *v* publish
publique *adj* public
puce *f* flea
pudding *m* pudding

pudique *adj* bashful
puer *v* stink
puéril *adj* puerile
puissant *adj* mighty
puit *d* well
pulpe *f* pulp
pulse *f* pulse
pulser *v* pulsate
pulvériser *v* pulverize
punaise *f* thumbtack
punir *v* punish
punissable *adj* punishable
punission *f* punishment
pupitre *m* lectern
pur *adj* pure
purée *f* puree
pureté *f* purity
purgatoire *m* purgatory
purge *f* purge
purger *v* purge
purification *f* purification
purifier *v* purify
pus *m* pus
putride *adj* putrid
puzzle *m* puzzle
pyjama *m* pajamas
pyramide *f* pyramid
pyromane *m* arsonist
python *m* python

P

Q

qualifier *v* qualify
qualité *f* quality
quand *adv* when
quantité *f* amount, quantity, volume
quantre-vingt *adj* eighty
quarante *adj* forty
quart *m* quarter
quartier général *m* headquarters
quatorze *adj* fourteen
quatre *adj* four
quatre-vingt-dix *adj* ninety
quatrième *adj* fourth
que *adj* that
quel *adj* what, which
quelque *adj* few
quelque chose *pro* something
quelquefois *adv* sometimes
quelques *adj* some
quelqu'un *pro* someone
querelle *f* feud, quarrel
quereller *v* quarrel
querelleur *adj* quarrelsome
question *f* question
questionnaire *m* questionnaire
questionner *v* question
quête *f* quest
queue *f* queue, tail
qui *pro* who, whom

quilt *m* quilt
quincaillerie *f* hardware
quinze *adj* fifteen
quitter *v* vacate
quotidien *adv* daily
quotient *m* quotient

R

rabais *m* discount, rebate
rabaisser *v* belittle
rabbi *m* rabbi
raccourci *m* shortcut
raccrocher *v* hang up
race *f* breed, race
races *f* species
racheter *v* buy off
racine *f* root
racisme *m* racism
raciste *adj* racist
racket *m* racketeering
racommoder *v* mend
raconter *v* tell
radar *m* radar
radeau *m* raft
radiateur *m* heater
radiation *f* radiation
radical *adj* radical

Q
R

radin *adj* stingy
radio *f* radio
radiographie *f* X-ray
radis *m* radish
radius *m* radius
rafale *f* gust
raffiner *v* refine
raffinerie *f* refinery
raffut *m* racket
rafraîchir *v* chill, cool
rafraîchissant *adj* refreshing
rage *f* rage
rage de dent *f* toothache
ragot *m* gossip
ragoter *v* gossip
ragoût *m* stew
raid *m* raid
raide *adj* steep, stiff
raideur *f* stiffness
raidir *v* stiffen
rail *m* rail
railler *v* scoff
rainure *f* groove
raisin *m* grape
raisin sec *m* raisin
raison *f* purpose, reason
raisonnable *adj* reasonable
raisonnement *m* reasoning
raisonner *v* reason
rajeunir *v* rejuvenate
ralenti *m* slow motion
ralentir *v* slow down

râler *v* grouch, grumble
râleur *adj* grumpy
rallier *v* muster
ramasser *v* pick up
rame *f* oar
ramer *v* row
ramification *f* ramification
rampant *adj* rampant
rampe *f* handrail
ramper *v* crawl
ranch *m* ranch
rancœur *f* rancor
rançon *n* ramson
rancune *f* grudge, spite
rancunier *adj* spiteful
randonnée *f* hike
rang *m* row, rank
ranger *v* put away
ranimer *v* revive
rapatrier *v* repatriate
rapeller *v* recall
rapide *adj* fast, prompt
rapidement *adv* quickly
rapiécer *v* patch
rappel *m* reminder
rappeller *v* remember
rapport *m* report, review
rapporter *v* report
rapports *m* relationship
raquette *f* racket
rare *adj* uncommon
rarement *adv* rarely, seldom

R

rareté f scarcity
raser v raze, shave
rasoir m razor
rassembler v congregate
rassis adj stale
rassurer v reassure
rat m rat
râteau m rake
rater v flunk
ratification f ratification
ratifier v ratify
ratio m ratio
ration f ration
rationaliser v rationalize
rationnel adj rational
rationner v ration
raton laveur m raccoon
rattraper v make up, catch
rauque adj hoarse
ravage m ravage
ravager v ravage
ravageur adj devastating
ravin m ravine
ravir v delight
rayé adj striped
rayer v cross out
rayon m beam, ray
rayonnage m shelves
rayure f stripe
raz-de-marée m tidal wave
razzia f raid
réactif adj responsive

réaction f reaction
réaction violente f backlash
réagir v react
réaliser v realize
réalisme m realism
réalité f reality
réanimer v resuscitate
réapparaître v recur
rebelle m rebel
rebeller v rebel
rebellion f rebellion
rebondir v rebound
rebuffade f rebuff
récapituler v recap
recapturer v recapture
recensement m census
récent adj recent
réceptif adj receptive
réception f desk, reception
réceptioniste f receptionist
récession f recession
recette f recipe
recevoir v receive
recharger v recharge
réchauffer v warm up
rêche adj rough
recherche f search
rechercher v research
rechute f relapse
récif m reef
récipient m container
réciproque adj reciprocal

R

récital m recital
réciter v recite
réclamer v reclaim
reclure f louse
reclus m recluse
récolte f crop, harvest
récolter v harvest
recommandé adj advisable
recommander v recommend
récompense f reward
récompenser v reward
recomptage m recount
réconcilier v reconcile
reconnaissant adj grateful
reconnaître v recognize
reconsidérer v reconsider
reconstituer v replenish
reconstitution f reenactment
reconstruire v rebuild
recourir v resort to
recours m recourse
recouvrir v recover
recréation f recreation
recréer v recreate
recru m recruit
recrutement m recruitment
recruter v recruit
rectangle m rectangle
rectangulaire adj rectangular
rectifier v rectify
rectum m rectum
reçu m sale slip

recueil m compendium
reculer v retreat
récupération f retrieval
récupérer v recoup
récurer v scour
récurrence f recurrence
recycler v recycle
rédemption f redemption
rédiger adj engrossed
redondant adj redundant
redonner v give back
redoubler v redouble
redoutable adj dreaded
redouter v dread
redresser v straighten out
réduire v reduce
réel adj real
réélire v reelect
refaire v redo, remake
référence f reference
référendum m referendum
refeter v shift
réfléchi adj reflexive
reflet m reflection
refléter v reflect
refluer v ebb
réforme f reform
réformer v reform
refroidir v cool down
refuge m haven, refuge
réfugié m refugee
refus m refusal

refuser v rebuff, reject

réfuter v rebut, refute

regarder v look, watch

régénération f regeneration

régent m regent

régime m diet

régiment m regiment

région f area, region

régional adj regional

registe v register

registre m record

règle f rule

régler v sort out

règne m reign

régner v reign

regret m regret

regrettable adj regrettable

regretter v regret

regrouper v aggregate

régularité f regularity

régulation f regulation

réguler v regulate

régulier adj steady

régulièrement adv regularly

réhabiliter v rehabilitate

réimpression f reprint

réimprimer v reprint

rein m kidney

reine f queen

réitérer v reiterate

rejet m rejection

rejeter v overrule

rejoindre v rejoin

réjouir v rejoice

relâché adj lax

relâcher v slacken

relatif adj relative

relaxant adj relaxing

relaxation f relaxation

relaxer v relax

relayer v relay

reléguer v relegate

relever v relieve

relier v link

religieuse f nun

religieux adj religious

religion f religion

relique f relic

remarier v remarry

remarquable adj outstanding

remarque f remark

remarquer v remark, notice

rembourrage m padding

rembourrer v pad, stuff

remboursement m refund

rembourser v refund, repay

remède m remedy

remèdier v remedy

remerciement m appreciation

remerciements m thanks

remercier v thank

remettre v postpone, put back

rémission f remission

remodeler v remodel

R

remontée *f* upturn
remonter *v* hitch up
remorque *f* trailer
remorquer *v* tow
remors *m* remorse
remplacement *m* replacement
remplacer *v* replace
rempli *adj* full
remplir *v* fill
remue-ménage *m* fuss
remuer *v* wag, stir
rémunérer *v* remunerate
renaissance *f* rebirth
renard *m* fox
rencontre *f* encounter
rencontrer *v* encounter
rendement *m* output
rendez-vous *m* date
rendre *v* turn in
rêne *f* rein
renfermé *adj* withdrawn
renfocer *v* strengthen
renfort *m* reinforcements
renfrogné *adj* disgruntled
renifler *v* sniff
renne *m* reindeer
renommée *f* fame
renoncer *v* renounce
renonciation *f* defection
renouveau *m* renewal
renouveler *v* renew
rénovation *f* renovation

rénover *v* renovate
rentrée *f* reentry
rentreprendre *v* undertake
rentrer *v* get back
renversement *m* overthrow
renverser *v* overthrow
renvoi *mm* belch
réorganiser *v* reorganize
répandu *adj* prevalent
reparaître *v* reappear
réparation *v* repair
réparer *v* fix
repas *m* meal
repasser *v* iron
repentance *f* repentance
repentir *v* repent
repérer *v* spot, find
répéter *v* repeat
répétition *f* repetition
répit *m* respite
réplique *f* replica
répliquer *v* replicate
répondre *v* answer
réponse *f* reply
reporter *m* reporter
repos *m* repose, rest
reposant *adj* restful
reposer *v* repose, rest
repoussant *adj* repulsive
repousser *v* repulse
reprendre *v* take back
représailles *f* reprisal

R

représentation *f* performance
représenter *v* represent
répression *f* repression
réprimande *f* scolding
réprimander *v* rebuke
réprimer *v* repress, stifle
reprise *f* resumption
repriser *v* darn
reproche *m* reproach
reprocher *v* reproach
reproduction *f* reproduction
reproduire *v* reproduce
reptile *m* reptile
république *f* republic
répudier *v* repudiate
répugnant *adj* repugnant
réputation *f* reputation
requérir *v* entreat
requin *m* shark
réseau *m* network
resembler *v* appear
réserve *f* reservation
réserver *v* reserve
réserves *f* supplies
réservoir *m* reservoir
résidence *f* residence
résider *v* reside
résidu *m* residue
résilient *adj* resilient
résistance *f* resistance
résister *v* resist
résolu *adj* resolute

résolution *f* resolution
résoudre *v* resolve
respect *m* respect
respecter *v* respect
respectif *adj* respective
respectueux *adj* respectful
respiration *f* breathing
respirer *v* breathe
responsabilité *f* liability
responsable *adj* responsible
responsible *adj* liable
ressemblance *f* likeness
ressembler *v* resemble
ressentiment *m* resentment
ressource *f* resource
restant *adj* remaining
restaurant *m* restaurant
restauration *f* restoration
reste *m* remainder
rester *v* remain, stay
restes *m* remains
restitution *f* restitution
restraindre *v* restrict
restriction *f* restraint
résultat *m* outcome
résumé *m* summary
résumer *v* resume, sum up
résurrection *f* resurrection
rétablir *v* restore
rétablissement *m* recovery
retardé *adj* retarded
retarder *v* delay

R

retenir v constrain, retain
rétention f retention
retentissant adj resounding
réticent adj reluctant
retiré adj secluded
retirer v withdraw, retire
retombées f fallout
retoucher v touch up
retouner v turn over
retour m return
retourner v return, revert
retourner contre v backfire
rétracter v recant, retract
retrait m withdrawal
retraite f retreat
retraiter v retire
rétrécir v shrink
rétroactif adj retroactive
rétrograder v demote
retrouver v regain
réunion f gathering
réunir v gather
réussi adj successful
réussir v succeed
réussite f success
rêvasser v daydream
rêve m dream
reveil m awakening
reveiller v awake
révélateur adj revealing
révélation f revelation
révéler v reveal

revenir v come back
revenu m revenue
rêver v dream
réverbère m lamppost
révérence f reverence
revérifier v double-check
revers m cuff
réversible adj reversible
revêtement m upholstery
réviser v revise
révision f revision
revivre v relive
révoltant adj appalling
révolte f revolt
révolter v revolt
revolver v revolver
révoquer v revoke
revue f review, revue
rez-de-chaussée m ground floor
rhinocéros m rhinoceros
rhum m rum
rhumatisme m rheumatism
ricaner v giggle
riche adj wealthy
richesse f wealth
ride f crease, wrinkle
rideau m curtain, drape
ridicule m ridicule
ridicule adj ridiculous
ridiculiser v ridicule
rien m nothing
rigueur f rigor

rigide *adj* rigid
rigoureux *adj* severe
rime *f* rhyme
rincer *v* rinse
riposter *v* counter
rire *v* laugh
rire *m* laugh
risible *adj* laughable
risque *m* risk
risqué *adj* risky
risquer *v* risk
rite *m* rite
rival *m* rival
rivaliser *v* compete
rivalité *f* rivalry
rive *f* shore
riveter *v* rivet
riz *m* rice
robe *f* dress
robe de chambre *f* robe
robe de nuit *f* nightgown
robe de soirée *f* gown
robinet *m* faucet, tap
robuste *adj* robust
rocade *f* bypass
roche *f* boulder
rocheux *adj* rocky
rôder *v* prowl
rôdeur *m* prowler
roi *m* king
roman *m* novel
romance *f* romance

romancier *m* novelist
rompre *v* break
ronchon *adj* grouchy
rond *adj* round
ronflement *m* snore
ronfler *v* snore
ronger *v* eat away, gnaw
rongeur *m* rodent
roquette *f* rocket
rosaire *f* rosary
rose *adj* pink, rosy
rose *f* rose
roseau *m* reed
rosée *f* dew
rossignol *m* nightingale
rot *m* burp
rotation *f* rotation
roter *v* burp
rôti *m* roast
rotin *m* cane
rôtir *v* roast
rôtissoire *m* broiler
rotule *f* kneecap
roue *f* wheel
rouge *adj* red
rougeole *f* measles
rougeurs *f* rash
rougir *v* blush, redden
rouille *f* rust
rouillé *adj* rusty
rouiller *v* rust
rouleau *m* scroll

R

rouler *v* cruise, roll
route *f* road, route
routier *m* trucker
routine *f* routine
royal *adj* regal, royal
royaume *m* kingdom
royauté *f* royalty
ruban *m* ribbon
rubis *m* ruby
ruche *f* beehive
rude *adj* rude
rudimentaire *adj* crude
rue *f* street
rugir *v* roar
rugissement *m* roar
ruine *f* downfall, ruin
ruiné *adj* bankrupt
ruiner *v* ruin
ruisseau *m* stream
rumeur *f* rumor
rupture *f* rupture
rural *adj* rural
ruse *f* ruse
rusé *adj* cunning
russe *adj* Russian
Russie *f* Russia
rustique *adj* rustic
rythme *m* rhythm, rate

S

sable *m* sand
sable mouvant *m* quicksand
sabord *m* bulwark
sabot *m* hoof
sabotage *m* sabotage
saboter *v* sabotage
sac *m* bag, sack
sac à dos *m* backpack
sac à main *m* purse
saccager *v* rampage
sacré *adj* sacred
sacrement *m* sacrament
sacrifice *m* sacrifice
sacrilège *m* sacrilege
sadiste *m* sadist
sage *adj* wise
sage-femme *f* midwife
sagesse *f* wisdom
saigner *v* bleed
sain *adj* sane
saint *adj* holy
saint *m* saint
sainteté *f* holiness
saisir *v* grab, seize
saison *f* season
saisonnier *adj* seasonal
salade *f* salad
saladier *m* bowl
salaire *m* salary, wage

sale *adj* dirty, soiled
salé *adj* salty
saleté *f* dirt
salir *v* soil
salive *f* saliva
saliver *v* spit
salle *f* room
salle à manger *f* dining room
salle de bains *f* bathroom
salle de classe *f* classroom
salle de danse *f* ballroom
salle de séjour *f* living room
salon *m* lounge
saloon *m* saloon
saluer *v* greet, bow, nod
salut *m* salvation
salutations *f* greetings
samedi *m* Saturday
sanctifier *v* sanctify
sanction *f* sanction
sanctionner *v* sanction
sanctuaire *m* sanctuary
sandale *f* sandal
sandwich *m* sandwich
sang *m* blood
sang-froid *m* poise
sanglant *adj* bloody
sanglier *m* boar
sanglot *m* sob
sangloter *v* sob
sangsue *f* leech
sanguinaire *adj* bloodthirsty

sans *pre* without
sans arrêt *adv* nonstop
sans but *adj* aimless
sans cesse *adv* ceaselessly
sans défaut *adj* flawless
sans défense *adj* helpless
sans emploi *adj* jobless
sans enfants *adj* childless
sans équivoque *adj* unequivocal
sans fil *adj* cordless
sans fin *adj* endless
sans fond *adj* bottomless
sans fondement *adj* baseless
sans limite *adj* boundless
sans manche *adj* sleeveless
sans merci *adj* merciless
sans plomb *adj* unleaded
sans pouvoir *adj* powerless
sans rapport *adj* irrelevant
sans sou *adj* penniless
sans valeur *adj* worthless
sans vie *adj* lifeless
sans-abri *adj* homeless
santé *f* health
saper *v* undermine
saphire *m* saphire
sarcasme *m* sarcasm
sarcastique *adj* sarcastic
sardine *f* sardine
satanique *adj* satanic
satellite *m* satellite
satire *f* satire

S

satisfaction *m* satisfaction
satisfaire *v* satisfy
satisfaisant *adj* satisfactory
satisfait *adj* content
saturer *v* saturate
sauce *f* gravy, sauce
saucisse *f* sausage
sauf *pre* except
sauf *adj* safe
saule *m* willow
saumon *m* salmon
saut *m* jump, leap
sauter *v* jump, skip
sautiller *v* hop
sauvage *adj* wild
sauvagerie *f* savagery
sauve *v* save
sauvegarde *f* backup
sauvègarder *v* save
sauver *v* rescue
sauveur *m* savior
savoir *v* know
savoir-faire *m* know-how
savourer *v* savor, relish
savoureux *adj* tasty
scandale *m* scandal
scandaliser *v* scandalize
scanner *v* scan
scarabée *m* beetle
sceau *m* seal
sceller *v* seal
scénario *m* scenario

scène *f* stage, scene
scénique *adj* scenic
sceptique *adj* skeptic
schisme *m* schism
scie *f* saw
scie sauteuse *f* jigsaw
science *f* science
scientifique *adj* scientific
scier *v* saw
scintiller *v* sparkle
scooter *m* scooter
score *m* score
scorpion *m* scorpion
scout *m* scout
script *m* script
scrupule *m* scruples
scrupuleux *adj* scrupulous
scruter *v* scan
scrutin *m* ballot
sculpteur *m* sculptor
sculpture *f* sculpture
séance *f* session, sitting
seau *m* bucket, pail
sec *adj* dry, dried
séche-linge *m* dryer
sécher *v* dry
sécheresse *f* drought
séchoir *m* dryer
second *m* second
secondaire *adj* secondary
secouer *v* shake, jerk
secours *m* rescue

S

secousse *f* tremor
secret *adj* covert
secret *m* secrecy, secret
secrétaire *m* secretary
secrètement *adv* secretly
secte *f* sect
secteur *m* sector
section *f* section
sectionner *v* sever
securiser *v* secure
sécurité *f* safety
sédation *f* sedation
séduction *f* seduction
séduire *v* seduce
séduisant *adj* attractive
segment *m* segment
seigle *m* rye
seigneur *m* lord
seigneurie *f* lordship
sein *m* breast
seize *adj* sixteen
séjour *m* stay
sel *m* salt
sélection *f* selection
sélectionner *v* select
selle *f* saddle
selon *pre* according to
semaine *f* week
sembler *v* seem, sound
semelle *f* sole
semer *v* sow
semestre *m* semester

séminaire *m* seminary
sénat *m* senate
sénateur *m* senator
sénile *adj* senile
sens *m* sense
sensation *f* sensation
sensibilité *f* tenderness
sensible *adj* sensible
sensuel *adj* sensual
sentiment *m* feeling
sentimental *adj* sentimental
sentiments *m* feelings
sentinelle *f* sentry
sentir *v* smell, taste, feel
séparation *f* separation
séparé *adj* separate
séparer *v* part, separate
sepenter *v* wind
sept *adj* seven
septembre *m* September
septième *adj* seventh
séquence *f* sequence
serein *adj* serene
sérénade *f* serenade
sérénité *f* serenity
sergent *m* sergeant
série *f* series
sérieux *m* grave, serious
sérieux *adv* gravely
seringue *f* syringe
serment *m* oath
sermon *m* sermon

S

serpent *m* serpent, snake
serre *f* greenhouse
serré *adj* tight
serrer *v* tighten, squeeze
serrurier *m* locksmith
sérum *m* serum
serveur *m* waiter
serveuse *f* waitress
service *m* service, favor
serviette *f* towel, napkin
servir *v* serve
serviteur *m* servant
seuil *m* threshold
seul *adj* alone
seul *adv* lonely
seulement *adv* only
sève *f* sap
sévère *adj* stern, severe
sévèrement *adv* sternly
sévérité *f* severity
sexe *m* sex
sexualité *f* sexuality
sexy *adj* foxy
sherry *m* sherry
shopping *m* shopping
short *m* shorts
si *c* if, whether
sidérant *adj* staggering
siècle *m* century
siège *m* seat, siege
siemment *adv* knowingly
sieste *f* nap

siffler *v* whistle, hiss
sifflet *m* whistle
signal *m* signal
signature *f* signature
signe *m* sign, gesture
signer *v* sign
significatif *adj* meaningful
signification *f* meaning
signifier *v* mean, signify
silence *m* silence
silencieux *adj* quiet, silent
silhouette *f* silhouette
sillon *m* furrow
similaire *adj* similar
similarité *f* similarity
simple *adj* simple, plain
simplement *adv* merely
simplicité *f* simplicity
simplifier *v* simplify
simuler *v* simulate
simultané *adj* simultaneous
sincère *adj* sincere
sincèrité *f* sincerity
singe *m* monkey
singulier *adj* queer
sinistre *adj* sinister
sirène *f* siren
sirop *m* syrup
siroter *v* sip
site *m* site
site web *m* web site
situation *f* situation, state

S

situé *adj* located
situer *v* locate
six *adj* six
sixième *adj* sixth
skier *v* ski
slip *m* briefs
slogan *m* slogan
sniper *m* sniper
sobre *adj* sober
sobrement *adv* plainly
sociable *adj* outgoing
socialiser *v* socialize
socialisme *m* socialism
socialiste *adj* socialist
société *f* society
soda *m* soda
soeur *f* sister
sofa *m* sofa
soie *f* silk
soigné *adj* tidy, neat
soigner *v* nurse
soi-même *pre* oneself
soin *m* care
soins *m* treatment
soirée *f* evening
soixante *adj* sixty
soixante-dix *adj* seventy
sol *m* soil, ground
solaire *adj* solar
soldat *m* soldier
solder *v* discount
soleil *m* sun

solennel *adj* solemn
soliciter *v* solicit
solidarité *f* solidarity
solide *adj* solid
solitaire *m* loner
solitaire *adj* lonesome
solitude *f* loneliness
solliciter *v* request
soluble *adj* soluble
solution *f* solution
solvant *adj* solvent
sombre *adj* somber
sombrer *v* lapse
somme *f* sum
sommeil *m* sleep
sommeiller *v* snooze
sommet *m* apex, climax
somptueux *adj* lavish
son *adj* her, his
son *m* sound
sondage *m* poll, survey
sonder *v* probe
sonner *v* ring, sound
sonnerie *f* ring, bell
sonnette *f* doorbell
sophistiqué *adj* fancy
sorcèlerie *f* witchcraft
sorcellerie *f* sorcery
sorcier *m* sorcerer
sorcière *f* witch
sordide *adj* squalid
sort *m* fate

S

sorte *f* way, kind, sort
sortie *f* exit, way out
sortir *v* get out, go out
souci *m* worry
soucier *v* care about, worry
soucoupe *f* saucer
soudain *adj* sudden
souder *v* solder, weld
soudeur *m* welder
soudoyer *v* bribe
souffir de *v* suffer from
souffle *m* shock
souffler *v* blow
souffrance *f* suffering
souffrant *adj* ailing
souffrir *v* suffer, hurt
soufre *m* sulphur
souhait *m* wish
souhaiter *v* wish
soul *adj* drunk
soulagement *m* relief
soulager *v* alleviate
soulèvement *m* uprising
soulever *v* arouse, rise up
souligner *v* emphasize
soumettre *v* subdue, submit
soumis *adj* submissive
soumission *f* meekness
soupçon *m* inkling
soupe *f* soup
souper *m* supper
soupir *m* sigh

soupirer *v* sigh
souple *adj* supple
source *f* source, spring
sourcil *m* eyebrow
sourd *adj* deaf
sourire *v* smile
sourire *m* smile
souris *f* mice, mouse
sournois *adj* devious, sly
sous *pre* beneath, under
souscrire *v* subscribe
sous-jacent *adj* underlying
sous-sol *m* basement
sous-terrain *adj* underground
sous-titre *m* subtitle
soustraction *f* subtraction
soustraire *v* subtract
sous-vêtements *m* underwear
soutane *f* cassock
soutenir *v* support, claim
soutien *m* backing
soutien gorge *m* bra
souvenir *v* recollect
souvenir *m* memento
souvent *adv* often
souverain *adj* sovereign
souveraineté *f* sovereignty
soviétique *adj* soviet
spa *m* spa
spacieux *adj* roomy
spasme *m* spasm
spécial *adj* special

S

spécialement *adv* particularly
spécialiser *v* specialize
spécialité *f* specialty
spécimen *m* specimen
spectacle *m* spectacle
spectateur *m* spectator
spéculation *f* speculation
spéculer *v* speculate
speech *m* speech
sperme *m* sperm
sphère *f* sphere
spirituel *adj* spiritual
splendeur *f* splendor
splendide *adj* splendid
sponsor *m* sponsor
spontané *adj* spontaneous
spontanéité *f* spontaneity
sporadique *adj* sporadic
sport *m* sport
sportif *adj* sporty
squelette *m* skeleton
stabilité *f* stability
stable *adj* secure, stable
stade *m* stage
stage *m* training
stagiaire *m* trainee
stagnant *adj* stagnant
stagnation *f* stagnation
stagner *v* stagnate
stand *m* stall
standard *m* standard
standardiser *v* standardize

station *f* station
statistique *f* statistic
statue *f* statue
status social *m* status
steak *m* steak
sténographie *f* shorthand
stérile *adj* infertile
stériliser *v* sterilize
stimulant *m* stimulant
stimulation *f* boost
stimuler *v* stimulate
stimulus *m* stimulus
stipuler *v* stipulate
stock *m* stock
stoïque *adj* stoic
stratagème *m* ploy
stratégie *f* strategy
stress *m* strain, stress
stressant *adj* stressful
strict *adj* strict
structure *f* framework
studieux *adj* industrious
stupéfiant *adj* astounding
stupéfier *v* astound
stupide *adj* stupid
stupidité *f* stupidity
stutter *v* stutter
style *m* style
stylo *m* pen
subir *v* undergo
sublime *adj* sublime
submergé *adj* swamped

S

submerger *v* submerge
subséquent *adj* subsequent
subsidiaire *adj* subsidiary
subsister *v* subsist
substance *f* substance
substantiel *adj* substantial
substitu *m* substitute
substituer *v* substitute
subtile *adj* subtle
subvention *f* subsidy
subventionner *v* subsidize
succès *m* hit
successeur *m* successor
succomber *v* succumb
succulent *adj* succulent
sucer *v* suck
sucre *m* sugar
sucrer *v* sweeten
sucreries *f* sweets
sud *m* south
sudest *m* southeast
sudiste *m* southerner
sudouest *m* southwest
Suède *f* Sweden
suèdois *adj* Sweedish
suffisamment *adj* sufficient
suffoquer *v* suffocate
suggérer *v* suggest
suggestif *adj* suggestive
suggestion *f* suggestion
suicide *m* suicide
suisse *adj* Swiss

Suisse *f* Switzerland
suite *f* sequel
suivant *adj* next
suivre *v* follow, tail
sujet *m* topic, subject
super *adj* great
superbe *adj* gorgeous, superb
superflu *adj* superfluous
supérieur *adj* superior, upper
supériorité *f* superiority
supermarché *m* supermarket
superstition *f* superstition
supervision *f* supervision
supplication *f* plea
supplier *v* plead
support *m* stand
supportable *adj* bearable
supporter *v* put up with
supposer *v* suppose
supposition *f* assumption, supposition
supposons que *c* supposing
supprimer *v* suppress
suppurer *v* fester
suprême *adj* supreme
sur *pre* on, upon
sûr *adj* confident
sur mesure *adj* custom-made
suranné *adj* outmoded
surcharge *f* surcharge
surcharger *v* overcharge
surdité *f* deafness

S

sure *adj* sure
surement *adv* surely
surestimer *v* overestimate
surface *f* surface
surfer *v* surf
surmonter *v* cope
surnom *m* surname
surpasser *v* exceed, surpass
surpeuplé *adj* overcrowded
surplus *m* surplus
surprenant *adj* amazing
surprendre *v* amaze
surpris *adj* startled
surprise *f* surprise
sursaut *m* jolt
sursauter *v* jolt, startle
surtout *adv* mostly
surveillance *f* surveillance
surveiller *v* supervise
survenir *v* arise, occur
survie *f* survival
survivant *m* survivor
survivre *v* survive
suspect *adj* fishy
suspect *m* suspect
suspecter *v* suspect
suspendre *v* suspend
suspense *m* suspense
suspension *f* suspension
suspicieux *adj* suspicious
suspicion *f* suspicion
susprendre *v* hover

sustenter *v* sustain
sweat *m* sweater
syllabe *f* syllable
symbole *m* symbol
symbolique *adj* symbolic
symétrie *m* symmetry
sympa *adj* nice
sympathie *m* sympathy
symphonie *m* symphony
symptome *m* symptom
synagogue *f* synagogue
synchroniser *v* synchronize
synode *f* synod
synonyme *m* synonym
synthèse *f* synthesis
syphilis *f* syphilis
systèmatique *adj* systematic
système *m* system

tabac *m* tobacco
table *f* table
tableau *m* chart, painting
tableau noir *m* blackboard
tablette *f* tablet
tablier *m* apron
tabouret *m* stool

S
T

tache *f* blot, smear, stain
tâche *f* task, chore
tacher *v* stain, defile
tact *m* tact
tactique *adj* tactical
tactique *f* tactics
taie d'oreiller *f* pillowcase
taille *f* height, size
taille-crayon *m* sharpener
tailler *v* prune, trim
tailleur *m* tailor
taire *v* shut up, silence
talent *m* ability, skill
talentueux *adj* skillful
talon *m* heel
tambour *m* eardrum, drum
tamiser *v* sift
tamponner *v* stamp
tandis que *c* whereas
tangente *f* tangent
tangible *adj* tangible
tante *f* aunt
tapageur *adj* rowdy
taper *v* type
tapis *m* mat, rug
tapisserie *f* tapestry
tard *adv* late
tardif *adv* tardy
tarentule *f* tarantula
tarif *m* tariff
tarnir *v* tarnish
tartare *m* tartar

tarte *f* pie, tart
tas *m* heap
tasse *f* cup, mug
taupe *f* mole
taureau *m* bull
taux *m* rate
taverne *f* tavern
taxe *f* tax
taxi *m* cab
technicien *m* technician
technicité *f* technicality
technique *adj* technical
technique *f* technique
technologie *f* technology
teindre *v* dye
teinter *v* color
teinture *f* dye
télégramme *m* telegram
télépathie *f* telepathy
téléphone *m* phone
téléphoner *v* phone
téléscope *m* telescope
téléviser *v* televise
télévision *f* television
témoignage *m* testimony
témoin *m* witness
témoin oculaire *m* eyewitness
tempérament *m* temper
température *f* temperature
tempête *f* storm, gale
temple *m* temple
temporaire *adj* temporary

T

temps *m* time, weather
tenace *adj* nagging
tenacité *f* tenacity
tenailles *f* pliers, pincers
tendance *f* tendency
tendre *adj* loving, tender
tendresse *f* tenderness
tendu *adj* strained, tense
tenir *v* fit
tenir bon *v* hold
tennis *m* tennis
ténor *m* tenor
tension *f* tension
tentacule *f* tentacle
tentant *adj* tempting
tentation *f* temptation
tentative *f* attempt
tentative *adj* tentative
tente *f* tent
tenter *v* attempt, tempt
terme *m* term
termes *m* terms
terminer *v* end, conclude
terminologie *f* terminology
termite *m* termite
ternir *v* blemish
terrain *m* terrain, land
terrasse *f* terrace
terre *f* earth
terre (a) *adv* ashore
terrestre *adj* terrestrial
terreur *f* terror

terrible *adj* terrible
terrier *m* burrow
terrifiant *adj* terrifying
terrifier *v* terrify
territoire *m* territory
terroriser *v* terrorize
terrorisme *m* terrorism
terroriste *m* terrorist
test *m* test
testament *m* last will
tester *v* quiz, test
testifier *v* testify
tête *f* head
texte *m* text
texture *f* texture
thé *m* tea
théâtre *m* theater
théière *f* teapot
thème *m* theme
théologie *f* theology
théologien *m* theologian
théorie *f* theory
thérapie *f* therapy
thermomètre *m* thermometer
thermostat *m* thermostat
thèse *f* thesis
thon *m* tuna
thrombose *f* thrombosis
thyroïde *f* thyroid
tiède *adj* lukewarm
tige *f* rod, stem
tigre *m* tiger

T

timbre *m* stamp
timide *adj* shy, timid
timidité *f* shyness
tir *m* shot
tirelire *f* piggy bank
tirer *v* haul, pull, shoot
tirer au sort *v* draw
tireur *m* gunman
tireur d'élite *m* marksman
tiroir *m* drawer
tissé *adj* woven
tisser *v* weave
tissu *m* cloth, fabric
titre *m* title
toast *m* toast
toboggan *m* chute
toile *f* web
toile d'araignée *f* spiderweb
toilette *f* lavatory
toilettes *f* rest room
toi-même *pro* yourself
toison *f* fleece
toit *m* roof
tolérable *adj* tolerable
tolérance *f* tolerance
tolérer *v* tolerate
tomate *f* tomato
tombe *f* tomb
tombée de la nuit *f* nightfall
tomber *v* fall, tumble
tombola *f* raffle
ton *m* shade, tone

ton *adj* your
tonalité *f* dial tone
tondre *v* mow, shear
tonique *m* tonic
tonne *f* ton
tonneau *m* barrel
tonnerre *m* thunder
torche *f* torch
tordre *v* twist
tordu *adj* twisted
toréador *m* bull fighter
tornade *f* twister
torrent *m* stream, torrent
torride *adj* torrid
torsade *f* twist
torse *m* torso
tortiller *v* wiggle
tortue *f* turtle
tortueux *adj* winding
torture *f* torture
torturer *v* torture
tôt *adv* early
total *m* count
total *adj* total
totalitaire *adj* totalitarian
totalité *f* totality
touchant *adj* touching
touche *f* touch
toucher *v* adjoin, touch
toujours *adv* always
tour *m* turn, trick, tour
tourbillon *m* whirlpool

tourelle *f* turret
tourisme *m* tourism
touriste *m* tourist
tourment *m* torment
tourmenter *v* tease, torment
tourner *v* circle, spin, turn
tourne-vis *m* screwdriver
tournois *m* tournament
tournoyer *v* whirl
tous les jours *adj* everyday
tousser *v* cough
tout *adj* all
tout le monde *pro* everybody
tout puissant *adj* almighty
toux *f* cough
toxine *f* toxin
toxique *adj* toxic
tracer *v* trace
traces *f* track
trachée-artère *f* windpipe
tracteur *m* tractor
tradition *f* tradition
traducteur *m* translator
traduire *v* translate
trafiquer *v* traffic
tragédie *f* tragedy
tragique *adj* tragic
trahir *v* betray
trahison *f* betrayal
train *m* train
traîner *v* drag, lurk, trail
trait *m* trait

trait d'union *m* hyphen
traité *m* treaty
traitement *m* treatment
traiter *v* deal, treat
traître *m* traitor
traître *adj* treacherous
trajectoire *f* trajectory
trajet *m* drive
tram *m* tram
trance *f* trance
tranchant *adj* sharp
tranche *f* slice
tranchée *f* trench
trancher *v* slice
tranquilité *f* tranquility
transaction *f* transaction
transcender *v* transcend
transcire *v* transcribe
transférer *v* transfer
transfert *m* transfer
transformation *f* transformation
transformer *v* transform
transfusion *f* transfusion
transgresser *v* overstep
transit *m* transit
transition *f* transition
transitoire *adj* transient
transmettre *v* transmit
transparaître *v* come across
transparant *adj* see-through
transparent *adj* clear
transpiration *f* sweat

T

transpirer *v* sweat
transplanter *v* transplant
transport *m* freight
transport *v* transport
transporter *v* cart
transprirer *v* perspire
traumatique *adj* traumatic
traumatiser *v* traumatize
travail *m* work, labor
travailler *v* work, toil
travailleur *m* worker
travers (a) *pre* through, across
traverse *f* crossing
traverser *v* cross
trébucher *v* stumble
treize *adj* thirteen
tremblement *v* quiver
trembler *v* quake, tremble
tremper *v* soak
tremplin *m* springboard
trendance *f* trend
trente *adj* thirty
très *adv* very
trésor *m* treasure
trésorier *m* treasurer
tressaillement *m* thrill
trêve *f* truce
triangle *m* triangle
tribu *f* tribe
tribunal *m* tribunal
tribune *f* grandstand
tricherie *f* treachery

tricheur *m* cheater
tricoter *v* knit
trimestre *m* trimester
trimestriel *adj* quarterly
triomphant *adj* triumphant
triomphe *m* triumph
triompher *v* overcome
triple *adj* triple
tripode *m* tripod
triste *adj* sad
tristesse *f* sadness
trois *adj* three
troisième *adj* third
trolley *m* trolley
trombonne *m* paperclip
trompe *f* trunk
tromper *v* deceive, cheat
trompette *f* trumpet
trompeur *adj* deceptive
tronçonneuse *f* chainsaw
trône *m* throne
trophée *m* trophy
tropical *adj* tropical
tropique *m* tropic
troquer *v* barter
trottoir *m* sidewalk
trou *m* hole, gap
trouble *adj* murky
troubler *v* trouble
troupe *f* troop
troupeau *m* cattle, flock
trouver *v* find

T

truand *m* hoodlum
truc *m* gimmick
truite *f* trout
tsar *m* czar
tu *pro* you
tuberculose *f* tuberculosis
tuer *v* kill, slay
tueur *m* killer
tuile *f* tile
tulipe *f* tulip
tumeur *f* tumor
tumulte *m* uproar
tumultueux *adj* tumultuous
tunique *f* tunic
tunnel *m* tunnel
turbine *f* turbine
turbulence *f* turbulence
turque *adj* Turk
Turquie *f* Turkey
tuteur *m* tutor
tuyau *m* hose
type *m* type
typique *adj* typical
tyran *m* tyrant
tyrannie *f* tyranny
tyrannisé *adj* downtrodden

ulcère *m* ulcer
ultérieur *adj* later
ultimatum *m* ultimatum
ultime *adj* ultimate
ultrasons *m* ultrasound
un *a* a, an
un *adj* one
un jour *adv* someday
un peu *m* bit, little bit
unanimité *f* unanimity
undésirable *adj* undesirable
une *a* a
une fois *adv* once
uni *adj* plain
unification *f* unification
unifier *v* unify
uniforme *m* uniform
uniformité *f* uniformity
unilatéral *adj* unilateral
union *f* union
unique *adj* unique
unir *v* unite
unité *f* unit, unity
univers *m* universe
universel *adj* universal
universitaire *adj* academic
université *f* university
unmarried *adj* unmarried
uphill *adv* uphill

urbain *adj* urban
urgence *f* urgency
urgent *adj* urgent
urine *f* urine
uriner *v* urinate
urne *f* urn
usage *m* usage, use
user *v* wear
usine *f* factory
ustensile *m* utensil
usure *f* wear
usurper *v* usurp
utérus *m* uterus
utile *adj* helpful, useful
utilisateur *m* user
utiliser *v* utilize, use
utilité *f* usefulness

V

vacance *f* vacancy
vacances *f* vacation
vacant *adj* vacant
vacarme *m* commotion
vaccin *m* vaccine
vacciner *v* vaccinate
vache *f* cow
vaciller *v* vacillate

vagabond *m* vagrant
vague *adj* vague
vague *f* wave
vague de chaleur *f* heatwave
vaillant *adj* valiant
vaincre *v* vanquish
vainqueur *m* victor
vaisseau *m* vessel
vaisselle *f* crockery
valable *adj* worthy
valeur *f* value
valide *adj* valid
valider *v* validate
validité *f* validity
valise *f* luggage
vallée *f* valley
vallonné *adj* hilly
valoir *adj* worth
valse *f* waltz
valve *f* valve
vampire *m* vampire
van *m* van
vandale *m* vandal
vandaliser *v* vandalize
vandalisme *m* vandalism
vanité *f* vanity
vaniteux *adj* vain
vanne *f* floodgate
vantardise *v* boast
vanter *v* brag
vapeur *f* steam
vapeurs *f* fumes

vaporiser *v* vaporize
variable *adj* variable
varicelle *f* chicken pox
varié *adj* varied
varier *v* vary
variété *f* variety
variole *f* smallpox
vase *m* vase
vaste *adj* vast
vautour *m* vulture
veau *m* calf, veal
végétarien *v* vegetarian
végétation *f* vegetation
véhicule *m* vehicle
veil *f* eve
veille *fm* vigil
veine *f* vein
vélo *mf* bike
vélocité *f* velocity
velours *m* velvet
vendeur *m* seller
vendre *v* sell
vendredi *m* Friday
vénéneux *adj* poisonous
vénérer *v* venerate
vengeance *f* revenge
venger *v* avenge, revenge
venin *m* venom
venir *v* come
vent *m* wind
vente *f* sale
vente en gros *f* wholesale

venteux *adj* windy
ventilateur *m* fan
ventilation *f* ventilation
ventiler *v* ventilate
ventre *m* belly
ver *m* worm
verbalement *adv* verbally
verbe *m* verb
verdict *m* verdict
verge *f* verge
verger *m* orchard
verification *f* verification
vérifier *v* verify
vérité *f* truth
verni *m* varnish
vernir *v* varnish
vérou *m* lock
vérouiller *v* lock
verre *m* glass
verrou *m* bolt
verrue *f* wart
vers *pre* towards
vers *m* verse
vers l'est *adv* eastward
versant *m* hillside
versatile *adj* versatile
versé *adj* versed
versement *m* remittance
verser *v* pour, shed
version *f* version
vert *adj* green
vertèbre *f* vertebra

vertiges *m* dizziness
vertu *f* virtue
vertueux *adj* virtuous
vésicule biliaire *f* gall bladder
vessie *f* bladder
veste *f* jacket
vestiaire *m* locker room
vestige *m* vestige
veston *m* vest
vêtement *m* garment
vêtements *m* clothes
vétéran *m* veteran
vétérinaire *m* veterinarian
vêtir *v* clothe
vétuste *adj* antiquated
veuf *m* widower
veuve *f* widow
viaduc *m* viaduct
viande *f* meat
viande hachée *f* mincemeat
vibration *f* vibration
vibrer *v* vibrate, rattle
vice *m* vice
vicieux *adj* vicious
victime *f* victim, casualty
victimiser *v* victimize
victoire *f* victory
victorieux *adj* victorious
vide *adj* void, empty
vide *m* emptiness
vider *v* empty
vie *f* life

vie privée *f* privacy
vieillesse *f* old age
vièrge *f* virgin
vieux *adj* old
vieux jeu *adj* old-fashioned
vif *adj* bright, brisk
vigilant *adj* watchful
vigne *f* vine
vignoble *m* vineyard
vigoureux *adj* vivacious
villa *f* cottage
village *m* village
villageois *m* villager
ville *f* city, town
ville natale *f* hometown
vin *m* wine
vinaigre *m* vinegar
vindicatif *adj* vindictive
vingt *adj* twenty
vingtième *adj* twentieth
viol *m* rape
violence *f* violence
violent *adj* violent
violer *v* rape, violate
violet *adj* purple
violette *f* violet
violeur *m* rapist
violon *m* fiddle, violin
violoniste *f* violinist
vipère *f* viper
virage *m* corner
virer *v* veer

virginité *f* virginity
virgule *f* comma
viril *adj* virile
virile *adj* manly
virilité *f* manliness
virtuellement *adv* virtually
virulent *adj* virulent
virus *m* virus
vis *f* screw
visage *m* face
viser *v* aim
visibilité *f* visibility
visible *adj* visible
vision *f* vision
visite *f* visit
visiter *v* visit
visiteur *m* visitor
visser *v* screw
visualiser *v* visualize
visuel *adj* visual
vital *adj* vital
vitalité *f* vitality
vitamine *f* vitamin
vitesse *f* speed
vitrine *f* cabinet
vivant *adj* alive, live
vivide *adj* vivid
vocabulaire *m* vocabulary
vocation *f* vocation
voeux *m* woes
vogue *f* vogue
voile *f* sail

voile *m* veil
voilier *m* sailboat
voir *v* behold, see
voisin *m* neighbor
voisinage *m* vicinity
voiture *f* car
voix *f* voice
vol *m* fly, flight, theft
vol à l'étalage *m* shoplifting
volaille *f* poultry
volatile *adj* volatile
volcan *m* volcano
voler *v* fly, steal
voleur *m* thief
volleyball *m* volleyball
volontaire *m* volunteer
volontaire *adj* willing
volonté *f* will
voltage *m* voltage
volume *m* volume
vomi *m* vomit
vomir *v* vomit, throw up
vote *m* vote
voter *v* vote
vouloi *v* want
voyage *m* voyage, trip
voyager *v* travel
voyageur *m* traveler
voyelle *f* vowel
voyou *m* thug
vrac *m* bulk
vrai *adj* truthful

vraiment *adv* really
vue *f* view, sight
vulgaire *adj* vulgar
vulgarité *f* vulgarity
vulnérable *adj* vulnerable

zèbre *m* zebra
zélé *adj* zealous
zèle *m* zeal
zéro *m* zero
zeste *m* zest
zinc *m* zinc
zone *f* zone
zoo *m* zoo
zoologie *f* zoology

wagon *m* wagon
watt *m* watt

Word to Word® Bilingual Dictionary Series

Language - Item Code - Pages ISBN #

Albanian - 500X - 306 pgs
ISBN - 978-0-933146-49-5

Amharic - 820X - 362 pgs
ISBN - 978-0-933146-59-4

Arabic - 650X - 378 pgs
ISBN - 978-0-933146-41-9

Bengali - 700X - 372 pgs
ISBN - 978-0-933146-30-3

Burmese - 705X - 310 pgs
ISBN - 978-0-933146-50-1

Cambodian - 710X - 376 pgs
ISBN - 978-0-933146-40-2

Chinese - 715X - 374 pgs
ISBN - 978-0-933146-22-8

Farsi - 660X - 372 pgs
ISBN - 978-0-933146-33-4

French - 530X - 320 pgs
ISBN - 978-0-933146-36-5

German - 535X - 352 pgs
ISBN - 978-0-933146-93-8

Gujarati - 720X - 334 pgs
ISBN - 978-0-933146-98-3

Haitian-Creole - 545X - 362 pgs
ISBN - 978-0-933146-23-5

Hebrew - 665X - 316 pgs
ISBN - 978-0-933146-58-7

Hindi - 725X - 362 pgs
ISBN - 978-0-933146-31-0

Hmong - 728X - 294 pgs
ISBN - 978-0-933146-31-0

Italian - 555X - 362 pgs
ISBN - 978-0-933146-51-8

All languages are two-way:
English-Language / Language-English.
More languages in planning and production.

Japanese - 730X - 372 pgs
ISBN - 978-0-933146-42-6

Korean - 735X - 374 pgs
ISBN - 978-0-933146-97-6

Lao - 740X - 319 pgs
ISBN - 978-0-933146-54-9

Pashto - 760X - 348 pgs
ISBN - 978-0-933146-34-1

Polish - 575X - 358 pgs
ISBN - 978-0-933146-64-8

Portuguese - 580X - 362 pgs
ISBN - 978-0-933146-94-5

Punjabi - 765X - 358 pgs
ISBN - 978-0-933146-32-7

Romanian - 585X - 354 pgs
ISBN - 978-0-933146-91-4

Russian - 590X - 334 pgs
ISBN - 978-0-933146-92-1

Somali - 830X - 320 pgs
ISBN- 978-0-933146-52-5

Spanish - 600X - 346 pgs
ISBN - 978-0-933146-99-0

Swahili - 835X - 308 pgs
ISBN - 978-0-933146-55-6

Tagalog - 770X - 332 pgs
ISBN - 978-0-933146-37-2

Thai - 780X - 354 pgs
ISBN - 978-0-933146-35-8

Turkish - 615X - 348 pgs
ISBN - 978-0-933146-95-2

Ukrainian - 620X - 337 pgs
ISBN - 978-0-933146-25-9

Urdu - 790X - 360 pgs
ISBN - 978-0-933146-39-6

Vietnamese - 795X - 366 pgs
ISBN - 978-0-933146-96-9

Order Information

To order our Word to Word® Bilingual Dictionaries or any other products from Bilingual Dictionaries, Inc., please contact us at (951) 296-2445 or visit us at **www.BilingualDictionaries.com**. Visit our website to download our current Catalog/Order Form, view our products, and find information regarding Bilingual Dictionaries, Inc.

 **Bilingual Dictionaries, Inc.**

PO Box 1154 • Murrieta, CA 92562 • Tel: (951) 296-2445 • Fax: (951) 461-3092
www.BilingualDictionaries.com

Special Dedication & Thanks

Bilingual Dicitonaries, Inc. would like to thank all the teachers from various districts accross the country for their useful input and great suggestions in creating a Word to Word® standard. We encourage all students and teachers using our bilingual learning materials to give us feedback. Please send your questions or comments via email to support@bilingualdictionaries.com.